Human Rights-Based Change

This book provides different analytical perspectives into how human rights-based approaches to development (HRBADs) contribute to *change*. Based on the understanding that HRBADs are increasingly integrated into development and governance discourse and processes in many societies and organisations, it explores how the reinforcement of human rights principles and norms has impacted the practices and processes of development policy implementation. To reflect on the nature of the change that such efforts may imply, this book examines critically traditional and innovative ways of mainstreaming and institutionalising human rights in judicial, bureaucratic and organisational processes in development work. Attention is also paid to the results assessment and causal debates in the human rights field. The authors discuss important questions concerning the legitimacy of and preconditions for change. What is the change that development efforts should seek to contribute to and who should have the power to define such change? What is required of institutional structures and processes within development organisations and agencies in order for human rights integration and institutionalisation to have transformative potential?

This book was originally published as a special issue of the *Nordic Journal of Human Rights*.

Maija Mustaniemi-Laakso works as a Researcher at the Åbo Akademi University Institute for Human Rights in Finland. Her current research interests include migration and asylum law, vulnerability, human rights-based approach to development, and extraterritorial human rights obligations.

Hans-Otto Sano is Acting Research Director at the Danish Institute for Human Rights. He has worked for three years at the Nordic Trust Fund, The World Bank, as Senior Program Officer. Dr Sano is currently involved in research projects on Poverty and Human Rights-Based Approaches and in drafting a report on The Economy of Human Rights. His recent publications span themes on human rights indicators, on the drivers of human rights change, on the methods of assessing the impact of social and economic rights, and on social accountability and human rights.

Human Rights-Based Change

The Institutionalisation of Economic and
Social Rights

Edited by
**Maija Mustaniemi-Laakso and
Hans-Otto Sano**

Routledge
Taylor & Francis Group

LONDON AND NEW YORK

First published 2017 by Routledge

2 Park Square, Milton Park, Abingdon, Oxfordshire OX14 4RN
52 Vanderbilt Avenue, New York, NY 10017

Routledge is an imprint of the Taylor & Francis Group, an informa business

First issued in paperback 2018

British Library Cataloguing in Publication Data
A catalogue record for this book is available from the British Library

ISBN 13: 978-1-138-20830-8 (hbk)
ISBN 13: 978-0-367-07662-7 (pbk)

Typeset in Adobe Garamond
by RefineCatch Limited, Bungay, Suffolk

Publisher's Note
The publisher accepts responsibility for any inconsistencies that may have
arisen during the conversion of this book from journal articles to book chapters,
namely the possible inclusion of journal terminology.

Disclaimer
Every effort has been made to contact copyright holders for their permission to
reprint material in this book. The publishers would be grateful to hear from any
copyright holder who is not here acknowledged and will undertake to rectify
any errors or omissions in future editions of this book.

Contents

Citation Information   vii
Notes on Contributors   ix

Introduction   1
Maija Mustaniemi-Laakso and Hans-Otto Sano

1. Failures and Successes of Human Rights-Based Approaches to Development:
   Towards a Change Perspective   5
   Wouter Vandenhole and Paul Gready

2. Participatory Approaches to Socio-Economic Rights Adjudication: Tentative
   Lessons from South African Evictions Law   26
   Sandra Liebenberg

3. Modernisation of Maternity Care in Malawi   45
   Alessandra Sarelin

4. Education in Pursuit of the Development Dream? Effects of Schooling on
   Indigenous Development and Rights in Bolivia   66
   Tiina Saaresranta

5. Mainstreaming Human Rights in Development Programmes and Projects:
   Experience from the Work of a United Nations Agency   86
   Sisay Alemahu Yeshanew

6. Evidence in Demand: An Overview of Evidence and Methods in Assessing
   Impact of Economic and Social Rights   101
   Hans-Otto Sano

Index   117

Citation Information

The chapters in this book were originally published in the *Nordic Journal of Human Rights*, volume 32, issue 4 (November 2014). When citing this material, please use the original page numbering for each article, as follows:

Introduction
Editorial Note
Maija Mustaniemi-Laakso and Hans-Otto Sano
Nordic Journal of Human Rights, volume 32, issue 4 (November 2014), pp. 287–290

Chapter 1
Failures and Successes of Human Rights-Based Approaches to Development: Towards a Change Perspective
Wouter Vandenhole and Paul Gready
Nordic Journal of Human Rights, volume 32, issue 4 (November 2014), pp. 291–311

Chapter 2
Participatory Approaches to Socio-Economic Rights Adjudication: Tentative Lessons from South African Evictions Law
Sandra Liebenberg
Nordic Journal of Human Rights, volume 32, issue 4 (November 2014), pp. 312–330

Chapter 3
Modernisation of Maternity Care in Malawi
Alessandra Sarelin
Nordic Journal of Human Rights, volume 32, issue 4 (November 2014), pp. 331–351

Chapter 4
Education in Pursuit of the Development Dream? Effects of Schooling on Indigenous Development and Rights in Bolivia
Tiina Saaresranta
Nordic Journal of Human Rights, volume 32, issue 4 (November 2014), pp. 352–371

Chapter 5

Mainstreaming Human Rights in Development Programmes and Projects: Experience from the Work of a United Nations Agency
Sisay Alemahu Yeshanew
Nordic Journal of Human Rights, volume 32, issue 4 (November 2014), pp. 372–386

Chapter 6

Evidence in Demand: An Overview of Evidence and Methods in Assessing Impact of Economic and Social Rights
Hans-Otto Sano
Nordic Journal of Human Rights, volume 32, issue 4 (November 2014), pp. 387–402

For any permission-related enquiries please visit:
http://www.tandfonline.com/page/help/permissions

Notes on Contributors

Sisay Alemahu Yeshanew is a development law specialist at the Food and Agriculture Organization of the UN, and Senior Researcher affiliated to the Institute for Human Rights, Åbo Akademi University, Finland.

Paul Gready is Professor of Applied Human Rights at the Centre for Applied Human Rights, University of York, UK.

Sandra Liebenberg is Professor and H.F. Oppenheimer Chair in Human Rights Law at the University of Stellenbosch Law Faculty, South Africa.

Maija Mustaniemi-Laakso is a PhD candidate at the Institute for Human Rights, Åbo Akademi University, Finland.

Tiina Saaresranta is a PhD candidate at the Institute for Human Rights, Åbo Akademi University, Finland.

Hans-Otto Sano is Senior Researcher in the Danish Institute for Human Rights, Copenhagen, Denmark.

Alessandra Sarelin is a Post-Doctoral Researcher affiliated to the Institute for Human Rights, Åbo Akademi University, Finland.

Wouter Vandenhole is Professor of Human Rights Law in the Faculty of Law, University of Antwerp, Belgium.

INTRODUCTION

Maija Mustaniemi-Laakso
PhD Candidate, Institute for Human Rights, Åbo Akademi University, Finland

Hans-Otto Sano
Senior Researcher, Danish Institute for Human Rights, Copenhagen

Ten years ago, the focus of human rights-based approaches to development (HRBADs) centred mainly on documenting and understanding the content of such approaches, their implementation and potential benefits. Current research is more empirical, operational and practical. The perspective of the articles in the present Special Issue is that human rights-based approaches, and human rights law more generally, are now, to a growing extent, integrated into development and other governance discourses in a large number of countries and organisations. The practices and results emerging from this deserve deeper analytical and critical scrutiny.

Human rights norms and principles are slowly becoming institutionalised across various sectors at state level and locally, both national and international organisations, and often co-exist and interact with other organisational norms and practices. Such interaction, in organisational processes and structures, produces changes in the processes of policy implementation. These processes are most sophisticated in the judicialisation of social rights which, especially in developing countries, takes place within new, experimental legal procedures. The integration of human rights also produces outcomes and impacts which are the subject of debates on measurement and implementation techniques. Further, methodology in human rights studies is an emerging subject, bringing human rights scholars closer to quantitative methods, results-based management and evidence analysis.

A deeper understanding of the reinforcement of human rights principles and norms in development contexts is the main goal of the articles in this Special Issue. The articles examine traditional as well as new and innovative ways of mainstreaming and institutionalising human rights in judicial, bureaucratic and organisational processes. At their core, the articles seek to provide insights into how human rights-based approaches have contributed to *change*, that is, the nature of social, legal and organisational changes that human rights implementation may entail in various sectors.

This Special Issue begins with a discussion on the premises of transformative development and the organisational requirements needed to make the HRBADs work. Wouter Vandenhole and Paul Gready's contribution problematises the assumption that the adoption of a HRBAD leads to organisational changes, both in terms of policies and practices. The authors find that, due to the inherently distinct character of the development and human rights approaches, results-based management (which has become more fashionable in recent development) and human rights-based approaches may be more difficult to merge than assumed.

Sandra Liebenberg focuses on new, experimental practices in human rights implementation. Her contribution centres on participatory models of adjudication such as generous rules of standing, class actions, public interest litigation and participatory models of review as potential solutions to the distributive and democratic deficits of litigation and adjudication. With a special focus on the doctrine on meaningful engagement which emerged within the realm of South African eviction laws, Liebenberg discusses the democratic and resource ramifications that the participatory models of adjudication may give rise to in terms of socio-economic rights realisation.

Alessandra Sarelin analyses the modernisation process of maternity care in Malawi from a biopolitical perspective, focusing on the normalising and rationalising aspects of the safety arguments underpinning the ban on traditional birth attendants. Sarelin's research adds to a developing scholarship of analysing "human rights practice". She argues that the logic behind human rights and development leads to increased regulation and homogenisation of what is considered a socially acceptable, correct, safe and normal way to handle birth, namely the normalisation of facility-based birth practices. Yet, underlying this is the multifaceted problem of maternal mortality. Any solution will require political, economic, social and cultural change. According to Sarelin, the transfer of childbirth from the village and home to the clinic amounts to a technical solution to a complex problem, one likely to sustain existing power structures within societies and villages.

Tiina Saaresranta pursues a similar line of critical inquiry into the education sector. Analysing the right to education in a case study on Bolivia, Saaresranta problematizes the fundamental assumption that education is an empowering and instrumental right which contributes to development and facilitates access to other rights. She notes that the effects of the education models implemented in Bolivia have largely resulted in assimilation, mono-linguism, and mono-culturalism. Traditionally, Latin American states have tended to offer types of education disconnected from assisting indigenous community traditions and, conversely, have served those in decision-making positions. These educational models have resulted in the socialisation of indigenous children into non-indigenous societies, as well as perpetuated the marginalisation, poverty and dispossession of the indigenous communities.

Turning our attention to the human right to adequate food, Sisay Alemahu Yeshanew reflects on organisational human rights mainstreaming in the Food and Agriculture Organisation of the United Nations (FAO), arguing that mainstreaming is one implication of the HRBADs. He emphasises that mainstreaming may result in better effectiveness, targeting and sustainability by placing focus on governance in matters that are most relevant to people suffering from food insecurity. Yeshanew also identifies the requisites of a coherent and effective integration of the right to adequate food within FAO's work: specialisation within the organisation, a comprehensive mainstreaming strategy, capacity development, organisational support and contextualisation.

Regarding economic and social rights specifically, Hans-Otto Sano examines different kinds of evidence established in the research literature. While reporting on the nature of the evidence, the article's main purpose is to scrutinise the distinct measurement methods in use when documenting the impact of social rights acceptance and implementation. What do we know about the results of institutionalising social rights and how we establish this evidence are the core questions of Sano's article. Other key questions include how causal linkages are established and how well quantitative evidence is coupled with qualitative data.

The use of indicators may be an important issue and has received much attention in human rights scholarship. Yet, the author holds of equal importance the availability of data, which is a paramount priority, alongside the realisation that we have yet to arrive at better methods of documenting the impact of social rights institutionalisation.

An important lesson that can be distilled from the articles is that, while mainstreaming and integration of human rights may improve governance and targeting, human rights integration into the political and judicial domains may also produce negative or adverse outcomes contrary to their very purpose. The articles raise questions concerning the legitimacy of change: what kind of change is it that the human rights actors seek to achieve, and who holds the defining power? Human rights institutionalisation in policies may, for example, bring about homogenising and universalist approaches in the use of modern technologies, effectively rendering vulnerable groups less independent and self-determined and with a diminished capacity for participation. This may run the risk of sustaining or perpetuating existing unequal power imbalances within societies. In addition, the way in which rights are interpreted in social rights implementation policies may not always be sensitive to the needs, identities, cultures or livelihoods of the most marginalised groups. Intended empowerment may therefore transpire to produce processes and outcomes of disempowerment.

Increased and more nuanced sensitivity for context-specificity and participation are suggested and analysed in the articles as important elements in anticipating and counteracting such negative impacts. Liebenberg cautions, however, that while participatory approaches hold much promise, further research and experimentation is needed to identify the conditions under which participatory methods of socio-economic rights enforcement can be empowering on an equal basis to all, and become effective in terms of addressing systemic socio-economic issues. The role of law, and the interplay between politics and law, gives rise to interesting questions in this regard. While, as Sarelin notes, law holds transformative potential and can, at its best, be a discursive site, the articles in this Special Issue remind us that human rights law may also be used as an instrument for advancing political interests or to sustaining prevailing structures of power and inequality.

The alleged change of human rights integration and institutionalisation is transformative in the sense that power relations are changed in favour of those rights-holders who are less influential. Despite this, certain assumptions, which have been implicit in studies on human rights-based approaches, tend to underestimate the degree to which both organisational change is needed, and capacity-building and sensitising within organisations, agencies and states is required in order to implement HRBADs effectively, coherently, and in a manner which reduces inequality. As underscored by Vandenhole and Gready, organisational change is typically a *process*, and ideological and operational confrontation may be a necessary catalyst for change to take place within an organisation. The political dimension of this process, and the interplay between law and politics in aspiring to change, should, according to the authors of this Special Issue, not be neglected or underestimated. In order to be sustainable it is apposite, as Yeshanew notes, that mainstreaming structures address not only an organisation's programming and implementation levels, but also its political and organisational decision-making levels.

The articles in this Special Issue are based on academic papers presented at the Seminar on Challenges in Integrating Human Rights and Development organised at the Åbo Akademi University, Institute for Human Rights, 25–26 November 2013. The seminar brought together researchers and practitioners to critically reflect on the human rights-based development strategies from the perspective of change and impact as well as the relevance and adaptability of human rights regimes both in local contexts and in continually changing and globalising development processes. The seminar was organised as the final event of the research project "Integrating Human Rights and Development: Strategies, Impact and Emerging Issues" (Academy of Finland 2010–2013).

Failures and Successes of Human Rights-Based Approaches to Development: Towards a Change Perspective

Wouter Vandenhole

Professor, Faculty of Law, University of Antwerp, Belgium

Paul Gready

Professor, Centre for Applied Human Rights, University of New York, USA

Human rights-based approaches to development (HRBADs) seem to be grounded in assumptions of change that remain implicit and therefore often undebated. These assumptions of change play at two levels, i.e. that of organisational change and that of social change. The main emphasis of this article is on organisational change as the logical precursor to social change. Explanatory factors for the challenges in introducing HRBADs in development organizations include the different legitimizing anchors that both use (normative versus empirical), as well as the differences in disciplinary backgrounds of staff and in role definition (confrontation versus collaboration with the state). An important finding is that result-based management and HRBADs may be more difficult to reconcile than often believed. The tension between both may be illustrative of the fundamental differences that continue to characterize development and human rights approaches, notwithstanding the rapprochement that has taken place over the past decade(s). We argue that more empirical work is needed in order to better understand organisational and social change through HRBADs.

The relationship between human rights and development has been framed in multiple ways.[1] From a legal perspective, there are three major conceptualisations: the right to development; transnational human rights obligations; and human rights-based approaches to development (HRBADs). The former two represent a rather fundamental overhaul of human rights thinking, as they introduce new substantive rights and corresponding obligations and, even more importantly, new duty-bearers.[2] HRBADs may be said to be more pragmatic and less ambitious, in that they

---

[1] SP Marks, "The Human Rights Framework for Development: Seven Approaches", in Basu Mushumi, Archna Negi and Arjun K. Sengupta (eds), *Reflections on the Right to Development* (Sage Publications, 2005), 23–60; L-H Piron with T O'Neil, "Integrating Human Rights into Development. A synthesis of donor approaches and experiences" (2005), available at storage.globalcitizen.net/data/topic/knowledge/uploads/2012091216108590063_%E6%96%B01%20Integrating%20Human%20Rights%20into%20Development.pdf (accessed 22 April 2014); D D'Hollander, A Marx and J Wouters, "Integrating Human Rights in Development Policy: Mapping Donor Strategies and Practices", Working Paper 108, June 2013, available at papers.ssrn.com/sol3/papers.cfm?abstract_id=2286204 (accessed 18 April 2014), 9–42.

[2] For more details, see W Vandenhole, "The Human Right to Development as a Paradox" (2003) *Verfassung und Recht in Übersee. Law and Politics in Africa, Asia and Latin America* 377–404; W Vandenhole, GE Türkelli and R Hammonds, "New Human Rights Duty-Bearers: Towards a Re-conceptualisation of the Human Rights Duty-Bearer Dimension" in Anja Mihr and Mark Gibney (eds), *The SAGE Handbook of Human Rights* (Sage, forthcoming).

do not envisage fundamental changes to the human rights framework. They are much more practice-orientated, i.e. they seek to introduce human rights principles into development thinking and practice.[3] This more practical orientation does not make HRBAs easier or more simple though. In particular, their interplay with change is complex and under-researched.

HRBADs seem to be grounded in assumptions of change that remain implicit and therefore often undebated. These assumptions of change play at two levels. First of all, it is often assumed that the formal adoption of an HRBAD by an organisation implies that that organisation really applies an HRBAD. What seems to be ignored is that the introduction of any new policy requires organisational change which often provokes considerable internal resistance or is met with lethargy and bureaucratic attitude. This challenge applies all the more to the introduction of an HRBAD which can be considered a rather legal or even legalistic approach to fundamental social or economic questions despite its focus on principles. Secondly, whether and how *social* change takes place depends on a complex interplay of actors, institutions and policies. A straightforward causal relationship between an HRBAD and the envisaged social change is often presumed, however, in particular within result-based paradigms. Whereas organisational and social change are to be distinguished analytically, in practice they are often intrinsically linked. For a start, it is unlikely that the envisaged social change will occur if the organisation fails to adopt and implement its HRBAD policy properly in the first place.[4] Secondly, the way an organisation thinks about effecting social change as part of the adoption of an HRBAD will inevitably impact on whether and how it achieves social change.

In what follows, we shall first succinctly introduce HRBADs and the role of law and legal institutions therein. We shall then look into the transformative potential of (human rights) law in society. Although much more empirical research is needed before anything meaningful can be said about the contribution of HRBADs to social change, we do not completely omit this point given its intrinsic link with organisational change in practice. However, logically, purposive social change may only be effected by an HRBAD to the extent that an organisation has really managed to introduce such an approach more or less successfully. The main emphasis of this article is therefore on organisational change as the logical precursor to social change. In section 3, we shall draw out what it took in particular for an international organisation like UNICEF to introduce an HRBAD, based on empirical case studies that have been conducted by others. By way of contextualisation, we include an exploratory investigation into the introduction of an HRBAD by the United Nations at the country level, by states (Norway and Sweden) and by non-governmental organisations (ActionAid) from the perspective of organisational change.

The nature and scope of the exercise is obviously limited due to the fact that we could only draw on existing empirical work (rather than undertake empirical work ourselves), but that methodological limitation does not pose a fundamental obstacle at this stage, where the main purpose is that of drawing more attention to the change perspective in understanding the limited headway HRBADs have made so far. To the extent that the available empirical

---

[3] They are nonetheless considered to be the most sophisticated way of linking human rights to development. The other categories are implicit human rights work; human rights projects; human rights dialogue; and human rights mainstreaming. See L-H Piron with T O'Neil, "Integrating Human Rights into Development. A synthesis of donor approaches and experiences" (2005), available at storage. globalcitizen.net/data/topic/knowledge/uploads/201209121610859063_%E6%96%B01%20Integrating %20Human%20Rights%20into%20Development.pdf (accessed 22 April 2014).

[4] Certainly, successful organisational change will not automatically translate into the envisaged social change.

data allow for it, we shall use a similar analytical matrix. In particular, we shall pay attention to internal reflection and planning, and leadership and true believers[5] as explanatory entry points for organisational change following the introduction of an HRBAD.[6] In addition to these drivers of change, we shall look into frequently mentioned spoilers of change, such as lack of capacity and staff turnover. At the interplay of organisational and societal change is the tension between result-based management and HRBADs.

By drawing attention to the (often naïve or simply wrong) assumptions of organisational and social change in HRBADs, we do not seek to dismiss them. Rather, this exercise seeks to gain a better understanding of when and why an HRBAD works. After two decades of mainly promotional literature on HRBADs stressing their added value,[7] the time may have come to strengthen the knowledge base on HRBADs and to address the hard questions more explicitly.[8] This piece is a modest attempt to contribute to that research agenda setting exercise. Further detailed empirical research will be needed to corroborate or dismiss the hypotheses that we advance here.

I. HRBADs and the Role of Law and Legal Institutions

There is no single or universal definition or practice of HRBAD, hence the word is used in the plural. Nevertheless, some common characteristics of HRBADs can be identified. The Office of the High Commissioner for Human Rights (OHCHR) correctly emphasises that HRBADs are both about process and outcomes: whereas HRBADs are operationally directed to promote and protect human rights as envisaged outcomes, their normative grounding in human rights standards also draws attention to the process through which the outcomes are achieved.[9] So, HRBADs claim to change the way development work is done (process), and also put forward full human rights realisation as the goal of development work (outcomes). In both respects, change is a central notion: a change is proposed as to how development is carried out (which has inevitable implications on organisations involved in development work), and the objective of full human rights realisation will require fundamental social change.

The grounding in human rights means first and foremost that HRBADs often draw on the legal codification of human rights norms and standards in United Nations and regional treaties,

---

[5]The expression is borrowed from Oestreich. True believers are persons within an organisation, not necessarily within the leadership, who make the case "that pursuing a principled idea … [is] worthwhile from an ethical as well as a practical point of view". See JE Oestreich, *Power and Principle. Human Rights Programming in International Organizations* (Georgetown University Press, Washington, DC, 2007), 8

[6]The external environment and new issues or approaches, the two other factors that are often mentioned in explaining organisational change, seem more relevant in explaining whether and why an HRBAD was introduced as a matter of policy.

[7]See, e.g., J Kirkemann Boesen and T Martin, "Applying a Rights-Based Approach. An Inspirational Guide for Civil Society" (Danish Institute for Human Rights, 2007), available at www.crin.org/docs/dihr_rba.pdf (accessed 22 April 2014).

[8]See, e.g., S Hickney and D Mitlin (eds) *Rights-Based Approaches to Development. Exploring the Potential and Pitfalls* (Kumarian Press, 2009); P Gready and J Ensor (eds), *Reinventing Development? Translating Rights-Based Approaches from Theory to Practice* (Zed Books, 2005).

[9]OHCHR, *Frequently Asked Questions on a Human-Rights Based Approach to Development Cooperation* (New York and Geneva, OHCHR, 2006), 15, available at www.ohchr.org/Documents/Publications/FAQen.pdf (accessed 22 April 2014). Compare LT Munro, "The 'Human Rights-Based Approach to Programming': A Contradiction in Terms?", in Sam Hickey and Diana Mitlin (eds), *Rights-Based Approaches to Development. Exploring the Potential and Pitfalls* (Kumarian Press, 2009), 193–94.

as well as in municipal law, and on the work of human rights monitoring bodies and courts. A degree of commonality may be found in the fact that HRBADS share some human rights principles, which may be aptly summarised by the acronym PANEL: participation, accountability, non-discrimination, empowerment and linkage to human rights norms. The last of these (i.e., linkage to human rights norms) has been labelled "normativity" in a recent report, so an alternative acronym is PANEN.[10] Whereas these principles are not necessarily new to development, nor exclusively legal principles, they do have a specific human rights and even legal meaning (except for empowerment which has no legal equivalent). Moreover, the linkage to human rights norms or normativity intrinsically has a strong legal component, although it is not necessarily reducible to (human rights) law. The legal preponderance in HRBADs is borne out by the fact that staff with a legal background "tend to quickly grasp the implications of a rights-based approach".[11] The reference to human rights norms almost inevitably brings human rights monitoring bodies into the picture, be it at universal, regional or national level. At the universal level, expert bodies (called committees) monitor the implementation of the core United Nations human rights treaties through reporting (and sometimes also complaints and inquiry) procedures. At the regional level, a judicial monitoring regime is in place for the Americas, Africa and Europe. Domestically, human rights monitoring is typically undertaken by human rights institutions and courts.

Certainly, HRBADs are not the monopoly of the legal discipline, but law and the legal discipline can hardly be ignored or completely side-lined, which brings us to the question of what the transformative potential of human rights law is, and what can be learned more generally from social change theories. So far, these questions have seldom been explicitly addressed in HRBAD literature, notwithstanding their central importance to a good understanding of when and how HRBADs may work.[12] Although this article focuses on the logical precursor to effecting social change, i.e. organisational change, the intrinsic links in practice between both make it necessary to touch upon social change for a short while. Moreover, the views held on effecting social change may have a bearing on or intersect with the way organisational change is broached.

II. The Transformative Potential of Human Rights and Social Change Theories

Gready and Ensor had already pointed out in 2005 that "[h]ow structural change might be achieved requires much greater clarification, both conceptually and practically". As a minimum, underlying implicit assumptions of change need to be rendered explicit. Ideally, a *theory* rather than assumptions of change underpin HRBADs. Such a theory should be

---

[10]UNICEF, "Global Evaluation of the Application of the Human Rights-Based Approach to UNICEF Programming. Final Report – Volume I" (UNICEF, 2012), available at www.unicef.org/policyanalysis/rights/files/UNICEF_HRBAP_Final_Report_Vol_I_11June_copy-edited_translated.pdf (accessed 16 April 2014), 13 and 15–16. Moreover, in this report, empowerment is not mentioned as a human rights principle, but conceptualised as the goal for HRBAD. Instead, transparency is upgraded from an element of accountability to a separate principle (13–19). Another acronym used, for example, is PANTHER (FAO).

[11]UNICEF, "Global Evaluation of the Application of the Human Rights-Based Approach to UNICEF Programming. Final Report – Volume I" (UNICEF, 2012), available at www.unicef.org/policyanalysis/rights/files/UNICEF_HRBAP_Final_Report_Vol_I_11June_copy-edited_translated.pdf (accessed 16 April 2014), 40.

[12]BA Andreassen and G Crawford (eds), *Human Rights, Power and Civic Action. Comparative Analyses of Struggles for Rights in Developing Societies* (Routledge, 2013).

grounded as much as possible in empirical evidence, spelling out how it conceptualises change (causation, influences, directions of change) and which actors and institutions it deems instrumental in bringing about social change, and clarifying how power is understood.[13]

Elsewhere, Gready with Vandenhole have clarified the archetypical similarities and differences between human rights and development theories and practice through the prism of what they call five "key entry point[s] to change: 1) the state; 2) the law; 3) transnational and international collaboration; 4) localism and bottom-up approaches; and 5) multiple and complex methods".[14] In what follows, we mainly summarise the findings on the state and the law.

In development, the role of the state (should it be an interventionist, managerial, or "small" state) is seen as a pre-eminently political question. In human rights, formally, a politically neutral stance on the role of the state is often taken,[15] although the tripartite typology of state obligations (respect, protect, fulfil) clearly reveals that the state is to respect human rights (which excludes authoritarianism) and is expected to take positive action (which excludes a minimalist, non-interventionist state). For international organisations like UNICEF, the adoption of an HRBA has meant that it moved beyond service delivery to also "shifting great responsibility on to governments",[16] which seems to confirm that human rights require more than a minimalist state. As to the relationship of the state with human rights actors and development actors, a reverse tendency is noticeable; human rights actors have or are perceived to have a mainly adversarial relationship with the state as they seek to expose violations, whereas development actors tend to be seen more as partners of the state.[17] This ties in with a third aspect, how actors define their own role (service delivery, capacity-building, advocacy), and what impact that role definition has, in particular on relationships with the state (cooperation versus confrontation).[18] Later in this article, we shall add some nuance to this binary thinking in terms of confrontation versus cooperation, by making an analytical distinction between political work and confrontation.

The role of law is often entirely ignored in development. Whenever development actors following the adoption of an HRBAD do pay some attention to legal reform and litigation, it

---

[13]BA Andreassen and G Crawford (eds), *Human Rights, Power and Civic Action. Comparative Analyses of Struggles for Rights in Developing Societies* (Routledge, 2013).

[14]P Gready with W Vandenhole "What are we Trying to Change? Theories of Change in Development and Human Rights", in Paul Gready and Wouter Vandenhole (eds), *Human Rights and Development in the New Millennium. Towards a Theory of Change* (Routledge, 2014), 3. For another account of the two, often contrasting, approaches to development, see LT Munro, "The 'Human Rights-Based Approach to Programming': A Contradiction in Terms?", in Sam Hickey and Diana Mitlin (eds), *Rights-Based Approaches to Development. Exploring the Potential and Pitfalls* (Kumarian Press, 2009), 182–93.

[15]LT Munro, "The 'Human Rights-Based Approach to Programming': A Contradiction in Terms?", in Sam Hickey and Diana Mitlin (eds), *Rights-Based Approaches to Development. Exploring the Potential and Pitfalls* (Kumarian Press, 2009), 3–5.

[16]JE Oestreich, *Power and Principle. Human Rights Programming in International Organizations* (Georgetown University Press, Washington, DC, 2007), 43.

[17]P Gready with W Vandenhole "What are we Trying to Change? Theories of Change in Development and Human Rights", in Paul Gready and Wouter Vandenhole (eds), *Human Rights and Development in the New Millennium. Towards a Theory of Change* (Routledge, 2014), 5–6.

[18]P Gready with W Vandenhole "What are we Trying to Change? Theories of Change in Development and Human Rights", in Paul Gready and Wouter Vandenhole (eds), *Human Rights and Development in the New Millennium. Towards a Theory of Change* (Routledge, 2014), 6–7.

represents a major shift in their work.[19] There are two basic positions on the role of law in change: those who argue that the law follows change, and those who believe that law may lead change. In the latter category, there is a strong tendency towards legal instrumentalism and social engineering through law. An inherent risk of approaching the law as a mere *instrument* for social change is the instrumentalisation of law by political power. There is also little empirical evidence that law "works", that is to say that it brings about the intended effects.[20] Using the law in development thus raises questions of instrumentalisation and effectiveness.

Emphasis on the inherent normativity of law, as reflected for example in human rights law, may shield the law to some extent from outright political instrumentalisation, but exposes it to more radical critique on the inherently ideological (i.e. liberal) nature of the law. The liberal nature of the law is reflected in the understanding of empowerment as putting citizens in a position to "make political demands that lead to better service provision and to the sort of situation where citizens can provide services for themselves".[21] Nonetheless, human rights law is generally believed to have transformative potential because of its check on power and its focus on accountability. Likewise, human rights *litigation* has been assigned transformative potential under certain preconditions and in close interaction with policy and legislation.[22]

Another entry point to change is the role of participation and empowerment in bottom-up and localised approaches.[23] Of key importance in these approaches is the way in which human rights are primarily seen as a struggle rather than as pre-conceived legal rules, which makes it clear that human rights are not the privileged nor the exclusive domain of the law. Whereas this does not exclude the use of human rights legal tools and norms, it does introduce a different starting point (local struggles, not international norms), a different prioritisation (processes rather than outcomes) and a different end-goal (change in power relations rather than the implementation of international standards).[24] In turn, these differences cast a light on the fundamentally opposite ways in which external actors can attempt to bring about social change, i.e. by drawing on pre-conceived norms or on local struggles.

---

[19]See e.g. JE Oestreich, *Power and Principle. Human Rights Programming in International Organizations* (Georgetown University Press, Washington, DC, 2007), 54–55, who reports on the paradigm shift for UNICEF in working on legal reform

[20]P Gready with W Vandenhole "What are we Trying to Change? Theories of Change in Development and Human Rights", in Paul Gready and Wouter Vandenhole (eds), *Human Rights and Development in the New Millennium. Towards a Theory of Change* (Routledge, 2014), 7–8.

[21]JE Oestreich, *Power and Principle. Human Rights Programming in International Organizations* (Georgetown University Press, Washington, DC, 2007), 58.

[22]P Gready with W Vandenhole "What are we Trying to Change? Theories of Change in Development and Human Rights", in Paul Gready and Wouter Vandenhole (eds), *Human Rights and Development in the New Millennium. Towards a Theory of Change* (Routledge, 2014), 8–9.

[23]P Gready with W Vandenhole "What are we Trying to Change? Theories of Change in Development and Human Rights", in Paul Gready and Wouter Vandenhole (eds), *Human Rights and Development in the New Millennium. Towards a Theory of Change* (Routledge, 2014), 12–15.

[24]P Gready with W Vandenhole "What are we Trying to Change? Theories of Change in Development and Human Rights", in Paul Gready and Wouter Vandenhole (eds), *Human Rights and Development in the New Millennium. Towards a Theory of Change* (Routledge, 2014), 14.

Distinguishing factors	Human rights approach	Development approach
Legitimising anchor	norm-based	evidence-based
Views on the role of and relationship with the state	• neutral on political system • own role: advocacy • adversarial relationship	• role state is political issue • own role: service delivery • partnership
Views on the role of law	transformative potential thanks to accountability/check on power	• legal instrumentalism – social engineering through law
Views on the role of human rights litigation	potentially effective in interaction with policies/legislation	

Figure 1. Main archetypical differences in human rights and development approaches

A fundamental difference between human rights and development actors and their approach to change is that they use different "legitimizing anchors"[25]: whereas human rights actors tend to use (legal) norms as their legitimising anchor, development actors seek it more in empirical observations. In other words, human rights approaches tend to be norm-based whereas development approaches take an evidence-based approach.[26] Figure 1 summarises these differences.

In social change theories, causal chain theories are arguably under the greatest doubt. This may explain the tension between a result-based approach, as is now central to much development cooperation work on the one hand, and a complex approach to (social) change on the other.[27] No linear cause and effect relationship can be assumed in bringing about change, given the complex nature of change in particular in the field of human rights. There are no really quick fixes, results may be difficult to quantify and it may be even more difficult to claim credit for outcomes.[28] Result-based management (RBM), which seems to assume a direct causal chain between interventions and results, may paradoxically be a spoiler rather than a driver or facilitator of change.[29] A more careful account was put forward in a 2012 report on UNICEF's HRBAD, in which it was argued that HRBADs and RBM are compatible, but that "there are obstacles to their being applied concurrently". The main reason for these obstacles was reported to be that the perceived drive for results in RBM

---

[25]BE Simmons, *Mobilizing for Human Rights. International Law in Domestic Politics* (Cambridge University Press, Cambridge, 2009), 8.

[26]This is not to say that evidence-based approaches are value-free or neutral.

[27]R Eyben, T Kidder, J Rowlands and A Bronstein, "Thinking about Change for Development Practice: a Case Study from Oxfam GB", (2008) 18/2 *Development in Practice*, 201–212, 210.

[28]WG O'Neill, "The Current Status of Human Rights Mainstreaming Review of Selected CCA/UNDAFs and RC Annual Reports" (2003), available at www.undg.org/archive_docs/3070-Human_rights_review_of_selected_CCA_UNDAF_and_RC_reports.doc (accessed on 22 April 2014), 6.

[29]Compare M Darrow and L Arbour, "The Pillar of Glass: Human Rights in the Development Operations of the United Nations" (2009) 103 *AJIL* 446–501, 457.

impeded the application of HRBAD.[30] One such impediment may be that the "emphasis on producing quick results [leads] to advocacy activities being disadvantaged".[31] A more fundamental tension is that the

> human rights tradition finds itself in full-blown contradiction to the classical planning and programming tradition. The human rights-based approach to development denies that any prioritization of rights is possible … But if there can be no hierarchy of rights, can a human rights-based organization choose its strategic priorities? The question became acute as UNICEF professed to be a rights-based organization while at the same time embracing "results-based management", the latest version of the classical planning and programming tradition.[32]

RBM is at the intersection of social and organisational change. It focuses on the social change achieved, but has a strong bearing on how an organisation works. We therefore include the tension between RBM and an HRBAD in the organisational change analysis in the next section.

III. HRBADs and Organisational Change

Logically preceding a solid understanding of the complexity of social change is the need to better understand what it takes for an organisation to introduce an HRBAD with a view to bring about social change successfully in the first place. Both in change theory and organisations theory, it has been emphasised that views on change and on how organisations change are very often based on implicit assumptions. Both sets of theories also point out the complexity of (organisational) change, and the existence of many different and often competing approaches or "schools", with some emphasising structural constraints (i.e. constraints based on durable social structures) and others individual agency. Both dimensions are important and often operate in tandem.[33] Moreover, a distinction is to be made between formal structure and actual day-to-day activities, for the assumption that organisations function according to formal blueprints is not supported by empirical research,[34] hence the emphasis again on the need for much more empirical work. In the case example of UNICEF that follows, we look in particular into internal reflection and planning, and leadership and true believers as explanatory entry points for the (lack of) organisational change accompanying the introduction of an HRBAD. In addition to these drivers of change, we

---

[30]UNICEF, "Global Evaluation of the Application of the Human Rights-Based Approach to UNICEF Programming. Final Report – Volume I" (UNICEF, 2012), available at www.unicef.org/policyanalysis/rights/files/UNICEF_HRBAP_Final_Report_Vol_I_11June_copy-edited_translated.pdf (accessed 16 April 2014), iv and 47–48.

[31]A Tostensen and others, "Supporting Child Rights. Synthesis of Lessons Learned in Four Countries" (2011), available at www.cmi.no/publications/file/3947-supporting-child-rights.pdf (accessed 16 April 2014), 103; compare LT Munro, "The 'Human Rights-Based Approach to Programming': A Contradiction in Terms?", in Sam Hickey and Diana Mitlin (eds), *Rights-Based Approaches to Development. Exploring the Potential and Pitfalls* (Kumarian Press, 2009), 200.

[32]LT Munro, "The 'Human Rights-Based Approach to Programming': A Contradiction in Terms?", in Sam Hickey and Diana Mitlin (eds), *Rights-Based Approaches to Development. Exploring the Potential and Pitfalls* (Kumarian Press, 2009), 198.

[33]For a proposal to rather focus on their interaction, through the concept of structuration, see WR Scott, *Institutions and Organizations. Ideas and Interests* (Sage Publications, 2008), 48 and 76–79.

[34]JW Meyer and B Rowan, "Institutionalized Organisations: Formal Structure as Myth and Ceremony" (1977) 83/2 *Am J of Soc*, 340–363, 341–42.

shall pay attention to the spoilers of change, such as lack of capacity or staff turnover, and to the tension between HRBAD and RBM. Attempts at introducing HRBAD by the UN at the country level by states and by non-governmental organisations seem to show similar trends at first sight, though much more research is needed before firm conclusions can be reached.

III.1 UNICEF: Between adaptation and transformation

UNICEF's experience with HRBAD is considered as one of the more successful examples, and has been well documented over a longer period of time. UNICEF has evolved from a technical organisation with a focus on service provision to one that uses children's rights as codified in the Convention on the Rights of the Child (CRC) in all its programming. A congruence of external and internal forces, including NGO and executive board pressure, changed UNICEF's policy towards the CRC.[35] True believers and the executive director of the organisation took it further, and the "CRC became a key strategic priority".[36] Oestreich has concluded that a group of "true believers" and even more strong leadership are the variables with the highest explanatory power.[37] Central to the change in attitude towards the CRC was the perception that human rights language would not place UNICEF in "confrontational, political situations vis-à-vis states parties", but rather add legitimacy to UNICEF's work.[38] This reflects a more nuanced take on the more general tension in role definition in human rights versus development work that we flagged in the previous section: the former is understood by traditional development organisations to be political and confrontational, whereas the latter is claimed to be neutral and pragmatic.

> Staff remain wary of promoting new policies, or changing existing ones, in ways that appear to violate the sovereignty of states or that risk so angering states that they will curtail cooperation with UNICEF. There remains a sense of there being a fine line between those CRC aspects that will actually help UNICEF pursue its goals and those that will ultimately undermine its ability to work cooperatively with states.[39]

> The organization, in fact, has shown considerable latitude in choosing which elements of the CRC it wishes to pursue and which it deems to fall outside its mandate. They all receive rhetorical support, but only those deemed to be both central to UNICEF and politically viable are actually incorporated into program planning.[40]

---

[35]JE Oestreich, *Power and Principle. Human Rights Programming in International Organizations* (Georgetown University Press, Washington, DC, 2007), 31–32.

[36]JE Oestreich, *Power and Principle. Human Rights Programming in International Organizations* (Georgetown University Press, Washington, DC, 2007), 33.

[37]JE Oestreich, *Power and Principle. Human Rights Programming in International Organizations* (Georgetown University Press, Washington, DC, 2007), 6–10.

[38]JE Oestreich, *Power and Principle. Human Rights Programming in International Organizations* (Georgetown University Press, Washington, DC, 2007), 33.

[39]JE Oestreich, *Power and Principle. Human Rights Programming in International Organizations* (Georgetown University Press, Washington, DC, 2007), 42.

[40]JE Oestreich, *Power and Principle. Human Rights Programming in International Organizations* (Georgetown University Press, Washington, DC, 2007), 43.

At the same time, Oestrich points out that UNICEF has not just added children's rights as an additional goal to its operational agenda (which Oestrich, with reference to Haas, labels adaptation), it has sought transformation of the organisation.[41] The results have been mixed, with more progress in relatively new programming areas that were introduced simultaneously with or because of the HRBA. In his analysis, a key to success "is the need for dedication among the top management to creating such change".[42] Other drivers of change have been "the intellectual development of a rights-based paradigm" (which comes close to internal reflection and planning) prior to organisational change, in particular by clarifying what the added value of HRBAD was (what Oestrich calls the "argument from effectiveness"),[43] true believers and the hiring of staff with legal or similar backgrounds to build capacity in rights issues.[44] Obstacles to organisational change have been the limited ambitions of the leadership (who saw HRBAD mainly as a rhetorical device); scepticism among staff ("the problem of convincing staff with technical backgrounds and extensive field experience")[45] and lack of consensus within the organisation;[46] the lack of a "clear organizational line of authority";[47] and the lack of capacity and bureaucratic inertia.[48] For the 1990–1997 period, this meant that there was a change mainly in rhetoric, not in operational practice, and that organisational change primarily took place in field offices, to the extent that true believers took up the challenge.[49] In the 1997–2005 period,

---

[41]JE Oestreich, *Power and Principle. Human Rights Programming in International Organizations* (Georgetown University Press, Washington, DC, 2007), 44. There seem to be similarities between the notion of adaptation and the language of layers and organisational archaeologies used by Gready in his analysis of ActionAid's introduction of HRBA, see below

[42]JE Oestreich, *Power and Principle. Human Rights Programming in International Organizations* (Georgetown University Press, Washington, DC, 2007), 45.

[43]JE Oestreich, *Power and Principle. Human Rights Programming in International Organizations* (Georgetown University Press, Washington, DC, 2007), 47.

[44]JE Oestreich, *Power and Principle. Human Rights Programming in International Organizations* (Georgetown University Press, Washington, DC, 2007), 50.

[45]E Oestreich, *Power and Principle. Human Rights Programming in International Organizations* (Georgetown University Press, Washington, DC, 2007), 46, compare 48.

[46]LT Munro, "The 'Human Rights-Based Approach to Programming': A Contradiction in Terms?", in Sam Hickey and Diana Mitlin (eds), *Rights-Based Approaches to Development. Exploring the Potential and Pitfalls* (Kumarian Press, 2009), 200.

[47]JE Oestreich, *Power and Principle. Human Rights Programming in International Organizations* (Georgetown University Press, Washington, DC, 2007), 48; compare LT Munro, "The 'Human Rights-Based Approach to Programming': A Contradiction in Terms?", in Sam Hickey and Diana Mitlin (eds), *Rights-Based Approaches to Development. Exploring the Potential and Pitfalls* (Kumarian Press, 2009), 200, who argues that the organisational structure, i.e. the fact that the Medium-Term Strategic Plan was developed at headquarters, but that the country offices were supervised by the Regional Directors, was one of the reasons why the MTSP did not "stick in any meaningful way"

[48]UNICEF, "Global Evaluation of the Application of the Human Rights-Based Approach to UNICEF Programming. Final Report – Volume I" (UNICEF, 2012), available at www.unicef.org/policyanalysis/ rights/files/UNICEF_HRBAP_Final_Report_Vol_I_11June_copy-edited_translated.pdf (accessed 16 April 2014), 50.

[49]UNICEF, "Global Evaluation of the Application of the Human Rights-Based Approach to UNICEF Programming. Final Report – Volume I" (UNICEF, 2012), available at www.unicef.org/policyanalysis/ rights/files/UNICEF_HRBAP_Final_Report_Vol_I_11June_copy-edited_translated.pdf (accessed 16 April 2014), 48.

major organisational change took place towards programmatic integration at headquarters in New York through the introduction of HRBA responsibility in the programme division, where policy development is mainly located.[50] In the same period, rights advisers were created in the regional offices, with a mandate covering all UNICEF activities (mainstreaming).[51] This lead to changes in the programmatic activities of field offices, i.e. changes in the way the organisation spoke with host governments, as well as changes in new and traditional programming areas.[52] The technical areas seemed to be the hardest case for organisational change. This may be explained by the fact that the technical work has to be placed "within the context of the larger political and social themes" such as empowerment, participation and equality, which require political change.[53] However, within UNICEF, HRBA was not perceived "as requiring a major overhaul in what UNICEF [was] doing in the more traditional, technical work sectors",[54] which may show that the introduction of HRBA has not really challenged the organisation to genuinely transform itself. Munro, who has argued that HRBA reaches its limits and potential when it comes to "the selection of priorities and the allocation of scarce resources between competing ends"[55] may even be read as welcoming that limited transformative impact on UNICEF, at least as far as the technical developmental work as understood by development people is concerned. This raises the question whether HRBAD requires an organisation to transform, even when that is possible, or whether adaptation is the mode of organisational change to be pursued.

The 2007–2011 period has been assessed in the *Global Evaluation of the Application of the Human Rights-Based Approach to UNICEF Programming* of March 2012. This external evaluation zoomed in on the country level, examining the situation in 38 Country Offices.

---

[50]UNICEF, "Global Evaluation of the Application of the Human Rights-Based Approach to UNICEF Programming. Final Report – Volume I" (UNICEF, 2012), available at www.unicef.org/policyanalysis/rights/files/UNICEF_HRBAP_Final_Report_Vol_I_11June_copy-edited_translated.pdf (accessed 16 April 2014), 49.

[51]UNICEF, "Global Evaluation of the Application of the Human Rights-Based Approach to UNICEF Programming. Final Report – Volume I" (UNICEF, 2012), available at www.unicef.org/policyanalysis/rights/files/UNICEF_HRBAP_Final_Report_Vol_I_11June_copy-edited_translated.pdf (accessed 16 April 2014), 49.

[52]UNICEF, "Global Evaluation of the Application of the Human Rights-Based Approach to UNICEF Programming. Final Report – Volume I" (UNICEF, 2012), available at www.unicef.org/policyanalysis/rights/files/UNICEF_HRBAP_Final_Report_Vol_I_11June_copy-edited_translated.pdf (accessed 16 April 2014), 50 *et seq.* For a more sceptical account, LT Munro, "The 'Human Rights-Based Approach to Programming': A Contradiction in Terms?", in Sam Hickey and Diana Mitlin (eds), *Rights-Based Approaches to Development. Exploring the Potential and Pitfalls* (Kumarian Press, 2009), 197–200.

[53]UNICEF, "Global Evaluation of the Application of the Human Rights-Based Approach to UNICEF Programming. Final Report – Volume I" (UNICEF, 2012), available at www.unicef.org/policyanalysis/rights/files/UNICEF_HRBAP_Final_Report_Vol_I_11June_copy-edited_translated.pdf (accessed 16 April 2014), 58–59.

[54]UNICEF, "Global Evaluation of the Application of the Human Rights-Based Approach to UNICEF Programming. Final Report – Volume I" (UNICEF, 2012), available at www.unicef.org/policyanalysis/rights/files/UNICEF_HRBAP_Final_Report_Vol_I_11June_copy-edited_translated.pdf (accessed 16 April 2014), 60.

[55]LT Munro, "The 'Human Rights-Based Approach to Programming': A Contradiction in Terms?", in Sam Hickey and Diana Mitlin (eds), *Rights-Based Approaches to Development. Exploring the Potential and Pitfalls* (Kumarian Press, 2009), 201.

Spoilers of organisational change were identified: implementation staff's overall limited understanding of HRBAD;[56] conceptual confusion between the focus on equity[57] and HRBAD;[58] the location of the focal point for gender and human rights within the Division for Policy and Practice (rather than in the Programme Division), which created some distance between policy and programming; insufficient practical guidance on the approach for sector-specific application; human resources-management practices that neither emphasised nor supported competency in HRBAD; minimal and informal accountability for HRBAD; lack of attention paid to effective implementation of HRBAD in staff performance reviews; lack of support from management; and lack of systematic reporting on HRBAD implementation.[59]

As to the degree of application of human rights principles, the findings were mixed, with good results on normativity, mixed application with regard to participation and accountability, and satisfactory to weak on non-discrimination and transparency. Although the degree of application of human rights principles is not entirely in the hands of the organisation, it is to a large extent determined by factors internal to the organisation.[60] In a more temporal perspective, i.e. through the lens of the programming cycle stages, HRBAD application was found to be strongest in the preparation phase and weakest in the monitoring and evaluation phase.[61] The strong performance on normativity and weaker on other human rights principles may be open to different interpretations. One is to consider UNICEF successful in integrating human rights language but, in fact, it mainly just pays lip service to it. Of course, integrating explicit language on human rights may be the easiest part of introducing an HRBAD.

---

[56]UNICEF, "Global Evaluation of the Application of the Human Rights-Based Approach to UNICEF Programming. Final Report – Volume I" (UNICEF, 2012), available at www.unicef.org/policyanalysis/rights/files/UNICEF_HRBAP_Final_Report_Vol_I_11June_copy-edited_translated.pdf (accessed 16 April 2014), 39 *et seq.*

[57]For a succinct introduction to the notion of equity in UNICEF's work, see UNICEF, "Global Evaluation of the Application of the Human Rights-Based Approach to UNICEF Programming. Final Report – Volume I" (UNICEF, 2012), available at www.unicef.org/policyanalysis/rights/files/UNICEF_HRBAP_Final_Report_Vol_I_11June_copy-edited_translated.pdf (accessed 16 April 2014), 4–5.

[58]UNICEF, "Global Evaluation of the Application of the Human Rights-Based Approach to UNICEF Programming. Final Report – Volume I" (UNICEF, 2012), available at www.unicef.org/policyanalysis/rights/files/UNICEF_HRBAP_Final_Report_Vol_I_11June_copy-edited_translated.pdf (accessed 16 April 2014), 46–47.

[59]UNICEF, "Global Evaluation of the Application of the Human Rights-Based Approach to UNICEF Programming. Final Report – Volume I" (UNICEF, 2012), available at www.unicef.org/policyanalysis/rights/files/UNICEF_HRBAP_Final_Report_Vol_I_11June_copy-edited_translated.pdf (accessed 16 April 2014), 110–36.

[60]UNICEF, "Global Evaluation of the Application of the Human Rights-Based Approach to UNICEF Programming. Final Report – Volume I" (UNICEF, 2012), available at www.unicef.org/policyanalysis/rights/files/UNICEF_HRBAP_Final_Report_Vol_I_11June_copy-edited_translated.pdf (accessed 16 April 2014), 60–72.

[61]UNICEF, "Global Evaluation of the Application of the Human Rights-Based Approach to UNICEF Programming. Final Report – Volume I" (UNICEF, 2012), available at www.unicef.org/policyanalysis/rights/files/UNICEF_HRBAP_Final_Report_Vol_I_11June_copy-edited_translated.pdf (accessed 16 April 2014), 72–81.

In sum, whereas the introduction of HRBAD by UNICEF may have led to adaptation, it has not transformed the organisation. Key drivers of change have been leadership and true believers in combination with internal reflection. Obstacles and spoilers of change have been identified in considerable detail. Different disciplinary backgrounds and diverging views on role definition, competing agendas, lack of capacity and learning processes, and deficiencies in the accountability and incentive structure stand out. The tension between RBM and an HRBAD became particularly acute in the discussion on whether or not prioritisation of certain rights is permissible, but also in the short-term focus of RBM versus the long-term project of realising human rights.[62]

III.2 Comparative perspectives

In what follows, we briefly explore whether some of the trends that we have identified with UNICEF can also be traced with other actors that have introduced HRBADs. Again drawing on available empirical work, we shall look at the United Nations Development Group (UNDG), Norwegian and Swedish development cooperation and ActionAid. It goes without saying that drawing parallels between actors that are so different in law and practice should be done with utmost care. One may wonder, for example, whether it is not much easier for an international organisation like UNICEF to fully embrace the normativity of an HRBAD by explicitly incorporating the CRC in its work, given the potential for UNICEF to really identify itself with children's rights. For international organisations like the United Nations Development Programme or for states or non-governmental organisations, it may be less obvious to self-identify with a particular treaty or human rights of a particular group. This may in turn make organisational buy-in more challenging.

III.3 UNDG at the country level

Vandenhole has studied organisational change following the introduction of HRBADs within UNDG at the country level. Since 1997, UNDG has been the vehicle for coordination and alignment of UN development activities.[63] Empirical evaluations of HRBADs at the level of United Nations Country Teams (UNCTs), on which this assessment draws, again tend to emphasise actor-centred criteria rather than structures in explaining (lack of) organisational change.

UNCTs have several instruments at their disposal. The Common Country Assessment (CCA) is the main analytical tool, though no longer mandatory. The United Nations Development Assistance Framework (UNDAF) is a programming tool, i.e. the UN common response to a country's situation and priorities. For present purposes, the question is whether and how the integration of an HRBAD in CCA/UNDAF has led to organisational change. Four

---

[62]LT Munro, "The 'Human Rights-Based Approach to Programming': A Contradiction in Terms?", in Sam Hickey and Diana Mitlin (eds), *Rights-Based Approaches to Development. Exploring the Potential and Pitfalls* (Kumarian Press, 2009), 198–200.

[63]UNDG unites the 32 UN funds, programmes, offices and specialised agencies that play a role in development, such as the United Nations Development Programme (UNDP), UNICEF, the United Nations Educational, Scientific and Cultural Organization (UNESCO), the Food and Agriculture Organisation (FAO), the World Health Organization (WHO), the Office of the High Commissioner for Human Rights (OHCHR) and many others.

main issues have been identified as drivers or spoilers of organisational change within UNCTs: leadership; capacity; accountability and role definition.[64] Leadership and clear direction by the Resident Coordinator have been identified as the single most important factor.[65] A second element is mutual accountability among UNCT members (who represent one of the UN programmes, funds or agencies) regarding their responsibilities for applying a HRBA.[66] Capacity-building within the UNCT has equally been flagged as an important factor of failure or success.[67] Capacity-building requires the involvement of specialised human rights staff,[68] as well as concrete methodologies of participation and monitoring, and information packages for use in everyday work.[69] Capacity extends beyond a basic understanding of HRBA, to include "the advocacy and negotiating skills to raise "unpleasant news" in a constructive way that leads to change, and does

---

[64]In addition, there is disagreement whether UNCTs have managed to understand and apply an HRBA. While O'Neill believes that "core human rights concepts have percolated into the CCA/UNDAF process" (WG O'Neill, "The Current Status of Human Rights Mainstreaming Review of Selected CCA/UNDAFs and RC Annual Reports" (2003), available at www.undg.org/archive_docs/3070-Human_rights_review_of_selected_CCA_UNDAF_and_RC_reports.doc (accessed on 22 April 2014), 1), Haugen is more in doubt (HM Haugen, "UN Development Framework and Human Rights: Lip Service or Improved Accountability" (2014) *Forum for Development Studies*, available at http://dx.doi.org/10.1080/08039410.2014.901244 (accessed 23 April 2014).

[65]"Third Interagency Meeting on Implementing a Human Rights-Based Approach 1–3 October 2008, Tarrytown, New York, Overview of a Human Rights Based Approach in Selected 2007/2008 Common Country Assessment/UN Development Assistance Frameworks", available at www.undg.org/docs/9405/HRBA_in_CCA-UNDAF-26Sept[1].doc, 22 April 2014, 6; "Report Second Interagency Workshop on Implementing a Human Rights-based Approach in the Context of UN Reform, Stamford, USA, 5–7 May, 2003", www.undg.org/archive_docs/2568-2nd_Workshop_on_Human_Rights__Final_Report_-_Main_report.doc (accessed 22 April 2014), 10; WG O'Neill, "The Current Status of Human Rights Mainstreaming Review of Selected CCA/UNDAFs and RC Annual Reports" (2003), available at www.undg.org/archive_docs/3070-Human_rights_review_of_selected_CCA_UNDAF_and_RC_reports.doc (accessed on 22 April 2014), 5; "Report of the UN Inter-Agency Workshop on Implementing a Human Rights-based Approach in the Context of UN Reform, January 24-26, 2001, Princeton", 6.

[66]"Report Second Interagency Workshop on Implementing a Human Rights-based Approach in the Context of UN Reform, Stamford, USA, 5–7 May, 2003", www.undg.org/archive_docs/2568-2nd_Workshop_on_Human_Rights__Final_Report_-_Main_report.doc (accessed 22 April 2014), 2 and 9–10.

[67]"Report Second Interagency Workshop on Implementing a Human Rights-based Approach in the Context of UN Reform, Stamford, USA, 5–7 May, 2003", www.undg.org/archive_docs/2568-2nd_Workshop_on_Human_Rights_Final_Report_-_Main_report.doc (accessed 22 April 2014), 11; "Report of the UN Inter-Agency Workshop on Implementing a Human Rights-based Approach in the Context of UN Reform, 24–26 January 2001, Princeton" 6.

[68]"Third Interagency Meeting on Implementing a Human Rights-Based Approach 1–3 October 2008, Tarrytown, New York, Overview of a Human Rights Based Approach in Selected 2007/2008 Common Country Assessment/UN Development Assistance Frameworks", available at www.undg.org/docs/9405/HRBA_in_CCA-UNDAF-26Sept[1].doc, 22 April 2014, 6–8; HM Haugen, "UN Development Framework and Human Rights: Lip Service or Improved Accountability" (2014) *Forum for Development Studies*, available at http://dx.doi.org/10.1080/08039410.2014.901244 (accessed 23 April 2014), 20.

[69]"Third Interagency Meeting on Implementing a Human Rights-Based Approach 1–3 October 2008, Tarrytown, New York, Overview of a Human Rights Based Approach in Selected 2007/2008 Common Country Assessment/UN Development Assistance Frameworks", available at www.undg.org/docs/9405/HRBA_in_CCA-UNDAF-26Sept[1].doc, 22 April 2014, 8.

not cut off dialogue".[70] Dialogue (i.e. persuasion or socialisation), rather than naming and shaming (confrontation), takes centre-stage in the role definition. For example, the Resident Coordinator is understood to have no role to play in reporting and monitoring human rights violations.[71] This role definition is in line with the traditional division of labour between human rights organisations and development organisations, whereby the former are said to have a more adversarial role with governments, and the latter usually work in partnership with governments. Whether this is a driver or a spoiler of changes is a matter of debate. Some have argued that for HRBAD to be successful, UNCTs need to be willing to assume a more confrontational role.[72] Others suggest that there is a natural division of labour between the human rights bodies of the UN, including the OHCHR, who have an advocacy role, and the UNCT as a problem-solver.[73]

At the UN agency level, lack of support and high staff turnover have been identified as two major obstacles for change.[74] The spoilers within the UN system as a whole relate more to internal and institutional elements, such as the short time-frame used and the lack of ability to support risk-taking.[75]

All in all, the degree of organisational change brought about by the introduction of HRBAD into UN development analysis and programming within UNCTs has remained limited. Role definition is a key explanatory factor. The role definition of UNDGs and RCs has been very much in line with the development approach, i.e. partnership with governments, which in turn has reinforced rather than challenged the disconnect of the UN development players with the work of the UN human rights actors, as exemplified in the promotion-protection dichotomy at the organisational level. Key to challenging that

---

[70]WG O'Neill, "The Current Status of Human Rights Mainstreaming Review of Selected CCA/ UNDAFs and RC Annual Reports" (2003), available at www.undg.org/archive_docs/3070-Human_rights_review_of_selected_CCA_UNDAF_and_RC_reports.doc (accessed on 22 April 2014), 7.

[71]UNDP, *Human Rights for Development news brief*, vol. 1, available at www.undp.org/content/undp/en/home/libraryp age/democratic-governance/human_rights.html, 2009, 11 (accessed on 15 September 2014).

[72]WG O'Neill, "The Current Status of Human Rights Mainstreaming Review of Selected CCA/ UNDAFs and RC Annual Reports" (2003), available at www.undg.org/archive_docs/3070-Human_rights_review_of_selected_CCA_UNDAF_and_RC_reports.doc (accessed on 22 April 2014), 15.

[73]WG O'Neill, "The Current Status of Human Rights Mainstreaming Review of Selected CCA/ UNDAFs and RC Annual Reports" (2003), available at www.undg.org/archive_docs/3070-Human_rights_review_of_selected_CCA_UNDAF_and_RC_reports.doc (accessed on 22 April 2014), 24; for a critique, see M Darrow and L Arbour, "The Pillar of Glass: Human Rights in the Development Operations of the United Nations" (2009) 103 *AJIL* 446–501, 447–50.

[74]"Third Interagency Meeting on Implementing a Human Rights-Based Approach 1–3 October 2008, Tarrytown, New York, Overview of a Human Rights Based Approach in Selected 2007/2008 Common Country Assessment/UN Development Assistance Frameworks", available at www.undg.org/docs/9405/HRBA_in_CCA-UNDAF-26Sept[1].doc, 22 April 2014, 8; "Report Second Interagency Workshop on Implementing a Human Rights-based Approach in the Context of UN Reform, Stamford, USA, 5–7 May, 2003", www.undg.org/archive_docs/2568-2nd_Workshop_on_Human_Rights__Final_Report_-_Main_report.doc (accessed 22 April 2014), 9; WG O'Neill, "The Current Status of Human Rights Mainstreaming Review of Selected CCA/UNDAFs and RC Annual Reports" (2003), available at www.undg.org/archive_docs/3070-Human_rights_review_of_selected_CCA_UNDAF_and_RC_reports.doc (accessed on 22 April 2014), 5.

[75]"Report Second Interagency Workshop on Implementing a Human Rights-based Approach in the Context of UN Reform, Stamford, USA, 5–7 May, 2003", www.undg.org/archive_docs/2568-2nd_Workshop_on_Human_Rights__Final_Report_-_Main_report.doc (accessed 22 April 2014), 10.

promotion-protection dichotomy is the realisation that operational theories of change in the human rights field do not exclusively focus on naming and shaming; some place processes of persuasion or socialisation. Moreover, human rights treaty bodies typically do not adopt a confrontational approach in their monitoring of state parties' performance, but engage in a constructive dialogue.[76] The role definition reflects the way Resident Coordinators perceive of the relationship with the state, i.e. a partnership.

III.4 Donor states: Sweden and Norway

In 2011, a report was published that evaluates SIDA's[77] and NORAD's[78] aid policies in support of children's rights.[79] Both development cooperation agencies have longstanding experience with children's rights-based approaches in their development cooperation. SIDA has opted for a combination of mainstreaming and child-targeted interventions; NORAD has privileged child-targeted interventions.

Whereas the report focuses mainly on outputs and outcomes, it also contains some interesting conclusions on organisational change required for the successful introduction and implementation of an HRBA. What is peculiar in this setting is that the specificity of a *children's* HRBA was taken into account by incorporating the four general principles of the Convention on the Rights of the Child (non-discrimination; best interests of the child; right to life, survival and development; and the right of the child to be heard) into the assessment.

The report flags the organisational challenges posed by the mainstreaming of children's rights as part of an HRBAD:

> Mainstreaming is a very ambitious approach indeed. Its underlying rationale is that certain policy issues are of such paramount importance that they need to inform all undertakings. In principle, mainstreaming requires the entire organisation to be capable of implementing it, e.g. the requisite knowledge and practical skills to infuse every intervention with a child rights perspective. At that, the endeavour needs to be continuous to be effective, not a one-off exercise.[80]

In line with other findings, here, too, considerable emphasis is put on capacity-building within the organisation, on an on-going basis, as an important driver of change. Another element mentioned is the presence of true believers ("interest and commitment of individual staff members").[81] On the other hand, the lack of capacity and an overload of policies and

---

[76]W Vandenhole, "Overcoming the Protection Promotion Dichotomy. Human Rights Based Approaches to Development and Organisational Change within the UN at Country Level" in Paul Gready and Wouter Vandenhole (eds), *Human Rights and Development in the New Millennium. Towards a Theory of Change* (Routledge, 2014), 109–30.

[77]Swedish International Development Cooperation Agency.

[78]Norwegian Agency for Development Cooperation.

[79]A Tostensen, H Stokke, S Trygged and K Halvorsen, "Supporting Child Rights. Synthesis of Lessons Learned in Four Countries" (2011), available at www.cmi.no/publications/file/3947-supporting-child-rights.pdf (accessed 16 April 2014).

[80]A Tostensen, H Stokke, S Trygged and K Halvorsen, "Supporting Child Rights. Synthesis of Lessons Learned in Four Countries" (2011), available at www.cmi.no/publications/file/3947-supporting-child-rights.pdf (accessed 16 April 2014), 96.

[81]A Tostensen, H Stokke, S Trygged and K Halvorsen, "Supporting Child Rights. Synthesis of Lessons Learned in Four Countries" (2011), available at www.cmi.no/publications/file/3947-supporting-child-rights.pdf (accessed 16 April 2014), 96.

guidelines (referred to as a "crowded" policy agenda), the absence of clarity about goals and systems for follow-up and learning (including policy compliance procedures) as well as frequent staff turnover are identified as spoilers of organisational change. A gap between the headquarters and the embassies as part of the implementation machinery was also pinpointed.[82]

Interestingly, the recommendations in the report draw on both the development and the human rights approach: they are based on empirical evidence gathered through four country studies, but also on "the normative imperatives of the Convention".[83] On the latter point, it is observed that, in particular, the participation of children needs to be better thought through and operationalised.[84] In other words, the recommendations draw on the two legitimising anchors that were earlier identified: empirical evidence and human rights norms. The tension between results-based management and an HRBAD with an emphasis on advocacy was found also in SIDA's and NORAD's sponsored work on the ground.[85]

A fairly comprehensive study of HRBADs as adopted by donors flags broadly similar drivers and spoilers of organisational change to those we have identified in this and the previous section.[86]

III.5 Non-governmental organisations: ActionAid

A third actor that has introduced HRBADs are non-governmental organisations (NGOs). The introduction of an HRBAD by ActionAid has been well studied, and is therefore taken here by way of example.[87]

In their 2009 account, Chapman in collaboration with V Miller, A Campolina Soares and J Samuel focus mainly on social change and questions of power, but they also develop some ideas on organisational change. They argue that

> development NGOs must shift, in their primary role, from being implementers and drivers of development to being allies with people's organizations and social movements in a collective struggle for change. Such a shift means a much more complex mix of roles involving sharing and

---

[82] A Tostensen, H Stokke, S Trygged and K Halvorsen, "Supporting Child Rights. Synthesis of Lessons Learned in Four Countries" (2011), available at www.cmi.no/publications/file/3947-supporting-child-rights.pdf (accessed 16 April 2014), 96.

[83] A Tostensen, H Stokke, S Trygged and K Halvorsen, "Supporting Child Rights. Synthesis of Lessons Learned in Four Countries" (2011), available at www.cmi.no/publications/file/3947-supporting-child-rights.pdf (accessed 16 April 2014), 100.

[84] A Tostensen, H Stokke, S Trygged and K Halvorsen, "Supporting Child Rights. Synthesis of Lessons Learned in Four Countries" (2011), available at www.cmi.no/publications/file/3947-supporting-child-rights.pdf (accessed 16 April 2014), 92 and 101.

[85] A Tostensen, H Stokke, S Trygged and K Halvorsen, "Supporting Child Rights. Synthesis of Lessons Learned in Four Countries" (2011), available at www.cmi.no/publications/file/3947-supporting-child-rights.pdf (accessed 16 April 2014), 103.

[86] D D'Hollander, A Marx and J Wouters, "Integrating Human Rights in Development Policy: Mapping Donor Strategies and Practices", Working Paper 108, June 2013, available at papers.ssrn.com/sol3/papers.cfm?abstract_id=2286204 (accessed 18 April 2014), 48–49.

[87] Some empirical work has also been undertaken with regard to Plan's HRBAD in the field, see K Arts, "Countering Violence against Children in the Philippines: Positive RBA Practice Examples from Plan", in Paul Gready and Wouter Vandenhole (eds), *Human Rights and Development in the New Millennium. Towards a Theory of Change* (Routledge, 2014) 149–76.

negotiating power in new ways, challenging assumptions, and taking clear, often risky, political stands in favor of people marginalized by poverty and the privilege of others.[88]

As to the adoption of an HRBAD by ActionAid, it has been pointed out that changes within ActionAid that facilitated the implementation of the approach were *inter alia* the shift to southern leadership "and a related change in governance structures as the organisation shifted from being a northern NGO to a more international one".[89] Other drivers of organisational change that were identified are senior management, staff skills to critically think and reflect, also about power and change, and to engage in cross-disciplinarity.[90] As spoilers of organisational change were *inter alia* mentioned: the fact that the organisation was large and diffuse, that there was no coherent change strategy, and that there were insufficient resources and support for staff.[91]

Gready puts particular emphasis on the "organisational archaeologies and alignments" that characterise ActionAid: the organisation moved from a charity, through a participatory to a rights-based approach. These approaches did not replace each other; rather, they are layers that mutually influence each other.[92] As the transition to a new approach remains incomplete, two challenges for organisational alignment arise: part of the work and of the staff commitment still lies with service delivery and community development work, and HRBAD has been only operationalised fully for local programming, not, for example, for fundraising.[93] Whereas it may be tempting to label these challenges of misalignment "spoilers of change", that could be deceptive, as they may in fact be necessary to trigger organisational change.[94] The analysis in terms of a cycle of misalignment and realignment brings in a dynamic perspective on organisational change; it shows how organisational change is an on-going, dynamic process, not a one-off event. It also brings to the fore the question of what

---

[88] J Chapman, in collaboration with V Miller, A Campolina Soares and J Samuel, "Rights-Based Development: The Challenge of Change and Power for Development NGOs", in Sam Hickey and Diana Mitlin (eds), *Rights-Based Approaches to Development. Exploring the Potential and Pitfalls* (Kumarian Press, 2009), 167.

[89] J Chapman, in collaboration with V Miller, A Campolina Soares and J Samuel, "Rights-Based Development: The Challenge of Change and Power for Development NGOs", in Sam Hickey and Diana Mitlin (eds), *Rights-Based Approaches to Development. Exploring the Potential and Pitfalls* (Kumarian Press, 2009), 169 and 174.

[90] J Chapman in collaboration with V Miller, A Campolina Soares and J Samuel, "Rights-Based Development: The Challenge of Change and Power for Development NGOs", in Sam Hickey and Diana Mitlin (eds), *Rights-Based Approaches to Development. Exploring the Potential and Pitfalls* (Kumarian Press, 2009), 170 and 175.

[91] J Chapman in collaboration with V Miller, A Campolina Soares and J Samuel, "Rights-Based Development: The Challenge of Change and Power for Development NGOs", in Sam Hickey and Diana Mitlin (eds), *Rights-Based Approaches to Development. Exploring the Potential and Pitfalls* (Kumarian Press, 2009), 177.

[92] P Gready, "ActionAid's Human Rights-Based Approach and its Impact on Organisational and Operational Change", in Paul Gready and Wouter Vandenhole (eds), *Human Rights and Development in the New Millennium. Towards a Theory of Change* (2014, Routledge), 177, 180.

[93] P Gready, "ActionAid's Human Rights-Based Approach and its Impact on Organisational and Operational Change", in Paul Gready and Wouter Vandenhole (eds), *Human Rights and Development in the New Millennium. Towards a Theory of Change* (2014, Routledge), 181.

[94] P Gready, "ActionAid's Human Rights-Based Approach and its Impact on Organisational and Operational Change", in Paul Gready and Wouter Vandenhole (eds), *Human Rights and Development in the New Millennium. Towards a Theory of Change* (2014, Routledge), 181.

degree of organisational change is needed: is organisational adaptation sufficient or even desirable or do we need transformation? Other elements of organisational change that were flagged earlier, i.e. the need to provide concrete guidance for programming and for dealing with dilemmas, and for capacity-building of staff, tend to be confirmed.[95] A distinctive element is the identification of the need for an overarching "identity narrative",[96] though UNICEF's ambiguity whether to use children's rights or equity discourse instead as its legitimising anchor may reflect a similar challenge.

As to role definition, it is argued that HRBADs, given their inherently political nature, demand the taking of sides, and so conflicts may have to be dealt with within alliances and with external actors.[97] This is not to say that service delivery and HRBAD are on two different planets; for Chapman, it is more a matter of "integrating service delivery and rights-based aspects of … programs".[98] Nevertheless, Gready, in his analysis, confirms ActionAid's "more confrontational relationship with the state".[99]

In sum, key to organisational change within ActionAid have been the cycles of internal reflection and planning, in response to misalignment challenges. Other elements that impact on organisational change, such as leadership, were channelled through these cycles.[100] ActionAid's relationship with the state seems to have become more confrontational, possibly commensurate with the degree to which the organisation has started to push for fundamental social change. The tension between RBM and HRBAD is less evident.

IV. Starting Points for Reflection

The ambition of this article was not to present a grand theory of change about HRBADs, nor to offer an encyclopaedic mapping of studies on change in HRBADs, nor even to report on own empirical research. Instead, it seeks to trigger more explicit acknowledgement of the often implicit assumptions of change in HRBADs. We have mainly focused on organisational change, for two reasons in particular. First, the implementation of an

---

[95]P Gready, "ActionAid's Human Rights-Based Approach and its Impact on Organisational and Operational Change", in Paul Gready and Wouter Vandenhole (eds), *Human Rights and Development in the New Millennium. Towards a Theory of Change* (2014, Routledge), 183–86 and 188.

[96]P Gready, "ActionAid's Human Rights-Based Approach and its Impact on Organisational and Operational Change", in Paul Gready and Wouter Vandenhole (eds), *Human Rights and Development in the New Millennium. Towards a Theory of Change* (2014, Routledge), 182 and 187, citing L David Brown and others, "ActionAid International Taking Stock Review 3. Synthesis Report" (2010) www.actionaid.org/sites/files/actionaid/tsr3_synthesis_report_final.pdf (accessed 23 April 2014).

[97]J Chapman in collaboration with V Miller, A Campolina Soares and J Samuel, "Rights-Based Development: The Challenge of Change and Power for Development NGOs", in Sam Hickey and Diana Mitlin (eds), *Rights-Based Approaches to Development. Exploring the Potential and Pitfalls* (Kumarian Press, 2009), 165, 179.

[98]J Chapman in collaboration with V Miller, A Campolina Soares and J Samuel, "Rights-Based Development: The Challenge of Change and Power for Development NGOs", in Sam Hickey and Diana Mitlin (eds), *Rights-Based Approaches to Development. Exploring the Potential and Pitfalls* (Kumarian Press, 2009), 181.

[99]P Gready, "ActionAid's Human Rights-Based Approach and its Impact on Organisational and Operational Change", in Paul Gready and Wouter Vandenhole (eds), *Human Rights and Development in the New Millennium. Towards a Theory of Change* (2014, Routledge), 177, 179.

[100]P Gready, "ActionAid's Human Rights-Based Approach and its Impact on Organisational and Operational Change", in Paul Gready and Wouter Vandenhole (eds), *Human Rights and Development in the New Millennium. Towards a Theory of Change* (2014, Routledge), 189.

HRBAD has often been only piecemeal, due to an underestimation of the implications for an organisation to properly introduce an HRBAD, so that it may be too early to study social change through HRBAD. Secondly, and closely related to the first reason, empirical evidence on the social impact of HRBADs remains fairly limited. Nonetheless, organisational and social change are closely intertwined in practice, as has been illustrated in particular with regard to the tension between RBM and HRBAD.

Somewhat paradoxically, when it comes to assessing results, result-based management (RBM) as a fashionable tool in development approaches seems to assume quite naïvely and without much empirical support a linear cause and effect relationship between interventions and outcomes. In the field of human rights, given the complex nature of (bringing about) social change, no such linear causal relationship can be assumed. Hence, RBM and HRBADs may be more difficult to reconcile than often believed, and that tension may be illustrative of the fundamental differences that continue to characterise development and human rights approaches, notwithstanding the rapprochement that has taken place over the past decade(s).

A fundamental difference between human rights and development actors and their approaches to change is that they use different "legitimising anchors": whereas human rights actors tend to use legal norms as their legitimising anchor, development actors seek it more in empirical observations. In other words, human rights approaches are norm-based whereas development approaches take an evidence-based approach. This should not come as a surprise, since normativity is a key feature of HRBADs. But what if the norms are in tension with empirical findings? And how can we ensure that these norms themselves are grounded in struggles on the ground? These questions clearly open up a whole field of research questions that need to be addressed (anew) in light of HRBADs.

Human rights-based change may pose particular challenges to change agents, as compared with other attempts to bring about change, since convincing development staff with a technical training to accept a normative framework may be a challenging task. Human rights-based change thus poses specific challenges to leadership, capacity-building and role definition, in that it tends to be considered by development actors as imposed from the outside, and to deviate from what they consider to be good development practice (being value rather than evidence-based and having its legitimising anchor in norms rather than in ownership or effectiveness). At the same time, HRBADs should remain sufficiently open to engage with empirical findings, in particular the more exacting ones.

With regard to capacity-building, for example, this clash of disciplines means that far more than just legal or technical training on HRBADs, what is needed is staff that are capacitated to engage in interdisciplinary reflection and work.

As to role definition, more work needs to be done on the dichotomies that are currently used. Quite often, the development-human rights dichotomy is equated with the promotion-protection dichotomy, which is in turn equated with cooperation-confrontation and political-neutral dichotomies. However, experience with human rights work shows that political work, in the sense of raising and addressing issues of power and social change, does not automatically mean outright confrontation. This is illustrated in UNICEF's experience. Through the adoption of an HRBAD, the organisation got involved in political activities, but it has looked for cooperative channels and avoided conflict and confrontation.[101] Whereas

---

[101]JE Oestreich, *Power and Principle. Human Rights Programming in International Organizations* (Georgetown University Press, Washington, DC, 2007), 56–57.

political work is undoubtedly more amenable to confrontation, it is not necessarily so, though that too may come at the price of not pressing too hard for social change.

An important lesson is that organisational change never implies a clean slate. Old and new approaches represent layers of "organisational archaeologies". This may be a comforting message for staff who are rather reluctant to embrace a new approach, but it also indicates that the introduction of a new approach takes time and effort to really sink in. Success is not guaranteed: at best, the organisation may transform, in many instances adaptation may be the more likely scenario. More empirical work is therefore needed to assess which level of organisational change (adaptation, transformation) is needed and/or desirable for successfully introducing an HRBAD in an organisation, and for the HRBAD to be successful in achieving social change.

The language of drivers and spoilers of change, while forceful, may carry normative connotations on good and bad elements for change that, at a deeper level of analysis, turn out not be as unequivocal as suggested. So-called spoilers of change may be needed to push an organisation to a point where it is willing and able to change. The perspective of cycles of misalignment and realignment brings in a dynamic perspective on organisational change. It shows how organisational change is an on-going, dynamic process, not a one-off event, and how misalignment may be a necessary precondition to bring about change. How these cycles function once again requires careful empirical work.

Participatory Approaches to Socio-Economic Rights Adjudication: Tentative Lessons from South African Evictions Law

Sandra Liebenberg

Professor, H.F. Oppenheimer Chair in Human Rights Law, University of Stellenbosch Law Faculty
South Africa

This article explores the potential of participatory modes of adjudicating socio-economic rights to mitigate the democratic and distributive deficits of adjudication, particularly in the context of the structural reforms required to fulfil the positive duties imposed by these rights. It traces a particular application of a participatory model of adjudication through the doctrine and remedy of meaningful engagement which has emerged in the context of South African evictions law. The benefits of meaningful engagement in advancing direct participation by communities and organisations in the processes of socio-economic rights realisation are considered. However, attention is also drawn to the ways in which engagement orders can limit participatory systemic reforms that advance the normative goals of these rights. The article is intended as a contribution to the broader global debate on models of participatory adjudication in the context of socio-economic rights.

I. Introduction

The role of adjudication in the context of socio-economic rights has gained remarkable prominence and traction in both domestic constitutional law and international human rights law over the past decade.[1] However, the increased judicialisation of processes aimed at realising people's material needs co-exists uneasily with the emphasis on citizen participation

---

[1] There has been a trend towards incorporating socio-economic rights in the wave of new constitutions drafted in Africa, South America and Eastern Europe. In a number of jurisdictions inestablished democracies, courts are gradually becoming more assertive in protecting people's material needs, relying on constitutionally recognised directive principles of state policy or expansive interpretations of traditional civil and political rights. International and regional human rights treaties protecting economic, social and cultural rights have also witnessed their supervisory bodies playing a more robust oversight role in relation to social rights, or the creation of new individual communication procedures, culminating in the landmark adoption and subsequent entry into force of the Optional Protocol to the International Covenant on Economic, Social and Cultural Rights on 5 May 2013 (General Assembly Resolution A/RES/63/117, 10 December 2008). For academic analyses of these trends under various national and international law jurisdictions, see R Gargarella, P Domingo and T Roux (eds) *Courts and Social Transformation in New Democracies* (Ashgate, Aldershot, 2006); M Langford, *Social Rights Jurisprudence: Emerging Trends in International and Comparative Law* (Cambridge University Press, Cambridge, 2008); V Gauri and DM Brinks (eds) *Courting Social Justice: Judicial Enforcement of Social and Economic Rights in the Developing World* (Cambridge University Press, Cambridge, 2008).

which lies at the heart of modern development discourse and praxis.[2] Courts, litigation and legal discourse traditionally do not constitute broadly participatory processes or spaces. They involve a limited range of parties, and the specialised, expert discourse of legal rules and processes constitute a barrier to meaningful participation by those whose rights are affected.[3] Yet, the global emphasis and growth on litigation to protect not only traditional civil and political rights, but also economic, social and cultural rights suggests that rights beneficiaries and communities are increasingly resorting to the courts despite the exclusionary tendencies of the legal medium.

This article examines the potential of participatory models of socio-economic rights adjudication to mitigate the tension between participatory development and the exclusionary effects of litigation and adjudication. It does so through the lens of recent experiments in participatory modalities of reviewing and enforcing socio-economic rights by the South African Constitutional Court. It is well known that South Africa entrenches a range of justiciable socio-economic and cultural rights in the Bill of Rights of the 1996 Constitution,[4] and that a sophisticated jurisprudence on these rights has developed.[5] It thus provides a valuable context for exploring the tension described above.

The article commences with an examination of the challenges which a transformative interpretation of socio-economic rights poses for traditional conceptions of the judicial role. It proceeds to consider the turn in a number of jurisdictions to participatory models of adjudication as a potential response to these concerns. Thereafter, a specific application of the participatory model of adjudication in the context of the meaningful engagement jurisprudence of the South African Constitutional Court is considered. Although this model has subsequently been extended to education rights disputes, it developed primarily in the context of disputes concerning the eviction of people from their homes, and the latter set of cases will be the primary focus of this study. Finally, some tentative conclusions are drawn from the evictions case study in South Africa regarding the challenges posed by participatory models of socio-economic rights adjudication to transformative interpretations of socio-economic rights.

---

[2] The centrality of "active, free and meaningful" individual and collective participation in development is underscored in various articles of the UN Declaration on the Right to Development (General Assembly A/RES/41/128, 4 December 1986): see articles 1 and 2. For a historical overview of conceptions of participation in development, see S Hickey and G Mohan, "Towards Participation as Transformation: Critical Themes and Challenges", in S Hickey and G Mohan (eds), *Participation from Tyranny to Transformation* (Zed Books, London, 2004), 3–24.

[3] A leading sceptical account from the perspective of the United States of the ability of courts and litigation to catalyse social change is GN Rosenberg, *The Hollow Hope: Can Courts Bring About Social Change?* (University of Chicago Press, Chicago, 1991). For a sophisticated analyses of the factors affecting the ability of courts to play a meaningful role in social transformation across a range of jurisdictions, see S Gloppen "Courts and Social Transformation: An Analytical Framework", in R Gargarella, P Domingo and T Roux (eds) *Courts and Social Transformation in New Democracies* (Ashgate, Aldershot, 2006), 35–57.

[4] The Constitution of the Republic of South Africa, 1996, chapter 2 (hereafter "the Constitution").

[5] See generally S Liebenberg, *Socio-Economic Rights: Adjudication Under a Transformative Constitution* (Juta & Co, Cape Town, 2010); M Langford, B Cousins, J Dugard and T Madlingozi, *Socio-Economic Rights in South Africa: Symbols or Substance?* (Cambridge University Press, Cambridge, 2014).

II. Transformative Interpretations of Socio-Economic Rights: Adjudicative Challenges

The path tracing the traditional concerns to the judicial enforcement of social rights has been well-trodden. The familiar landmarks are the institutional legitimacy, competence and security of courts to enforce the resource-intensive, polycentric and policy-laden commitments underpinning socio-economic rights.[6]

One response to these dilemmas is to seek to minimise the differences between civil and political rights (in relation to which there is broad acceptance of judicial enforcement) and socio-economic rights. Thus it is argued that the differences between the resource implications of the two sets of rights is primarily one of degree, and that, like civil and political rights, socio-economic rights also impose negative obligations which are less resource intensive and can be accommodated within the traditional model of review applied to civil and political rights. This typically entails a court striking down legislation or executive or administrative conduct which infringes upon a right. In such cases, the court usually provides a clear definition of the right and the nature of the violation in the specific case, and issues remedial orders which have immediate and final effect. The converse argument is that civil and political rights such as the rights to a fair trial, to security of the person, to free, fair and regular elections and equality rights also impose positive duties on the state. Adjudicatory bodies have developed a range of strategies for assessing compliance with these positive duties such as deploying a reasonableness or "due diligence" review standard,[7] as well as remedial strategies such as declaratory orders, "reading in", or mandatory positive orders requiring the inclusion of groups excluded from public programmes.[8]

Nevertheless, in most contemporary democracies the policy and resource implications of civil and political rights are less extensive as they are regarded as core features of liberal democracies and the state has usually already made the primary investments in terms of the infrastructure, personnel and institutions necessary for these rights. In contrast, the fulfilment of people's socio-economic needs has historically been relegated to the market or other private institutions such as the family or charitable institutions with the state playing a residual and regulatory role. The growth of the modern welfare state, with the state assuming a central role in ensuring the social and economic well-being of its population and a fair distribution of the benefits of development, is a relatively recent phenomenon spurred by the cataclysms of the Great Depression and Second World

---

[6]For recent evaluations of these constraints and their implications, see P O'Connell, *Vindicating Socio-Economic Rights: International Standards and Comparative Experiences* (Routledge, Abingdon, 2012), 1–20; J King, *Judging Social Rights* (Cambridge University Press, Cambridge, 2012), 119–286.

[7]See, for example, *Velásquez Rodríguez Case*, Judgment of 29 July 1988, Inter-Am.Ct.H.R. (Ser C) No. 4, paras 174–75 (State of Honduras held to a reasonableness and due diligence standard to prevent, investigate, identify, punish and compensate for human rights violations arising from forced disappearances).

[8]See, for example, the range of cases decided in terms of the rights to equality and non-discrimination in a number of jurisdictions: *Schachter v Canada* (1992) 2 SCR 679 (extension of parental benefits accorded to adoptive parents to natural parents); *Eldridge v British Columbia (Attorney General)* (1997) 3 SCR 624 (suspended declaratory order that deaf patients entitled to the provision of sign language interpreters in the publicly funded health insurance system); *National Coalition for Gay and Lesbian Equality v Minister of Home Affairs* 2000 (2) SA 1 (CC) (reading in order extending immigration benefits accorded to married couples to couples in permanent same sex relationships); *Minister of Home Affairs v Fourie* 2006 (1) SA 524 (CC) (requiring the status and benefits of marriage to be extended to same sex couples).

War.[9] Since the 1980s, the expansive role of the state in creating social entitlement programmes has come under increasing pressure from structural adjustment programmes imposed by international financial institutions, neoliberal economic policies, various forms of privatisation of formerly publicly-provided services, and austerity measures adopted in the wake of the financial crisis.[10]

A developmental state with the objective of redressing the underlying conditions which generate on-going patterns of material deprivation and inequality must of necessity assume a more proactive, interventionist role in relation to national and international market institutions and processes. This is necessary to ensure that socio-economic rights are realised on a sustainable basis, and to give effect to their transformative purposes of promoting a social and economic order capable of fostering human dignity, freedom and equality. Such an expansive interpretation of social rights thus seeks to do more than guarantee a minimal floor of social protection, but rather aims to afford impoverished groups meaningful tools with which to challenge the structural barriers which undermine their full and equal participation in society.

However, this transformation-orientated interpretation of socio-economic rights entailing far-reaching positive duties intensifies the challenges of litigation and adjudication alluded to above.[11] Not only must a court adjudicating this vision of socio-economic rights acquire a range of specialised information, but it runs risks of incurring distributional and democratic deficits in making far-reaching substantive rulings with polycentric ramifications.[12]

---

[9]On the rise and forms of the modern welfare state and its associated social entitlement programmes, see generally G Esping-Andersen, *The Three Worlds of Welfare Capitalism* (Princeton University Press, Princeton, 1990); F-X Kaufmann, *European Foundations of the Welfare State* (Berghahn Books, New York, Oxford, 2012); CR Sunstein, *The Second Bill of Rights: FDR's Unfinished Revolution and Why We Need it More than Ever* (Basic Books, New York, 2004); K Rittich "Social Rights and Social Policy: Transformations on the International Landscape", in D Barak-Erez and AM Gross (eds), *Exploring Social Rights: Between Theory and Practice* (Hart Publishing, Oxford and Portland, Oregon, 2007), 107.

[10]See generally M Pieterse, "Beyond the Welfare State: Globalisation of Neo-Liberal Culture and the Constitutional Protection of Social and Economic Rights in South Africa", (2003) 13 *Stellenbosch LR* 3–28; P O'Connell "The Death of Social Rights", (2011) 74 *Modern Law Rev* 532–52; A Nolan (ed), *Economic and Social Rights after the Global Economic Crisis* (Cambridge University Press, Cambridge, forthcoming 2014); D Harvey, *A Brief History of Neoliberalism* (Oxford University Press, Oxford, 2005), 64–86; A Greig, D Hulme and M Turner, *Challenging Global Inequality: Development Theory and Practice in the 21st Century* (Palgrave MacMillan, Basingstoke, 2007), 100–28.

[11]Applying the conceptual apparatus of the UN Committee on Economic, Social and Cultural Rights, the expansive interpretation of socio-economic rights is broadly analogous to the obligation to "achieve progressively the full realization" of the rights recognised in the International Covenant on Economic, Social and Cultural Rights (993 UNTS 3, 16 December 1966). This obligation extends beyond the core obligation to ensure "minimum essential levels" of the relevant rights. General Comment No 3 (Fifth session, 1990) The nature of states parties obligations (art 2(1) of the Covenant) UN Doc. E/1991/23 paras 9–10. The expansive interpretation also resonates with the obligations of the state to eliminate systemic discrimination and advance the achievement of substantive equality. See General Comment No 20 (Forty-second session, 2009) Non-discrimination in economic, social and cultural rights (art 2(2) of the Covenant), UN Doc. E/C.12/GC/20, paras 8–9 and 39.

[12]For the classic description of the problem of polycentricity in adjudication, see L Fuller, "The Forms and Limits of Adjudication", (1978) 92 *Harvard LR* 353–409. For responses in the context of socio-economic rights adjudication, see S Liebenberg, *Socio-Economic Rights: Adjudication Under a Transformative Constitution* (Juta & Co, Cape Town, 2010), 71–75; J King, *Judging Social Rights* (Cambridge University Press, Cambridge, 2012), 189–210.

Distributive inequities may arise as a court is not well placed to foresee the implications of its rulings for other groups and rights not represented before the court. The consequence may be that those with the resources to access the courts gain preferential access to social benefits ahead of groups in a worse-off position.[13]

Closely related to the above is the fact that the traditional form of litigation involves a dispute between a limited range of parties. Courts sympathetic to a transformative interpretation of socio-economic rights may hand down judgments which have major policy implications without the opportunity for large sections of the population who may be affected by the decision to be heard. This gives rise to democracy deficits in the judicial enforcement of socio-economic rights. One of the major virtues of adjudication is to develop interpretations of rights that are attuned and responsive to the lived experiences of those affected by a particular social and economic problem. To the extent that these experiences are not reflected in the litigation, the interpretations by a court of the rights at stake will run the risk of not being perceived as fair and inclusive. In this respect, the democratic deficit extends beyond the well-worn counter-majoritarian dilemma of judicial review which is squarely located in a representative conception of democracy.[14] It encompasses the ideal of a participatory democracy, described by Robert Dahl as follows:

> Throughout the process of making binding decisions, citizens ought to have adequate opportunity, and an equal opportunity, for expressing their preferences as to the final outcome. They must have adequate and equal opportunities for placing questions on the agenda and for expressing reasons for endorsing one outcome rather than another.[15]

We thus find ourselves on the horns of a dilemma. By embracing a more expansive, transformative vision of socio-economic rights, we run the risk of intensifying the distributive and democratic deficits of socio-economic rights adjudication. If we seek refuge in a more

---

[13]O Ferraz, "Harming the Poor through Social Rights Litigation", (2010–2011) 89 *Texas LR* 1643–68; KG Young and J Lemaitre, "The Comparative Fortunes of the Right to Health: Two Tales of Justiciability in Colombia and South Africa", (2013) 26 *Harvard Human Rights J* 179–216; HA García, "Distribution of Resources Led by Courts: A Few Words of Caution", in H Alviar García, K Klare, LA Williams (eds), *Social and Economic Rights in Theory and Practice: Critical Inquiries* (Routledge, Abingdon 2015), 67–84. However, at least some of the distortions arising from the social rights litigation documented in this literature arise from the particular nature of the writ of protection (*tutela* or *amparo*) proceedings in the relevant South American jurisdictions. The individualised, *inter partes* effect of these procedures does not make it easy for a court to consider the systemic impact of the litigation on groups not represented before the court. The Colombian Constitutional Court has developed various devices to address systemic issues, for example, through "unification judgments" (consolidating a large number of *tutelas* dealing with the same complaint) and the development of the doctrine of an unconstitutional state of affairs (*estado de cosas inconstitucional*). See generally on these developments, M Sepúlveda, "Colombia: The Constitutional Court's Role in Addressing Social Injustice", in M Langford, *Social Rights Jurisprudence: Emerging Trends in International and Comparative Law* (Cambridge University Press, Cambridge, 2008), 144–62, 146–149.

[14]On the constraints of an institutional conception of democracy in socio-economic rights litigation, see D Brand, "Judicial Deference and Democracy in Socio-economic Rights Cases in South Africa", in S Liebenberg and G Quinot (eds), *Law and Poverty: Perspectives from South Africa and Beyond* (Juta & Co, Cape Town, 2012), 172–96.

[15]RA Dahl *Democracy and its Critics* (Yale University Press, New Haven, 1989), 109. See also his critique of the concept of the guardianship model for making binding decisions on the citizenry (at 65–79).

minimalist, judicially modest interpretation of socio-economic rights, we may "abate the nuisance of obvious destitution in the lowest ranks of society",[16] but enfeeble the response of these rights to the structural causes of poverty and inequality. One way to escape the dilemma may be to accept a minimalist interpretation of socio-economic rights by the courts, and pursue broader transformative approaches to socio-economic rights through mobilisation and advocacy strategies beyond the courts. However, a minimalist judicial interpretation of these rights will have broader political and social ramifications, and may exert a restraining influence on an attempt to expand the meaning of these rights in other arenas and processes. As Danie Brand notes,

> courts also occupy a symbolic, or perhaps more accurately, an exemplary role with respect to poverty and need discourses – their vocabulary, the conceptual structures they rely on, the rhetorical strategies they employ infiltrate and so influence and shape the political discourses around poverty and need.[17]

The question thus arises as to whether there are adjudicative methods that can assist in resolving this dilemma. It is to this question we now turn.

III. Seeking a Resolution through Participatory Models of Adjudication

Courts around the world, sensitive to the justice and democratic deficits of judicial review of socio-economic rights described above, have developed various strategies to mitigate these deficits. These include broadening the range of parties that enjoy access to courts, and developing models of review that are responsive to the polycentric and systemic impacts of judicial interventions. Participation by a broader range of parties in litigation is facilitated through strategies such as developing generous rules of legal standing and permitting class actions, public interest actions, *amici curiae* ("friends of the court) briefs, and ordering the joinder of non-parties.[18] Sensitivity to the systemic impacts of litigation is promoted through the adoption of flexible models of judicial review such as the well-known reasonableness standard adopted by the South African Constitutional Court for assessing the positive obligations. Reasonableness review amounts to a multi-factor balancing test incorporating a

---

[16]TH Marshall, "Citizenship and Social Class", in *Class, Citizenship and Social Development* (University of Chicago Press, Chicago, 1963), 106 cited by K Rittich "Social Rights and Social Policy: Transformations on the International Landscape", in D Barak-Erez and AM Gross (eds), *Exploring Social Rights: Between Theory and Practice* (Hart Publishing, Oxford, 2007), 133.

[17]D Brand, "The 'Politics of Need Interpretation' and the Adjudication of Socio-economic Rights Claims in South Africa", in AJ Van Der Walt (ed), *Theories of Social and Economic Justice* (Sun Press, Stellenbosch, 2005), 17–36 at 24.

[18]On the development of public interest litigation in the context of Indian Constitutional law, see S Muralidhar, "India: The Expectations and Challenges of Judicial Enforcement of Social Rights", in M Langford (ed), *Social Rights Jurisprudence: Emerging Trends in International and Comparative Law* (Cambridge University Press, Cambridge, 2008), 102–24, at 106–9. The South African courts have routinely required the joinder of local authorities to eviction applications brought by private landowners against unlawful occupiers to enable the authorities to facilitate a context-sensitive resolution of the conflict between property and housing rights. See G Muller and S Liebenberg, "Developing the Law of Joinder in the Context of Evictions of People from their Homes", (2013) 29 *SA J on Human Rights* 554–70.

consideration of the particular circumstances of the complaint,[19] the broader social context, including those similarly placed or worse off than the complainant,[20] and the available resources and capacity which the state can marshal at the particular juncture.[21]

A further strategy which is increasingly deployed by a range of national courts and enjoying increased academic attention is a turn to dialogic and participatory modalities of rights review and remedies. Dialogic models of adjudication aim to alleviate separation of powers concerns by consciously fostering mutual responsiveness and cooperation between the courts, legislatures and executives in the enforcement of socio-economic rights. This necessarily involves a departure from strong forms of judicial review where courts provide definitive and final interpretations of rights to encourage shared, iterative constitutional interpretation of rights by the other branches.[22]

Dialogic models operate largely within the paradigm of representative democracy whereas the primary objective of participatory models of review is to induce the direct participation of a broad range of affected citizens and organisations of civil society in the processes of defining and implementing socio-economic rights. Whilst not displacing the institutions of representative democracy, it seeks to open them up to the participation of rights beneficiaries and a broad range of stakeholders in the hope of increasing the responsiveness of social policy to those affected by it. Rather than conceiving of socio-economic rights as commodities to be delivered by the institutions of representative democracy to a passive citizenry, participatory models of enforcement conceive of socio-economic rights as a set of values relating to the material dimensions of people's lives. These values must be concretised in law, policy and institutions through active engagement between government and citizenry.

Participatory adjudication methods encompass the modest meaningful engagement review and remedial mechanism of the South African Constitutional Court (which will constitute the focus of the remainder of this article), participatory structural injunctions (known as a continuing mandamus in Indian constitutional law),[23] and the more

---

[19]See, for example, the linkages between reasonableness, human dignity and the meeting of urgent human needs drawn by the Constitutional Court in *Government of the Republic of South Africa v Grootboom* 2001 (1) SA 46 (CC), para 44 (hereafter "*Grootboom*"); *Minister of Health v Treatment Action Campaign (no 2)* 2002 (5) SA 721, paras 72–78 (hereafter "*Treatment Action Campaign*").

[20]*Soobramoney v Minister of Health, Kwa-Zulu Natal* 1998 (1) SA 765 (CC), paras 30–31; *Mazibuko v City of Johannesburg* 2010 (4) SA 1 (CC), paras 7, 48–68, 87–89.

[21]*Grootboom* 2001 (1) SA 46 (CC), paras 45–46; *Treatment Action Campaign*, paras 115–121; *Khosa v Minister of Social Development; Mahlaule v Minister of Social Development* 2004 (6) SA 505 (CC), paras 58–62.

[22]On dialogic review, see generally K Roach, "Dialogic Judicial Review and its Critics", (2004) 23 *Supreme Court LR* 49–104; C Bateup, "The Dialogic Promise: Assessing the Normative Potential of Theories of Constitutional Dialogue", (2006) 71 *Brooklyn LR* 1109–80; R Dixon, "Creating Dialogue about Socio-economic Rights: Strong-Form versus Weak Form-Judicial Review Revisited", (2007) 5 *I. CON* 391–418.

[23]On structural injunctions in the context of the US school desegregation litigation, see M Tushnet, *Weak Courts, Strong Rights: Judicial Review and Social Welfare Rights in Comparative Constitutional Law* (Princeton University Press, Princeton, 2008), 254–56; On the continuing mandamus in Indian constitutional law, see S Parmer and N Wahi, "India: Citizens, Courts and the Right to Health: Between Promise and Progress?", in AE Yamin and S Gloppen (eds), *Litigating Health Rights: Can Courts Bring More Justice to Health?* (Harvard University Press, Cambridge, MA, 2011), 155–89, at 172–74. Finally, for an assessment of structural interdicts in the context of socio-economic rights litigation in South African, see C Mbazira, *Litigating Socio-economic Rights: A Choice Between Corrective and Distributive Justice* (Pretoria University Law Press, Pretoria, 2009), 165–225; S Liebenberg, *Socio-Economic Rights: Adjudication Under a Transformative Constitution* (Juta & Co, Cape Town, 2010), 424–438.

far-reaching democratic experimentalist models of adjudication gaining traction in various national and international forums.[24] Although there are no bright lines distinguishing these models, they can usefully be viewed as representing a continuum ranging from the more modest to the more extensive forms of participation in socio-economic rights realisation and implementation.

For courts, participatory modes of socio-economic rights enforcement offer a number of attractive features.[25] First, they lower the heat of democratic legitimacy concerns by decentring the judicial role in rights definition and enforcement. Instead of the court playing a pre-emptive role in defining the detailed policy entailments of a particular socio-economic right, participatory models of adjudication aim to stimulate a process of deliberation between state institutions, rights beneficiaries, civil society organisations and even business entities. Through such deliberations, the stakeholders attempt to reach agreement on what specific policy measures the right requires in the particular context, and the reforms and policies that would give optimal effect to the right. In due course, as the deliberative process unfolds and increased consensus is generated, the court may assume a stronger normative role. However, at least during the initiative phases of the litigation, the court takes a back seat, focusing rather on the procedural conditions for equal voice and participation.

Secondly, participatory enforcement mechanisms can mitigate polycentricity and judicial competence concerns by broadening the range of parties participating in the litigation, and expanding the information available to the court through the detailed record generated by the deliberations described above. Information can be garnered through the involvement of experts, human rights commissions/ombuds, and the convening of public hearings.[26] Novel solutions to seemingly intractable problems may be generated as parties analyse the root causes of rights violations, share local knowledge, deliberate and test policies through processes of trial and error.

Finally, participatory enforcement methods are sensitive to institutional security concerns of courts by reducing the scope for direct conflicts with the other branches of government, and increasing their popular legitimacy by requiring the participation of citizen groups in resolving socio-economic rights disputes. Policies developed through broad public participation are likely to enjoy greater legitimacy than those developed through unilateral legislative, executive or judicial action.

These advantages are particularly significant when courts seek to enforce the more expansive obligations entailed in the transformative vision of socio-economic rights discussed above. In such cases, there is typically no single, obvious policy solution to cure the socio-

---

[24]See M Dorf and C Sabel, "A Constitution of Democratic Experimentalism", (1998) 98 *Columbia LR* 267–473; C Sabel and W Simon, "Destabilization Rights: How Public Law Litigation Succeeds", (2004) 117 *Harv LR* 1016–1101; O Gerstenberg, "Negative/Positive Constitutionalism, 'Fair Balance' and the Problem of Justiciability", (2012) 10 *I. CON* 904–25; K Young, *Constituting Economic and Social Rights* (Oxford University Press, Oxford, 2012), 256–87.

[25]See generally B Ray "Demosprudence in Comparative Perspective", (2011) 47 *Stan. J. Int. Law* 111–73.

[26]For accounts of such broad participatory processes in social rights adjudication in the South American context, see: N Angel-Cabo and DL Parmo, "Latin American Social Constitutionalism: Courts and Popular Participation", in HA García, K Klare, LA Williams (eds), *Social and Economic Rights in Theory and Practice: Critical Inquiries* (Routledge, Abingdon, 2015), 85–104; R Gargarella, "Deliberative Democracy, Dialogic Justice and the Promise of Social and Economic Rights", H Alviar García, K Klare, LA Williams (eds), *Social and Economic Rights in Theory and Practice: Critical Inquiries* (Routledge, Abingdon, 2015), 105–120.

economic rights violation, the underlying causes of the violation are complex, and redress requires a series of structural reforms over a period of time. Participatory adjudication methods offer the courts a way to stimulate and oversee the overall direction of these reforms without usurping the policy-making role of the other branches of government or the right of people themselves to have a meaningful voice in the policies and programmes through which their socio-economic rights are realised.

However, in order to arrive at a more balanced assessment of these purported virtues as well as the potential weaknesses of participatory models of socio-economic rights adjudication, close attention must be paid to their practical operation in various jurisdictions. The following analysis of the doctrine of meaningful engagement in South African evictions disputes is intended as a contribution to this broader project.

IV. Meaningful Engagement in South African Evictions Jurisprudence: A Case Study

IV.1 Evictions law as structural reform litigation

The Bill of Rights in the South African Constitution includes a property rights clause prohibiting arbitrary deprivation of property, stipulating the conditions subject to which expropriations may occur, as well as imposing various obligations on the state in relation to restitution and land reform.[27] Significantly, it also incorporates a clause relating to housing rights which includes a prohibition against the eviction of persons from their homes without an order of court made without considering "all the relevant circumstances".[28] Due to apartheid-era forced removals and discriminatory land and housing policies, a large housing backlog and deeply entrenched patterns of spatial injustice exist in South Africa. In urban areas, impoverished, overwhelmingly black communities live in overcrowded, poorly serviced informal settlements on poorly located land on the periphery of South African towns and cities. The redress of these deep structural housing problems requires far-reaching policy and budgetary initiatives.[29]

Evictions have often served as a locus of tension between the long-term structural reforms required in the housing sector and the need to respond to the urgent needs and circumstances of those who are evicted from their homes for a variety of reasons. Such reasons may include evictions on the basis of unlawful occupation, health and safety reasons, disaster management, or to enable the upgrading of an informal settlement.

---

[27] Section 25. See generally AJ van der Walt, *Constitutional Property Law* (3rd edition, Juta & Co, Cape Town, 2011); JM Pienaar, Land Reform (Juta & Co, Cape Town, 2014).

[28] Section 26 of the Constitution reads as follows:

   (1) Everyone has the right to have access to adequate housing;
   (2) The state must take reasonable legislative and other measures, within its available resources, to achieve the progressive realisation of this right.
   (3) No one may be evicted from their home, or have their home demolished, without an order of court made after considering all relevant circumstances. No legislation may permit arbitrary evictions.

[29] A number of authors have noted the complex set of interventions required to redress the legacy of apartheid housing policy and planning. See, for example M Huchzermeyer, *Unlawful Occupation: Informal Settlements and Urban Policy in South Africa and Brazil* (Africa World Press, Trenton, 2004); JM Pienaar, "The Housing Crisis in South Africa: Will the Plethora of Housing Policies and Legislation have a Positive Impact?", (2002) 17 *SA Public Law* 336–70; S Berrisford, "Unravelling Apartheid Spatial Planning Legislation in South Africa", (2011) 22 *Urban Forum* 247–63.

The challenge for both local authorities and the courts is to ensure that in responding to the needs of disadvantaged groups who face evictions, the apartheid-inherited patterns of spatial injustice and under-development are not perpetuated. This can occur, for example, when groups or communities are evicted and relocated from well-located urban land close to their livelihood opportunities to already overcrowded informal settlements on the periphery of South Africa's towns and cities.[30] Evictions law in a context such as South Africa challenges the common perception that the negative enforcement of socio-economic rights (the duty to respect) is relatively uncomplicated and cost-free.[31] In fact, it entails extensive positive duties from various organs of state with myriad polycentric dimensions. These include balancing the property and housing rights of other affected groups; the nature and location of alternative accommodation for those evicted taking into account the spatial integration of previously racially segregated communities and ensuring their livelihood opportunities and sustainable development;[32] the provision and financing of services (such as water, electricity, sanitation and refuse removal); and the budgetary and administrative responsibilities of different spheres of government within the framework of co-operative governance. Given the complex, polycentric nature of evictions law in South Africa, the turn to participatory mechanisms in the adjudication of eviction disputes in the South African context thus offers fruitful insights into their practical implications in the context of socio-economic rights litigation.

IV.2 Meaningful engagement through the jurisprudence

An early decision of the Constitutional Court, *Port Elizabeth Municipality v Various Occupiers* (hereafter "*PE Municipality*"),[33] laid the foundations for the general approach to be adopted by the South African courts to eviction applications potentially resulting in homelessness. The eviction application was brought by a local authority against a group of 68 unlawful occupiers of privately owned land in terms of the Prevention of Illegal Eviction from and Unlawful Occupation of Land Act 19 of 1998 (hereafter "PIE").[34] The Court held that "a potentially dignified and effective mode" of achieving a sustainable resolution of the clash between property and housing rights in a case such as this was for courts "to encourage and require the parties to engage with each other in a proactive and honest endeavour to find mutually acceptable solutions".[35] In the words of Justice Sachs, who delivered the judgment:

---

[30]See M Strauss and S Liebenberg, "Contested Spaces: Housing Rights and Evictions Law in Post-Apartheid South Africa", (2014) 13 *Planning Theory*, 428–48.

[31]See, for example, E Riedel, "Economic, Social and Cultural Rights", in C Krause and M Scheinin (eds), *International Protection of Human Rights: A Textbook* (2nd revised ed, Åbo Akademi Institute for Human Rights, Turku/Åbo, 2012), 131–52 at 135.

[32]The duty to make short-term provision for those in urgent housing need was established in the *Grootboom* case, and laid the foundations for the subsequent evolution of the principle that alternative temporary accommodation should generally be made available by state authorities to those facing homelessness as a result of an eviction. This principle also applies where a private party brings an eviction application: *City of Johannesburg Metropolitan Municipality v Blue Moonlight Properties* 2012 (2) SA 104 (CC).

[33]2005 (1) SA 217 (CC).

[34]PIE was enacted by the post-apartheid government to give effect to section 26 of the Constitution. On PIE and the jurisprudence interpreting it, see generally S Liebenberg, *Socio-Economic Rights: Adjudication Under a Transformative Constitution* (Juta & Co, Cape Town, 2010), 268–93.

[35]*PE Municipality* 2005 (1) SA 217 (CC), para 39.

"Wherever possible, respectful face-to-face engagement or mediation through a third party should replace arms-length combat by intransigent opponents".[36]

The Court held that one of the relevant circumstances in determining whether it is just and equitable to make an eviction order is whether "serious negotiations had taken place with equality of voice for all concerned"[37] or mediation has been tried (in appropriate circumstances, to be ordered by the courts).[38] The *PE Municipality* judgment emphasises the need for courts to assume a more managerial, procedurally innovative role in seeking to facilitate creative solutions to the conflicting rights and interests at issue.[39] Ultimately, the Court dismissed the local authority's appeal against the refusal of an eviction order by the lower court, finding that it was not just and equitable to order the eviction. One of the factors in this judicial assessment was "the absence of any significant attempts by the Municipality to listen to and consider the problems" of the particular group of occupiers.[40]

The *PE Municipality* case was an important precursor to the meaningful engagement doctrine which was fully articulated and applied in the leading decision of the Constitutional Court in *Occupiers of 51 Olivia Road v City of Johannesburg* (hereafter "*Olivia Road*").[41] This case involved a constitutional challenge to provisions in the National Building Regulations and Building Standards Act 103 of 1977 (hereafter "the NBRSA"). The City of Johannesburg had issued a series of administrative notices in terms of this legislation requiring thousands of occupiers of so-called "bad buildings" (buildings which allegedly posed a threat to the health and safety of residents due to their poor conditions) in the inner city to vacate the buildings. Failure to comply with the notice constituted a criminal offence in terms of the legislation. A spate of evictions carried out by municipal law enforcement officials ensued in the wake of these notices. These evictions formed part of the City of Johannesburg's Inner City Regeneration Strategy which housing rights organisations perceived as an initiative to gentrify inner city areas preceded by the removal of impoverished residents whose livelihoods, including waste recycling, domestic work, and hawking, were closely tied to their residence within the hub of the city.[42]

The relevant provisions of the legislation were alleged to infringe section 26(3) of the Constitution. Specific relief was sought against the eviction of the particular applicants constituting over 400 occupiers of two buildings in the inner city of Johannesburg. In addition, the applicants challenged the city's failure to formulate a housing plan for all similarly affected residents living in desperate circumstances in Johannesburg's inner city. These latter two aspects of the case will be referred to as the applications for specific and for systemic relief respectively. The case was appealed all the way from the High Court,[43] to the

---

[36] *PE Municipality* 2005 (1) SA 217 (CC), para 39.

[37] *PE Municipality* 2005 (1) SA 217 (CC), para 30.

[38] *PE Municipality* 2005 (1) SA 217 (CC), para 45.

[39] *PE Municipality* 2005 (1) SA 217 (CC), paras 30–38.

[40] *PE Municipality* 2005 (1) SA 217 (CC), para 59.

[41] 2008 (3) SA 208 (CC).

[42] See Report of the Centre for Housing Rights and Evictions (COHRE), "Any Room for the Poor? Forced Evictions in Johannesburg, South Africa (8 March 2005)",available at http://www.escr-net.org/usr_doc/COHRE_Johannesburg_FFM_high_res.pdf (accessed 13 September 2014).

[43] *City of Johannesburg v Rand Properties (Pty) Ltd and Others* 2007 (1) SA 78 (W).

Supreme Court of Appeal,[44] before eventually coming before the South African Constitutional Court for final decision.

In a novel development for South African constitutional law, the Constitutional Court issued an interim order two days after the hearing in the application but prior to handing down its final judgment. The interim order required the parties to engage with each other meaningfully,

> in an effort to resolve the differences and difficulties aired in the application in the light of the values of the Constitution, the constitutional and statutory duties of the municipality and the rights and duties of the citizens concerned, including alleviating the plight of the applicants by rendering their buildings as safe and conducive to health as is reasonably practicable.[45]

The City and applicants were ordered to report back to the court on the outcomes of the engagement, and the Court indicated that it would take account of the contents of the reports in preparing its judgment and the issuing of further directions should this become necessary.[46]

The outcome of this meaningful engagement order was a comprehensive settlement agreement between the parties which included interim steps for rendering the buildings safer and more habitable, as well as detailed provision for the relocation of the occupiers to alternative accommodation within the inner city.[47] This included the identification of the relevant buildings for relocation, the nature and standard of the accommodation to be provided, and the calculation of the rental to be paid. The agreement stipulated that this alternative accommodation was being provided pending the provision of suitable permanent housing solutions which would be developed by the City in consultation with the occupiers concerned. This engagement agreement was endorsed and made an Order of the Court.

In its subsequent judgment, the Court provided its reasons for the engagement order together with its ruling on the challenges to the constitutionality of the NBRSA, specific relief for the applicants and the systemic challenge concerning the lack of a housing plan for those similarly affected by evictions from "bad buildings". The Court derived a general obligation on the City to engage meaningfully with those facing eviction from a range of constitutional provisions, but particularly section 26(2) of the Constitution which imposes a duty of reasonableness on the state in all steps taken in relation to the realisation of housing rights.[48] Meaningful engagement was furthermore held to be a "relevant circumstance" in terms of section 26(3) of the Constitution prior to making an eviction order. Thus a failure by a municipality to engage meaningfully, or an unreasonable

---

[44] *City of Johannesburg v Rand Properties (Pty) Ltd and Others* 2007 (6) SA 404 (SCA).

[45] *Olivia Road* 2008 (3) SA 208 (CC), para 5.

[46] *Olivia Road* 2008 (3) SA 208 (CC).

[47] Settlement agreement between City of Johannesburg and the Occupiers of 51 Olivia Road, Berea Township and 197 Main Street, Johannesburg dated 29 October 2007. See the summary in the *Olivia Road* judgment (2008 (3) SA 208 (CC)), paras 25–26. For an account of the engagement process by the lawyer for the residents, see S Wilson, "Planning for Inclusion in South Africa: The State's Duty to Prevent Homelessness and the Potential of 'Meaningful Engagement'", (2011) 22 *Urban Forum* 265–82.

[48] As noted by the Court: "Every homeless person is in need of housing and this means that every step take in relation to a potentially homeless person must also be reasonable if it is to comply with section 26(2)" (*Olivia Road* 2008 (3) SA 208 (CC), para 17).

response in the engagement process, would "ordinarily be a weighty consideration against the grant of an eviction order."[49]

The Court elaborated on a number of requirements pertaining to the subject-matter of meaningful engagement in an eviction dispute[50] as well as the processes of meaningful engagement. A central process requirement is that local authorities put in place structures managed by "competent sensitive council workers skilled in engagement" to facilitate engagement processes, particularly where a large number of people are potentially affected by evictions.[51] The process of engagement must further be characterised by reasonableness, flexibility and good faith on both sides. People in need of housing should not be regarded as "a disempowered mass" and should be encouraged to be proactive, and not purely defensive.[52] However, the Court also noted that groups facing eviction may be so vulnerable that they may not understand the significance of the engagement process and may withdraw from it. In these circumstances a municipality cannot simply walk away from the process, but must display sensitivity to the fact that the affected group may be poor, vulnerable and illiterate. In these circumstances, reasonable efforts should be made to maintain their involvement.[53] Civil society organisations should support and facilitate engagement processes.[54] Finally, engagement processes should be open and transparent, and a complete and accurate record of the process should be kept.[55] Although the Court had approved the engagement agreement, it held that it would not always be appropriate to do so. The *Olivia Road* engagement agreement was endorsed by the Court as it had been ordered while the proceedings were pending before it, and the parties had been specifically ordered to report back to the court on the outcome of the engagement process.[56] The Court emphasised that the process of engagement should usually take place prior to the commencement of litigation unless it is not possible or reasonable to do so because of urgency or some other compelling reason.[57]

The Court found it unnecessary to review the decision of the City to issue the "order to vacate" notices in terms of the NBRSA as it held that the eviction proceedings had been effectively settled through the meaningful engagement order.[58] However, it was in the interests of justice to consider the narrower issue of the constitutionality of the issuing of notices to vacate by the City on pain of criminal sanction pursuant to section 12 of the NBRSA. In this regard, the Court confirmed that a notice to vacate should not have been issued by the City or upheld by the lower courts without taking relevant circumstances into account, particularly the likely consequence of homelessness resulting from an eviction.[59] The Court affirmed that the availability of alternative accommodation was always a relevant consideration where people faced homelessness. Moreover, government departments should

---

[49] *Olivia Road* 2008 (3) SA 208 (CC), para 21.

[50] *Olivia Road* 2008 (3) SA 208 (CC), para 14.

[51] *Olivia Road* 2008 (3) SA 208 (CC), para 19.

[52] *Olivia Road* 2008 (3) SA 208 (CC), para 20.

[53] *Olivia Road* 2008 (3) SA 208 (CC), para 15.

[54] *Olivia Road* 2008 (3) SA 208 (CC), para 20.

[55] *Olivia Road* 2008 (3) SA 208 (CC), para 21.

[56] *Olivia Road* 2008 (3) SA 208 (CC), para 30.

[57] *Olivia Road* 2008 (3) SA 208 (CC), para 30.

[58] *Olivia Road* 2008 (3) SA 208 (CC), para 39.

[59] *Olivia Road* 2008 (3) SA 208 (CC), paras 42–43.

avoid working in silos where one department took a decision to evict people with "some other department in the bureaucratic maze determining whether housing should be provided".[60] Finally, the Court declared the provision in the NBRSA that imposed a criminal penalty for failure to comply with the order to vacate notice inconsistent with section 26(3) of the Constitution as it in effect amounted to an eviction without a court order. By way of remedy, the Court granted a "reading-in" order to the effect that the criminal sanction would only apply to people who, after service upon them of an order of court for their eviction, continue to occupy the property concerned.[61] Before such a court order was issued, the court would have to take into account all relevant circumstances, including whether there had been prior meaningful engagement and the availability of alternative accommodation.

Significantly, however, the Court declined to pronounce on the systemic component of the occupiers' case concerning whether the City had formulated and implemented a housing plan to deal with the long-term needs of the applicants as well the thousands of persons similarly facing eviction from unsafe and unhealthy buildings in the inner city. It held that this would amount to a generalised abstract review of the city's housing plan and it was not desirable that the Constitutional Court dealt with the issues as the court of first and last instance. The Court expressed confidence that the city would deal with the issue of permanent housing solutions for the applicants and those similarly affected through meaningful engagement. Moreover, it was always open to particular occupiers to bring a case before a lower court containing specific allegations regarding non-compliance with the housing obligations imposed by the Constitution in relation to them.[62]

Subsequently to *Olivia Road*, the concept of meaningful engagement has been evoked in a number of eviction-related disputes. In *Residents of Joe Slovo Community v Thubelisha Homes & Others* ("*Joe Slovo I*"),[63] the Court granted an eviction order against some 20,000 members of the Joe Slovo informal settlement in terms of PIE to facilitate the upgrading of the site, but imposed detailed conditions regarding the relocation of the community to a temporary resettlement area some 15 km away pending their return to the upgraded settlement. The authorities were required to engage meaningfully with the community concerning the details of the implementation of the eviction order and the relocation of the community to the temporary resettlement area. The parties were furthermore required to report back to the court on the process and implementation of the eviction and relocation. Ultimately, after numerous delays in the implementation of the Order, the eviction order was discharged by the Constitutional Court some 21 months after the original Order.[64] The authorities ultimately decided to pursue an *in situ* upgrade of the community which did not require the eviction and relocation of the community from the site of the informal settlement. The irony was that the feasibility of an *in situ* upgrade had been one of the reasons the community had resisted the original eviction application, arguing that it would disrupt their children's schooling as well as fragile networks and livelihood opportunities as an impoverished community.

---

[60] *Olivia Road* 2008 (3) SA 208 (CC), para 44.

[61] *Olivia Road* 2008 (3) SA 208 (CC), paras 47–54.

[62] *Olivia Road* 2008 (3) SA 208 (CC), paras 32–36.

[63] 2010 (3) SA 454 (CC).

[64] *Residents of Joe Slovo Community, Western Cape v Thubelisha Homes* 2011 (7) BCLR 723 (CC) ("*Joe Slovo II*").

Even though the judgment in *Joe Slovo I* imposed strong meaningful engagement requirements in implementing the eviction order, it sanctioned weak community engagement in the processes leading up to the decision to evict the community.[65] In his separate judgment, Justice Sachs described defects in the engagement processes concerning the upgrading of the settlement and the need for residents to relocate to a temporary resettlement area as follows:

> There can be no doubt that there were major failures of communication on the part of the authorities. The evidence suggests the frequent employment of a top-down approach where the purpose of reporting back to the community was seen as being to pass on information about decisions already taken rather than to involve the residents as partners in the process of decision-making itself.[66]

However, ultimately all these judgments delivered in *Joe Slovo I* concluded that the overall objectives of the project in promoting housing development outweighed the inadequacies in the engagement processes in relation to the development project as a whole and leading up to the decision to apply for an eviction order.[67] The judgments also emphasised the need not to impose unduly prolix and onerous burdens on government in relation to engagement processes.[68]

In *Abahlali base'Mjondolo Movement of South Africa v Premier of the Province of KwaZulu-Natal* ("*Abahlali*"),[69] the Constitutional Court declared a provision of provincial legislation, section 16 of the KwaZulu-Natal Elimination and Prevention of Re-emergence of Slums Act 6 of 2007, inconsistent with section 26 of the Constitution. Section 16 gave the Member of the Provincial Executive Council of the Province the power to publish a notice requiring an owner or person in charge of land or buildings occupied by unlawful occupiers to institute proceedings to evict the occupiers under PIE within a certain period of time, failing which the relevant municipality was obliged to bring eviction proceedings. The majority of the Court held that this provision introduced the coercive institution of eviction proceedings thereby undermining the "dignified framework" for evictions developed by the Court in terms of Constitution and relevant legislation.[70] This dignified framework included resorting to evictions of people from their homes as a last resort after meaningful engagement has been attempted.[71]

Finally, in *Schubart Park Residents Association v City of Tshwane Metropolitan Municipality* ("*Schubart Park*")[72] the remedy of meaningful engagement accompanied by judicial supervision was ordered to facilitate the right of return for some 3000–5000 persons removed from a residential complex close to Pretoria city centre. The residents had been

---

[65]For general criticisms of the Court's judgment in this regard, see K McLean, "Meaningful Engagement: One Step Forward or Two Back?" (2010) 3 *Constitutional Court Rev* 223–42; L Chenwi, "'Meaningful Engagement' in the Realisation of Socio-economic Rights: The South African Experience" (2011) 26 *Southern African Public Law* 128–56, at 146–147.

[66]*Joe Slovo I* 2010 (3) SA 454 (CC), para 378 (footnotes omitted). See also para 247 (*per* Ngcobo, J).

[67]2010 (3) SA 454 (CC), paras 379–384 (*per* Sachs, J).

[68]See, for example, 2010 (3) SA 454 (CC), para 117 (*per* Yacoob, J); para 296 (*per* O'Regan, J).

[69]2010 (2) BCLR 99 (CC).

[70]2010 (2) BCLR 99 (CC), para 122.

[71]2010 (2) BCLR 99 (CC), paras 113–115.

[72]2013(1) SA 323 (CC).

forcibly removed from the buildings they were occupying on grounds of alleged health and safety concerns by national and municipal law-enforcement and fire brigade officials. The Constitutional Court held that this amounted to an eviction of persons from their homes without a court order in contravention of section 26(3) of the Constitution. The Municipality's tender to the residents to restore possession of the building to them – or, if restoration proved to be impossible, the provision of "alternative habitable dwellings" – subject to various conditions[73] was held by the Court to constitute an inadequate basis for a proper order of engagement between the parties. As Justice Froneman for the Court held:

> It proceeds from a "top-down" premise, namely that the City will determine when, and for how long and ultimately whether at all, the applicants may return to Schubart Park.[74]

The Court also underscored that that the attitude of the City towards the residents – regarding them as "obnoxious social nuisances" – was inconsistent with the constitutional foundations for meaningful engagement which required respect for the dignity of each person as a bearer of rights.[75]

IV.3 Meaningful engagement: Tentative lessons

The jurisprudence on meaningful engagement of the South African Constitutional Court offers many of the advantages outlined above in relation to participatory modes of rights enforcement. Meaningful engagement is a weighty factor in determining whether an eviction would be just and equitable in terms of relevant legislation, and is ultimately grounded in the right of access to adequate housing enshrined in section 26 of the Constitution. It gives a particularly vulnerable group – those without lawful title and facing eviction from their home – a voice in proceedings that could leave them without a roof over their heads or relegated to informal settlements on the margins of the city far from sustainable livelihood opportunities. It invites a range of stakeholders – the occupiers, the landowner, the local authority, legal representatives, NGOs and experts – to deliberate on case-specific solutions to the conflict between the various rights and interests involved. Depending on the specific case, these rights and interests may involve various permutations of property rights, housing rights, the health and safety responsibilities of local authorities, environmental rights, and the interests of different groups in housing projects.

In *Olivia Road*, the Court set out the institutional features and normative objectives for meaningful engagement in an evictions context. These include the involvement of specially trained, skilled Council workers to facilitate engagements on a structured basis, a commitment to finding creative ways to avoid homelessness, good faith by all the parties, transparency, and the recognition of the agency of the poor. These features were also highlighted in the *Abahlali* and *Schubart Park* cases discussed above, particularly the need to respect the human dignity of vulnerable groups and to regard them as equal partners in resolving housing rights conflicts. This conception of meaningful engagement certainly advances the ideals of participatory rights-based development.

---

[73]The terms of the tender are set out in full in the *Schubart Park* judgment, 2013(1) SA 323 (CC), para 12. This order had been endorsed by the High Court in a legal challenge brought by the residents to their eviction.

[74]2013(1) SA 323 (CC), para 50.

[75]2013(1) SA 323 (CC), paras 46–50.

However, the application of the meaningful engagement doctrine in the jurisprudence reviewed also raises a set of closely interrelated concerns. The first concerns the scope of meaningful engagement. The judgments envisage meaningful engagement as a mechanism to resolve a particular eviction dispute either during or, preferably, prior to resorting to legal proceedings. Although these cases may be regarded as a prelude to a more extensive application of the doctrine, it has largely functioned to date as a mechanism for dispute resolution. The Court has not required that the meaningful engagement doctrine be applied to resolve the broader systemic issues pertaining to housing for the urban poor. This is pertinently illustrated by the Court's refusal to entertain the systemic component of the *Olivia Road* case concerning the absence of a broader housing plan for all those affected by health and safety evictions in the Johannesburg Inner City. In the *Joe Slovo* case, the Court also imposed stringent meaningful engagement requirements for the carrying out of the eviction and relocation orders, but allowed the authorities considerable leeway in the engagement processes with the community pertaining to the manner in which the informal settlement upgrade would take place. There was a lot at stake for the community as it entailed the question whether the upgrade could be carried on *in situ* with minimum disruption, or whether a large-scale removal of the community to a temporary resettlement area would be necessary.

This use of meaningful engagement purely as a dispute resolution mechanism does not fulfil its potential as a participatory vehicle for realising the more far-reaching positive duties imposed by socio-economic rights. It may be that meaningful engagement will evolve in this direction over time, not only as a doctrine in the context of socio-economic rights litigation, but also as a fundamental feature of governance and development practice in South Africa. In this way, the meaningful engagement doctrine developed in a litigation context will have contributed to a deepening of citizen participation in rights-based development in South Africa.[76] But the jury is still out on whether meaningful engagement will fulfil its true potential in this regard.

The second concern – closely related to the first – is that meaningful engagement as a dispute-settlement mechanism runs the danger of avoiding the normative purposes and values of socio-economic rights. Although the Court articulated the goals of meaningful engagement broadly in terms of alleviating the consequences of an eviction, it did not specifically link these objectives to housing as a human right and the implications thereof in an eviction context. While it may be argued that this linkage is implicit in the Court's grounding of meaningful engagement in section 26 of the Constitution, a more explicit link between the doctrine and the rights and obligations generated by the housing rights enshrined in section 26 seems important for ensuring that the overall objectives of the engagement process are informed by the normative goals and values of housing as a human right. The danger here is that the outcome of the engagement processes will not be consistent with leading international standards that have developed on what constitutes "adequate" housing.[77]

---

[76]See G Muller, "Conceptualising 'Meaningful Engagement' as a Deliberative Democratic Partnership", (2011) 22 *Stell LR* 742–58, at 753–56. In this regard, Muller draws on Sherry Arnstein's "ladder of citizen participation" developed in S Arnstein, "A Ladder of Citizen Participation", (1969) 35 *J of the American Institute for Planners* 216–24.

[77]See, for example, the factors developed by the UN Committee on Economic, Social and Cultural Rights in determining what constitutes "adequate" housing in terms of article 11(1) of the International Covenant on Economic, Social and Cultural Rights: General Comment No 4 (Sixth session, 1991) "The Right to Adequate Housing", UN doc. E/1992/23, para 8.

This leads to the final concern which not only affects meaningful engagement, but all participatory models for rights-based development – that of bargaining inequalities.[78] In all the cases discussed above, the ultimate outcomes of the litigation were favourable for the litigants. However, in these cases, the applicants were supported by expert and dedicated legal teams from strong public interest law organisations as well as by various housing rights NGOs. The majority of those facing evictions from their homes will not have these advantages. Vulnerable, marginal communities and groups will have to face powerful property owners, developers and local authorities. In these circumstances, the affected groups may benefit more from strong pronouncements by the courts of the procedural and substantive obligations imposed by housing rights on the public and private parties involved, than from the vicissitudes of engagement processes where they are in a very weak position. It will be recalled in this regard that the Court in *Olivia Road* underscored that judicial oversight of the engagement process would not always be appropriate. One way of diminishing the impact of bargaining inequalities is for a court to set firm procedural and normative parameters within which engagement processes must occur in a particular case and to maintain on-going supervisory oversight of the engagement process. The latter can be accompanied by protective interim orders as well as on-going directions as the engagement process unfolds and the parties report back to the court on proposed solutions. This, however, creates its own set of difficulties for the judicial role, and raises problems of judicial capacity and potential tensions with the executive and administrative branches of government as courts assume a managerial oversight role.[79]

There are no easy ways out of the predicament of unequal participatory spaces except to continue to strive to find innovative ways to level the playing field between parties so that the ideals of participatory development are at least approximated. This is the challenge facing social movements, courts, government officials, human rights institutions, civil society organisations and scholars if the new participatory modes of socio-economic rights enforcement are to fulfil their promise in catalysing transformative processes to advance the realisation of socio-economic rights.

V. Conclusion

Ultimately, participatory approaches to socio-economic rights hold much promise, particularly in seeking to combine the ideals of self-government with the objectives of rights-based social and economic development. But, as I have sought to demonstrate in the context of an analysis of meaningful engagement as an adjudicatory mechanism in South African evictions law, they are not a panacea. Their potential may be undermined by applying them solely as local dispute settlement mechanisms as opposed to vehicles for

---

[78]A Cornwell, "Spaces for Transformation? Reflections on Issues of Power and Difference in Participation in Development", in S Hickey and G Mohan, "Towards Participation as Transformation: Critical Themes and Challenges", in S Hickey and G Mohan (eds), *Participation from Tyranny to Transformation* (Zed Books, London, 2004), 75–91; S Liebenberg and K Young, "Adjudicating Social and Economic Rights: Can Democratic Experimentalism Help?", in H Alviar García, K Klare, LA Williams (eds), *Social and Economic Rights in Theory and Practice: Critical Inquiries* (Routledge, Abingdon, 2015), 237–57.

[79]For an extended critique of this managerial model of judicial oversight, see R Sandler and D Schoenbrod, *Democracy by Decree: What Happens When Courts Run Government* (Yale University Press, New Haven, 2003).

collaborative processes to redress the systemic causes of socio-economic rights deprivations; by the failure of courts to ensure their consistency with the broader normative purposes of socio-economic rights; and by pervasive bargaining inequalities. More experimentation with different models of right-based participation and empirical study is needed to identify the circumstances under which participatory methods of rights enforcement are effective and empowering. It is in this painstaking work that the hopes of participatory modes of socio-economic rights enforcement for advancing the realisation of the transformative commitments of socio-economic rights ultimately lie.

Acknowledgements

I thank the participants in the seminar on *Challenges in Integrating Human Rights and Development* convened by the Åbo Akademi Institute for Human Rights, Finland on 25–26 November 2013, for valuable comments on earlier drafts of this article. Helpful comments were also received from Gustav Muller and two anonymous referees. This article is based on research supported by the National Research Foundation. Any opinions or conclusions herein are those of the author and the NRF does not accept any liability in regard thereto.

Modernisation of Maternity Care in Malawi

Alessandra Sarelin

Post-doctoral researcher, Institute for Human Rights, Åbo Akademi University, Finland

Low-income countries have by and large adopted antenatal programmes and policies regarding childbirth of high-income countries. The logic behind human rights and development interventions leads to increased regulation and homogenisation of what is considered the socially acceptable, safe and normal way to handle birth. In an effort to decrease maternal and neonatal deaths and to modernise and institutionalise childbirth, the Government of Malawi, in cooperation with donors and the international community, is creating new regulatory regimes regarding where, how and under whose care to give birth. The government has made out-of-facility births with traditional birth attendants (TBAs) illegal by banning TBAs from practising. Customary legal mechanisms have been used to compel women to seek skilled birth attendance (i.e., modern practices) and to penalise TBAs who continue to practice. The traditional birth culture embodied in TBAs is portrayed as conservative, unchanging, primitive and impossible to control and monitor due to the oral tradition it is based upon and the low literacy rate. The ban on TBAs applies as a contribution to social norms on childbirth and normalisation practices of facility-based birth. As theorised by Michel Foucault, biopolitical governance means governing people's conduct within a framework and making use of traditional legal mechanisms. In the present case, a post-colonial state employs these means in order to change people's behaviour in the area of childbirth. The purpose of this article is to analyse the modernisation process of maternity care from a biopolitical perspective, focusing on the normalising and rationalising aspects that seem to underpin the safety arguments behind the TBA ban. The starting point is that the customary law represents a political battle over what it means to be a modern state concerned with the female population; law is a discursive site, as theorised by Ratna Kapur.

I. Introduction

I.1 The context: Hospitalisation of childbirth in Malawi

International agencies advocate as a key factor increasing the proportion of births with skilled attendants to reduce maternal and perinatal mortality and morbidity in low-income countries. Consequently, low-income countries have largely adopted the antenatal programmes and policies regarding childbirth of high-income countries.[1] Malawi was one of the first countries to sign up to the Campaign for Accelerated Reduction of Maternal Mortality (CARMMA) in 2009. One of CARMMA's objectives is to accelerate actions aimed at the reduction of maternal mortality in Africa. As a member state of the

---

[1] See T Kulmala, *Maternal Health and Pregnancy Outcomes in Rural Malawi* (Academic dissertation, University of Tampere, Tampere, 2000), 18. See also A Oakley, *The Captured Womb: A History of the Medical Care of Pregnant Women* (Basil Blackwell Publisher, New York 1984).

WHO, Malawi is also a signatory to the Ouagadougou Declaration on Primary Health Care (PHC) and Health Systems in Africa: Achieving Better Health for Africa in the New Millennium in which African countries reaffirmed their commitment to PHC as a strategy for delivering health services, and as an approach to accelerate the achievement of the MDGs as advocated by the World Health Report of 2008.

Following these commitments, the hospitalisation of birth is a rapid and increasing phenomenon in many countries in the global South, including Malawi. The percentage of births attended by a skilled birth attendant (SBA) in Malawi has increased from 55.6 per cent in 2000 to 73 per cent in 2011 (although this figure has declined in some areas in the past years).[2] However, the country continues to have a high maternal mortality ratio (MMR) of at least 675 deaths per 100,000 live births, which remains above the 2015 MDG target of 560 per 100,000.[3] In the early 1980s and 1990s, the MMR varied from 398 to 620.[4] Studies indicate that maternal mortality increased from 620 per 100,000 in 1992 to 1,120 in 2000.[5] However, long-term trends show a decrease from 910 per 100,000 in 1990 to 510 in 2008.[6] More recent figures presented in different sources vary between 984 and 510 per 100,000 live births,[7] which is still higher than the 1980s. (Of course, improved reporting might be behind these figures.) In contrast to the MMR, there seems to be less contradiction around the under-five mortality rate, which has dropped from 234 per 1000 live births in 1992 to 112 per 1000 in 2010.[8]

A historic overview of developments in maternity care in western countries indicates that a rise in MMR following efforts to increase institutionalisation is not unprecedented. In Scotland, the rate continued to rise between 1900 and 1930, and was higher than it had been between 1850 and 1920. A similar pattern of mortality was experienced in Australia, the USA, Belgium, and the Netherlands. All countries recorded rates as high or higher in the early 1930s as they had been 30 years before. At the same time, countries experienced an increase in the medical involvement of midwifery despite efforts to combat this trend.[9] Recall that some medical interventions at birth, although at times life-saving for mother and child, also have serious negative effects. It was, however, a fundamental advance in pharmacology that turned the trends in MMR in Europe and America. In the late 1930s,

---

[2]A Zonal Health Officer in Lilongwe who had conducted a study on usage of SBA and TBA noted a decrease in SBA in Lilongwe, i.e., an urban area (meeting of September 2013, Lilongwe).

[3]Malawi Growth and Development Strategy II 2011–2016. Also see Malawi Demographic Health Survey 2010.

[4]C Bowie and E Geubbels, *Epidemiology of Maternal Mortality in Malawi* (College of Medicine, Malawi, 2nd ed, 2013), 8.

[5]T Bisika, "The Effectiveness of the TBA Programme in Reducing Maternal Mortality and Morbidity in Malawi" (2008) 5 *East African Journal of Public Health* 103–.

[6]This figure is presented in A Nove, "Midwifery in Malawi: In-depth Country Analysis" (*State of the World's Midwifery 2011*) 3. Available at http://www.unfpa.org/sowmy/resources/docs/country_info/ in_depth/ Malawi_SoWMYInDepthAnalysis.pdf (accessed 20 March 2014).

[7]A report by the Ministry of Health and WHO from 2006 gives the figure of 984 deaths per 100,000 live births and writes: "the situation has remained largely the same over the past decades". See Ministry of Health, *Final Report: Assessment of Future Roles of Traditional Birth Attendants (TBAs) in Maternal and Neonatal Health in Malawi* (WHO Malawi, Lilongwe, August 2006), 7.

[8]F Bustero and P Hunt, *Women's and Children's Health: Evidence of Impact of Human Rights* (WHO, Geneva, 2013), 42.

[9]M Tew, *Safer Childbirth? A Critical History of Maternity Care* (Chapman & Hall, London, 2nd ed, 1995), 276.

this depressing scene was suddenly transformed, when aseptic techniques were introduced and sulphonamides became available to treat puerperal sepsis.[10] The high mortality was due to unnecessary interference through forceps using non-aseptic techniques.[11] Maternal mortality has continued to decrease in high-income countries, except for the USA where maternal mortality ratios have doubled in 1986–2006.[12] The purpose of this article is, however, not to draw conclusions about the safest place of birth, or the safest practices used by birth assistants, although these figures are presented as background information. The point pressed here is to understand that institutionalisation of childbirth does not *automatically* lead to positive outcomes.

In an effort to modernise maternity care, the government of Malawi has made out-of-facility births with traditional birth attendants (TBAs), also known as *azambas*, illegal and has banned TBAs from practising. Sierra Leone and Uganda have also banned TBAs.[13] The WHO defines TBA as "a person who assists the mother during childbirth and who initially acquired her skills by delivering babies herself or by working with other TBAs".[14] In contrast, the WHO defines a skilled birth attendant (SBA) as "trained to proficiency in the skills needed to manage normal (uncomplicated) pregnancies, childbirth and the immediate postnatal period, and in the identification, management and referral of complications in women and newborns".[15]

However, in spite of strongly held perceptions by Malawi health professionals that the care TBAs provide is of poor quality due to low literacy, poor supervision and their old age, TBAs tend to be highly respected in rural areas and a significant number of women in Malawi, particularly in the rural areas, prefer to seek their services.[16] Based on a long-standing tradition, TBAs have the spiritual and cultural authority to receive children into this world.

1.2 Purpose and method

The purpose of the article is to analyse the modernisation process of maternity care from a biopolitical perspective, focusing on the normalising and rationalising aspects of the safety arguments behind the TBA ban. The author reviews these arguments and argues that TBAs

---

[10]M Tew, *Safer Childbirth? A Critical History of Maternity Care* (Chapman & Hall, London, 2nd ed, 1995), 284–85.

[11]C Bowie and E Geubbels, *Epidemiology of Maternal Mortality in Malawi* (College of Medicine, Malawi, 2nd ed, 2013), 6.

[12]Amnesty International, *Deadly Deliveries: The Maternal Health Care Crises in the USA* (Amnesty International, London, 2010).

[13]See K Whitaker, "Is Sierra Leone Right to Ban Traditional Birth Attendants", *The Guardian* (London, 17 January 2012). Available at http://www.theguardian.com/global-development/poverty-matters/2012/jan/17/traditional-birth-attendants-sierra-leone (accessed 15 October 2013) and "Why Traditional Birth Attendants Will Keep Thriving", *Daily Monitor*, available at http://www.monitor.co.ug/artsculture/Reviews/Why-traditional-birth-attendants-will-keep-thriving/-/691232/1845284/-/12o3ca8z/-/index.html (accessed 15 October 2013).

[14]World Health Organization, *Traditional Birth Attendants: A Joint WHO/UNICEF/UNFPA Statement* (WHO, Geneva, 1992).

[15]A joint statement by WHO, ICM and FIGO, *Making Pregnancy Safer: The Critical Role of the Skilled Attendant* (WHO, Geneva, 2004).

[16]A Nove, "Midwifery in Malawi: In-depth Country Analysis" (*State of the World's Midwifery 2011*) 3. Available at http://www.unfpa.org/sowmy/resources/docs/country_info/in_depth/Malawi_SoWMY InDepthAnalysis.pdf (accessed 20 March 2014).

can be seen as a representation of the Other. Knowledge is used as a form of power and influence, and a way to create normalised and rationalised practices and ways of being. The process of knowledge-production is a site of tension and contest, and studying it is critical in understanding assumptions about how culture, difference and the Other are produced and continue to operate at the present time.[17] *Law* (e.g. the TBA ban) is a site on which to construct the subjectivity of the Other as distinct[18] – distinct from the normalised and superior practices embraced by modern medical knowledge. Law is a discursive site: "law is an important site of politics and the struggle over meaning".[19] The customary law initiated by the head of state and enforced by the village chiefs represents a political battle over what it means to be a modern state concerned with the female population.

The article is mainly based on literature review and document analysis. A short visit to Malawi took place in September 2013, during which the author had meetings with representatives of the Reproductive Health Unit at the Ministry of Health, the Christian Health Association of Malawi (CHAM), Malawi Human Rights Commission, human rights activists, nurse midwives and ordinary mothers. In addition, two group discussions were held in a village in the southern district: one with mothers, most of whom had also been assisting at births (12 women in total), and the other with a TBA (who was certified by the local church) and her three assistants who were also elders in the village. An interview guide was used during these group meetings but spontaneous questions were also raised.

The story that was told in these encounters was one about the modern being superior to the traditional. However, the article is not meant to be normative and is not advocating for either "traditional" or "modern" childbirth practices. The reality in Malawi is that both practices exist side by side. Yet, the strong dichotomisation between the two sets of practices was prevalent in all encounters with policy-makers and is reflected here. Moreover, as a birth doula, i.e., non-medical childbirth assistant, practising in Finland, the author has also developed a certain degree of critical scepticism of western, "modern", institution-based practices – simply for the reason that these practices are not women-centred but rather practitioner-, routine- and rule-centred. Having this perspective has undoubtedly had an impact on the narrative presented in the article.

Informed consent forms in Chichewa were used in the group meetings and the discussions were recorded. No recorder was used during the other meetings. During the research visit, the author was assisted by a Malawian lawyer and specialist in women's rights, Chisomo Kaufulu-Kumwenda, who also happened to be eight months pregnant. During the two group meetings with mothers and TBAs, she acted as interpreter between Chichewa and English.

II. Global Birth Politics and Governmentality: Some Examples

Maternity care is a good example of swift developments in relation to health and population policies, starting in high-income countries and moving to low-income countries. At the

---

[17] R Kapur, *Erotic Justice: Law and the New Politics of Postcolonialism* (The Glass House Press, London, 2005), 23.

[18] R Kapur, "The Citizen and the Migrant: Postcolonial Anxieties, Law, and the Politics of Exclusion/ Inclusion", (2007) 8 *Theoretical Inq. L.* 537–, 542.

[19] R Kapur, *Erotic Justice: Law and the New Politics of Postcolonialism* (The Glass House Press, London, 2005), 50.

beginning of the twentieth century, virtually all births took place at home; by the end of the same century the place of birth had changed in almost all industrialised countries (with the exception of the Netherlands) to large hospitals. This movement of the place of birth follows similar patterns in many industrialised countries, although changes occur at different times and according to a different pace.[20]

Today, illegalising home birth is a world-wide trend. The European Court of Human Rights has received appeals which hold that the right to private life is violated in post-communist Eastern European countries such as Lithuania, Hungary, and the Czech Republic where legislation and/or practice either interferes with or bans health professionals from taking part in home deliveries.[21] In all three countries, midwives have been imprisoned for assisting at home births.[22] In the USA, government restrictions prevent women from choosing midwife-assisted home birth in 15 states.[23]

These trends can be put into the theoretical framework of Foucault's scholarship on governmentality and biopolitics. With biopolitics, Foucault means "the attempt, starting from the eighteenth century, to rationalize the problems posed by governmental practice by phenomena characteristic of a set of living beings forming populations: health, hygiene, birth rate, life expectancy, race."[24] According to Foucault, "government" is to be understood as an activity that aims to "conduct individuals through their lives by putting them under the authority of a guide who is responsible for what they do and what happens to them."[25] In this context, "government" is not depicted as an institution but rather as an "activity that consists in governing people's conduct within the framework of, and using instruments of, a state".[26] Governmentality is not only concerned with discipline and regulation but has a primary *concern* with the population, with its health, longevity, happiness, productivity, and size.[27] A great amount is at stake in care at birth: the reproduction of society.[28] The state uses legal and political tools to direct the behaviour of people so as to optimise the process of reproduction. According to Carole Pateman, modern states take an enormous interest in the quantity and quality of their population, and women are the objects of this interest due to their childbearing capacity.

---

[20]E Declercq, R DeVries and K Viisainen et al, "Where to Give Birth: Politics and the Place of Birth", in R DeVries & S Wrede et al (eds), *Birth by Design* (Routledge, New York, 2001), 7–9.

[21]See *Ternovszky v Hungary* (App no 67545/09) (2010) ECHR 14 December 2010. The cases of *Dubská and Krejzová v Czech Republic* (App nos 28859/11 and 28473/12) are under review in the European Court of Human Rights. In Lithuania, the police has investigated 400 home births. See K Kunnas, "Epäilyttävä synnyttäjä", *Helsingin Sanomat* (Helsinki, 20 May 2013).

[22]See list provided at Our Sisters in Chains, available at http://www.sistersinchains.org/our-sisters-in-chains.html (accessed 10 October 2013).

[23]AF Cohen, "The Midwifery Stalemate and Childbirth Choice: Recognizing Mothers-to-Be as the Best Late Pregnancy Decisionmakers", (2005) 80 *Indiana Law Journal* 850–71.

[24]M Foucault, *The Birth of Biopolitics: Lectures at the Collège de France 1978–1979* (English translation, 2008; first published by Palgrave Macmillan, 1978–79), 317.

[25]M Foucault, *Security, Territory and Population: Lectures at the Collège de France 1977–1978* (English translation, Palgrave Macmillan, 2007), 363.

[26]M Foucault, *The Birth of Biopolitics: Lectures at the Collège de France 1978–1979* (English translation, 2008; first published by Palgrave Macmillan, 1978–79), 318.

[27]A Gupta, "Governing Population: The Integrated Child Development Services Program in India" in TB Hansen and F Stepputat (eds), *States of Imagination: Ethnographic Explorations of the Postcolonial State* (Duke University Press, Durham NC, 2001), 66–96, at 68–69.

[28]R DeVries, *A Pleasing Birth: Midwives and Maternity Care in the Netherlands* (Temple University Press, 2004), 15.

"Motherhood" has a patriarchal meaning in modern political life. Pateman holds that while it is men's duty to die for the state it is women's duty to give birth for it.[29]

It is also important to understand the function of *liberalism* in the context of biopolitical government. Foucault highlights that comparing the quantity of "freedom" between one political system and another does not make much sense. A regime that is liberal can take the task of "continuously and effectively taking charge of individuals and their well-being, health, and work, . . . even dying",[30] even when liberalism can be understood as a critique of excessive government (according to liberal values, it is always necessary to suspect that one governs too much). Dean points out that liberalism does not reject biopolitical regulation but is concerned with managing it. Coordinated and centralised administration of life needs to be weighed against the norms of the economic process as well as against the freedoms on which they depend.[31] A liberal *critique* might be the detailed regulation of the biological processes of the species, and racist tendencies found in biopolitics.[32] The best of biopolitical intentions can sometimes be used to justify acts such as forced sterilisation or removal of indigenous children from their parents and communities in the name of their own well-being.[33] The human rights framework is offered as one way of managing the darker sides of biopolitical administration, yet human rights is also an intrinsic part of the art of government of the modern state. Foucault calls the new regime of power that takes hold through this art of government "biopower". Biopower created the mechanisms of life as a category of explicit calculations and made knowledge-power an agent of the transformation of human life. This transformation implies that "modern man is an animal whose politics places his existence as a living being in question".[34] We will see how this plays out in the context of birth politics.

In Europe, attempts to govern people's conduct in the area of maternity and childbirth can be traced back to the eighteenth century when initiatives to offer midwives official training started in France and Germany.[35] Since the end of the nineteenth century in Finland, doctors, trained midwives and associations have tried to educate and change women's pregnancy and birth behaviour. Concrete actions to make motherhood a part of the protective functions of the state were taken soon after these awareness raising campaigns.[36] The greatest changes took place when birth moved from the home to the hospital, which in Finland was a swift

---

[29]C Pateman, *The Disorder of Women* (Polity Press, Cambridge, 1989), 11.

[30]M Foucault, *The Birth of Biopolitics: Lectures at the Collège de France 1978–1979* (English translation, 2008; first published by Palgrave Macmillan, 1978–79), 62.

[31]M Dean, "'Demonic Societies': Liberalism, Biopolitics and Sovereignty", in TH Hansen and F Stepputat (eds), *States of Imagination: Ethnographic Explorations of the Postcolonial State* (Duke University Press, Durham, NC, 2001), 51.

[32]M Dean, "'Demonic Societies': Liberalism, Biopolitics and Sovereignty", in TH Hansen and F Stepputat (eds), *States of Imagination: Ethnographic Explorations of the Postcolonial State* (Duke University Press, Durham, NC, 2001), at 50.

[33]M Dean, "'Demonic Societies': Liberalism, Biopolitics and Sovereignty", in TH Hansen and F Stepputat (eds), *States of Imagination: Ethnographic Explorations of the Postcolonial State* (Duke University Press, Durham, NC, 2001), 51.

[34]P Rabinow, "Introduction" in P Rabinow (ed), *The Foucault Reader* (Penguin Books, London, 1984), 3–29, at 17. Originally in M Foucault, *The History of Sexuality*, Vol. 1 (Pantheon Books, New York, 1978), 143.

[35]See U Paananen, S Pietiläinen et al (eds), *Kätilöntyö* [The work of the midwife] (Edita Publishing, Helsinki, 2007), 17.

[36]H Helsti, *Kotisynnytysten aikaan* [At the time of home birth] (Suomalaisen kirjallisuuden seura, Helsinki, 2000), 14.

transition, peaking in the post-war years of rapid urbanisation, industrialisation, and modernisation.[37] In the pre-industrial era, maternal mortality was around two per cent in Finland, i.e., higher than in Malawi today. Mortality started to decline quickly from the 1890s,[38] in fact, long before the general hospitalisation of birth.

Just as in Malawi today, Finnish midwives with official training struggled together with the medical establishment to exclude TBAs during the first decades of the twentieth century.[39] In 1920, legislation was adopted that forcefully banned the still prevalent practice of TBAs (55 per cent of childbearing women gave birth outside of the official system around this time). From then on, only formally trained midwives and physicians were allowed to assist at births. In the 1930s, hospital birth was supported in state policy first for pathological births, and gradually for all births in the country.[40] It was mainly professional associations of doctors and midwives who believed that birth practices needed to be reformed according to middle-class ideals.[41] Women in rural, remote areas resisted modern, trained assistants because the TBAs had a respected mystical and religious role,[42] a phenomenon still seen in many low-income countries where TBAs play a role today.

III. Modernisation of Maternity and Delivery Care in Malawi

III.1 Introduction: Policy framework and the ban of traditional birth attendants

Malawi is a country in the process of redefining itself after years of structural transformations. The history of the Structural Adjustment Programmes (SAPs) can be traced back to the early 1980s. Structural Adjustment Loans were given to the country during this decade, and involved cutting public expenditure, eliminating consumer price and fertiliser subsidies and promoting export.[43] After the shift in government from a one-party regime to multiparty democracy in 1994, the new government under President Bakili Muluzi implemented unprecedented liberalisation in both economics and politics. Extreme inequalities in the distribution of land and income translated into a severe crisis in health, a fact which is also visible in the high maternal death ratios presented in the introduction to this article. The second President, Bingu Wa Mutharika, initiated a change in rhetoric and policy, in favour of smallholder famers, making food security a priority.[44] The third and current President,

---

[37]E Declercq, R DeVries and K Viisainen et al, "Where to Give Birth: Politics and the Place of Birth", in R DeVries & S Wrede et al (eds), *Birth by Design* (Routledge, New York, 2001), 15.

[38]See H Helsti, *Kotisynnytysten aikaan* [At the time of home birth] (Suomalaisen kirjallisuuden seura, Helsinki, 2000), 63.

[39]S Wrede, *Decentering Care for Mothers: The Politics of Midwifery and the Design of Finnish Maternity Services* (Åbo Akademi University Press, Turku, 2001), 17.

[40]S Wrede, *Decentering Care for Mothers: The Politics of Midwifery and the Design of Finnish Maternity Services* (Åbo Akademi University Press, Turku, 2001), 87, 89.

[41]H Helsti, *Kotisynnytysten aikaan* [At the time of home birth] (Suomalaisen kirjallisuuden seura, Helsinki, 2000), 14.

[42]E Declercq, R DeVries and K Viisainen et al, "Where to Give Birth: Politics and the Place of Birth", in R DeVries & S Wrede et al (eds), *Birth by Design* (Routledge, New York, 2001), 13.

[43]G Abalu et al, "Comparative Analysis of Structural Adjustment Programmes in Southern Africa" (SD Publications Series, 1996), 11–14. Available at http://www.afr-sd.org/publications/23souafr.pdf (accessed 17 February 2014).

[44]H Englund, *Human Rights and African Airwaves: Mediating Equality on the Chichewa Radio* (Indiana University Press, Bloomington, 2011), 5–7.

Joyce Banda, who has led the government since April 2012, has made safe motherhood a priority.[45]

In an effort to decrease maternal and neonatal deaths and to modernise and institutionalise childbirth, the Foucauldian state, in cooperation with donors and the international community, is concerned with new regulatory regimes relating to where, how and under whose care to give birth. Foucault has claimed that when birth and death rates began to be measured as elements of the nation-state, sex moved from the private to the public sphere.[46] Malawi is now starting to attempt "public regulation of sex for the greatest good". Due to the high prevalence of HIV/AIDS, this regulation has taken the form of restriction and control.[47] In this discourse, the role of medical experts and professionals, who have knowledge and expertise, is strong. The power and surveillance over people is a subtle, continuous change which relies on institutions to raise awareness, educate and advocate behaviour change. Health centres, churches, NGOs, the government and other organisations try to motivate people to change their behaviour.[48] This applies to HIV/AIDS as well as to attempts to move childbirth from the villages to the maternity clinics and hospitals. According to Korpela, the second major form of power comes from traditional religion and witchcraft. Disobeying cultural beliefs is a serious issue; constant fear of the consequences of deviant behaviour gives control to traditional leaders,[49] which is why they have influence over women's reproductive choices and place of birth.

The banning of TBAs occurred for the first time in 2007, as part of the initiative to promote safe motherhood. In the National Sexual and Reproductive Health and Rights (SRHR) Policy of 2009, it was made clear that TBAs "shall not conduct deliveries as they have been given new roles".[50] This led to TBAs practising in secret and thus raising suspicion of unreported deaths as a result of maternal complications. Currently, the new administration under President Joyce Banda has taken a tough stance against TBA in child delivery services. The President has harnessed the support of the traditional leaders in banning TBAs.[51] She has met with 200 chiefs to "sensitize and empower them" to encourage their subjects to seek SBA. Therefore, at the village level, it is the chief that ensures that the ban against TBA delivery is implemented and monitored. A woman who gives birth with a TBA can be fined by the chief. The TBA is also fined, and sometimes taken to the police to face criminal charges.[52] The chief, who is both a political and religious leader,[53] is monitored by the group village headmen who

---

[45]See F Bustero and P Hunt, *Women's and Children's Health: Evidence of Impact of Human Rights* (WHO, Geneva, 2013), 43.

[46]M Foucault, *The History of Sexuality, Vol. 1: An introduction* (originally published in 1976); Vintage, 1990), 23.

[47]D Korpela, *The Nyau Masquerade: An Examination of HIV/AIDS, Power and Influence in Malawi* (Tampere University Press, Tampere, 2011), 48.

[48]D Korpela, *The Nyau Masquerade: An Examination of HIV/AIDS, Power and Influence in Malawi* (Tampere University Press, Tampere, 2011), 50.

[49]D Korpela, *The Nyau Masquerade: An Examination of HIV/AIDS, Power and Influence in Malawi* (Tampere University Press, Tampere, 2011), 50–51.

[50]Ministry of Health, *National Sexual and Reproductive Health and Rights (SRHR) Policy* (August 2009), 10.

[51]Meeting with TBAs, Southern District of Malawi (14 September 2013). This was confirmed in meetings with health professionals.

[52]Meeting with TBAs, Southern District of Malawi (14 September 2013).

[53]M Longwe, *Growing Up: A Chewa Girl's Initiation* (Kachere Series, Malawi, 2006), 68.

for their part serve under the Traditional Authority (TA). In failing to implement the ban, the chief suffers embarrassment and risks a fine (e.g. he could be asked to give a chicken or a goat) or a benefit could be taken away.[54] Thus, the new role of TBAs is limited to "referring" pregnant women to hospitals and not conducting actual deliveries. However, the referral system has always been a challenge in some cases given the great distances between the TBA locations and health centres as well as lack of transport. Ambulances also often lack fuel, and therefore, patients and their guardians often need either to find cash for the fuel or organise alternative transport.[55]

This, in other words, means that *customary legal mechanisms* are used to force women to seek SBA (i.e., modern practices) and to penalise TBAs who continue to practice despite the government's policy of SBA-assisted childbirth. In so far as applicable law is concerned, Malawi's legal system is pluralist in character. Constitutional law is the supreme form of law. Legislation, common law, customary law, and customary international law are all sources of law. Ideally, customary law is the traditional law. It is applied by traditional leaders in the determination of "traditional matters" in their areas of jurisdiction, but also formal courts can apply customary law.[56]

The Malawi Health Sector Strategy Plan 2011–2016 provides the framework that guides the efforts of the Ministry of Health and all stakeholders in contributing to the attainment of the Malawi Growth and Development Strategy (MGDS-II) and the MDGs. Furthermore, an action-orientated road map for accelerating the reduction of maternal and neonatal mortality and morbidity has been developed. The road map looks at the short-, medium- and long-term interventions that are believed to contribute to the improvement of maternal health care. The plan identifies several contributing factors to Malawi's high mortality rate, including: (1) staff shortages and weak human resource management; (2) limited availability and utilisation of maternal health care services; (3) low quality maternal health care services; (4) weak procurement and logistics system for drugs, supplies and equipment; (5) problems of infrastructure; (6) weak referral systems; (7) harmful social and cultural beliefs and practices.[57] The road map is silent on the role of TBAs, though emphasis is on creating awareness among women, men and community leaders of the importance of skilled delivery care.[58] Unsafe abortions are not mentioned in the road map list, but a study at a large facility in Malawi indicated that 24 per cent of maternal deaths in 1999 were attributable to post-abortion complications.[59] Another factor to consider is that the adolescent fertility rate is high: 177 per 1000 women aged 19–24. It is acknowledged that the younger the mother, the

---

[54]This fine system was confirmed in several meetings and is also used in Sierra Leone where TBAs have been banned.

[55]Meeting with group of mothers, Southern District of Malawi (14 September 2013). The commonality of this problem was confirmed in other meetings.

[56]RE Kapindu, "Malawi: Legal System and Research Resources", GlobaLex 2009, 19. Available at http://www.nyulawglobal.org/globalex/malawi.htm (accessed 8 October 2013).

[57]Ministry of Health, *Road Map for Accelerating the Reduction of Maternal and Neonatal Mortality and Morbidity in Malawi* (October 2005), 5.

[58]Ministry of Health, *Road Map for Accelerating the Reduction of Maternal and Neonatal Mortality and Morbidity in Malawi* (October 2005), at 33.

[59]See BA Levandowski et al., "The Incidence of Induced Abortions in Malawi", (2013) 39 *Int Perspectives on Sexual and Reproductive Health* 88–96. The authors refer to VM Lema et al., "Maternal Mortality at the Queen Elizabeth Central Teaching Hospital, Blantyre, Malawi", (2005) 82 *East African Medical J* 3–9.

higher the risk of death.[60] Thus the mortality rate can be more than twice as high for the age group 15–19 as for those aged 20–24, and between three and seven times as high for those aged 10–14.[61]

III.2 The rational assumption: Old, illiterate traditional birth attendants must have poor outcomes

When TBA care is favoured by women it is a flexible approach which seeks to offer women companionship and emotional support in labour. At least three or four women, in addition to the TBA, are present in the home during labour. This experience is not possible in the hospital setting because of strict policies on numbers of companions,[62] although this is changing as policies now encourage mothers to bring one female guardian to accompany them during births. Husbands have also recently been allowed into maternity wards. Moreover, TBAs are often favoured by women in the community because they respect the birthing woman, their fluency in local languages (Chichewa and others) and their relative status positions in the community.[63]

Malawian TBAs are lay midwives who have learned the craft through practical experience and oral tradition rather than formal learning. This allots TBAs great independence, but they also face similar challenges as the uneducated, working-class midwives of the late 1800s in Australia, who struggled to challenge medicine's claim that their practices are unsafe.[64] Midwives who learned their skills through practical experience and oral traditions also used to be the way to learn midwifery skills in industrialised countries until medicine took over birthing and the formal education of (nurse) midwives was initiated. In many contexts, both medicine and nursing opposed the training of independent midwives.[65]

In Malawi, training TBAs in the application of safe childbirth practices has been abandoned as a strategy to reduce maternal and neonatal mortality. Discarding this strategy has occurred after several decades of controversy around the position of TBAs in delivery care in low-income countries. In 1992, the WHO, UNICEF and UNFPA issued a joint statement stating that "because of the current shortage of professional midwives and institutional facilities to provide prenatal care, clean, safe deliveries as well as a variety of primary health care functions, WHO, UNICEF and UNFPA promote the training of TBAs in order to bridge the gap until there is access to acceptable, professional, modern health care services for all women and children".[66] Studies from the early 1980s revealed

---

[60]World Bank, "Reproductive health at a glance: Malawi" (April 2011). Available at http://siteresources. worldbank.org/INTPRH/Resources/376374-1303736328719/Malawi42211web.pdf (accessed 17 February 2014).

[61]See M Tew, *Safer Childbirth? A Critical History of Maternity Care* (Chapman & Hall, London, 2nd ed, 1995), 304.

[62]A Kumar, *The Examination of Traditional Birth Attendant Practices and their Role in Maternal Health Services in Mwandama Village Cluster* (College of Medicine Master's Thesis in Public Health, Blantyre, Malawi, 2007), 1.

[63]Ministry of Health, *Final Report: Assessment of Future Roles of Traditional Birth Attendants (TBAs) in Maternal and Neonatal Health in Malawi* (WHO Malawi, August 2006).

[64]K Fahy, "An Australian History of the Subordination of Midwifery", (2007) 4(1) *Women and Birth* 25–29.

[65]K Fahy, "An Australian History of the Subordination of Midwifery", (2007) 4(1) *Women and Birth* 25–29.

[66]World Health Organization, *Traditional Birth Attendants: A Joint WHO/UNICEF/UNFPA statement* (WHO, Geneva, 1992).

that most maternal deaths occurring among women attended by TBAs in Malawi would have been avoidable had the TBAs' skills been supplemented by those of modern midwifery. In 1982, a national TBA training programme was started and 2000 of the estimated existing 5000 TBAs had been trained by 2002.[67] Trained TBAs were given a delivery kit and were supervised by a TBA coordinator. Seeking the services of a trained TBA is sometimes the only way a woman in a rural community can have access to a clean delivery.[68]

Over the years, the WHO has shifted its policy regarding TBA training following evidence that is claimed to cast doubt on their effectiveness in improving outcomes for babies (the effect on maternal mortality has been too difficult to study). In one study from Mozambique, no significant differences in still birth, perinatal or infant mortality were found in women delivered in health facilities, by trained TBAs or untrained TBAs.[69] This study and other similar research[70] were used as evidence of the limited impact of training TBAs, but can also be seen as evidence of the limited impact of skilled birth attendance at health facilities. This is, however, not the way the results have been interpreted.

In line with the WHO, the Malawi government's focus has shifted towards the promotion of skilled attendants at birth. The justification for this shift is placed on the old age and illiteracy among TBAs and that "TBAs will [not] change their old practices to adopt new modern practices".[71] The automatic assumption is that "modern" practices are superior to "traditional" ones. The fact that some TBAs are also traditional healers makes the perception of them even more suspicious. "Harmful practices" used by TBAs that are listed both in written material and in my meetings with health professionals include the use of herbs to stimulate effective uterine contractions and to facilitate healing of a tear during the postpartum period.[72] Practices commonly applied in modern obstetric care in Malawi and elsewhere, such as fundal pressure and episiotomy, that have been shown in research[73] to be harmful for women, are not regarded as such. Not only is it unnecessary to inflict intentional vaginal trauma, it is harmful to woman on many levels. Cutting the perineum means severing

---

[67]Ministry of Health, *Final Report: Assessment of Future Roles of Traditional Birth Attendants (TBAs) in Maternal and Neonatal Health in Malawi* (WHO Malawi, August 2006), 16; A Kumar, *The Examination of Traditional Birth Attendant Practices and their Role in Maternal Health Services in Mwandama Village Cluster* (College of Medicine Master's Thesis in Public Health, Blantyre, Malawi, 2007), 1.

[68]T Bisika, "The Effectiveness of the TBA Programme in Reducing Maternal Mortality and Morbidity in Malawi" (2008) 5 *East African Journal of Public Health* 103–, 105, 109.

[69]S Gloyd, et al, "Impact of Traditional Birth Attendant Training in Mozambique: A Controlled Study", (2001) 46 *Journal of Midwifery & Women's Health* 210–16.

[70]Bergström and Goodburn have reviewed studies on training of TBAs and conclude: "None of these studies leads to a conclusion that TBA training as a single intervention can have a significant impact on maternal mortality." S Bergström and E Goodburn, *The Role of Traditional Birth Attendants in the Reduction of Maternal Mortality*, available at www.jsieurope.org/safem/collect/safem/pdf/s2933e/s2933e. pdf (accessed 14 October 2013), 10.

[71]Ministry of Health, *Final Report: Assessment of Future Roles of Traditional Birth Attendants (TBAs) in Maternal and Neonatal Health in Malawi* (WHO Malawi, August 2006), 20.

[72]Meeting with a perinatal nurse specialist (Blantyre, 13 September 2013); Meeting with nurse midwife and PhD student (Lilongwe 12 September 2013); Meeting with human rights lawyer (Lilongwe 9 September 2013). The use of herbs was also raised in the group meeting with TBAs.

[73]H Goer and A Romano, *Optimal Care in Childbirth: The Case for a Physiological Approach* (Pinter & Martin Ltd, London, 2013; first published in the USA by Classic Day Publishing, 2012) 327, 345, 365–372.

the sexual nerve system, which is a serious assailment of a woman's bodily and sexual integrity[74] and would deserve attention from a human rights perspective. This is especially considering that there is new research showing a connection between trauma to the vagina and the female brain. Vaginal trauma is not "just" physical. A fully functioning pelvic nerve system is crucial for producing the dopamine, oxytocin, and other chemicals that raise levels of perception, confidence, and feistiness.[75]

This is not to say that TBAs use safe practices, or to say that TBA practices are preferable to those of SBAs. Not all TBA practices are evidence-based – but this is also the case with SBA practices.[76] It should also be kept in mind that throughout the history of childbirth practices, there have been many incompetent birth attendants. These attendants could have been professional midwives, trained by apprenticeship with or without some formal, theoretical instruction; or self-trained handywomen who learnt their skills through practical experience; or untrained, unskilled helpers, relations, friends or neighbours.[77] However, there is also evidence that illiterate, untrained, yet very competent midwives can have excellent records.[78] There is no reason to doubt that this would not also be true in Malawi. There is no convincing evidence that TBAs alone can be blamed for the high toll of maternal deaths.

Since the tendency to celebrate modern obstetrics as superior to the birth customs embodied in the TBAs is so strong in Malawi, there is an equally strong assumption that the high maternal mortality rate is due to the low institutional delivery rate. However, studies that would compare the differences in outcomes between births attended by "skilled attendants" and "unskilled attendants" in Malawi are not available. What seems to be clear is that the majority of maternal deaths take place in hospitals,[79] though it is unclear whether these deaths are due to late referrals or sub-standard care. According to a study from Kamuzu Central Hospital in Lilongwe, maternal deaths were due to inadequate case management, non-availability of drugs, poor transport, unnecessary delays at peripheral health facilities and absence of qualified staff.[80]

According to the same study from Kamuzu Central Hospital, nearly 60 per cent of the women who died in hospitals were assisted by either a doctor or a clinical officer while 34 percent were attended by a nurse midwife. Unsafe abortions were also a major contributor to

---

[74]See HJ Baker, "'We Don't Want to Scare the Ladies': An Investigation of Maternal Rights and Informed Consent Throughout the Birth Process", (2010) 31 *Women's Rights Law Reporter* 538–93. Baker calls the episiotomy "a medically sanctioned female genital mutilation" (at 575).

[75]See N Wolf, *Vagina: A New Biography* (HarperCollins Publisher, New York, 2012), 24 and 88.

[76]A study reported that only one third of all of the American College of Obstetricians and Gynecologists guidelines, which form the basis of practice of obstetrics in the US, are based on scientifically sound evidence. See JD Wright et al., "Scientific Evidence Underlying the American College of Obstetricians and Gynecologists Practice Bulletins", (2011) 118 *Obstet & Gynecol* 505–12.

[77]M Tew, *Safer Childbirth? A Critical History of Maternity Care* (Chapman & Hall, London, 2nd ed, 1995), 7.

[78]See examples from the USA and England between the period of 1778 and 1890, provided in M Tew, *Safer Childbirth? A Critical History of Maternity Care* (Chapman & Hall, London, 2nd ed, 1995), 271.

[79]As a parallel, one can refer to a study about trends in maternal mortality in England in which the author finds no evidence for hospitalisation of birth being associated with lower mortality. If anything, hospitalisation was associated with higher mortality: the regions with more hospital births being the regions with higher mortality. See M Tew, *Safer Childbirth? A Critical History of Maternity Care* (Chapman & Hall, London, 2nd ed, 1995), 298.

[80]T Bisika, "The Effectiveness of the TBA Programme in Reducing Maternal Mortality and Morbidity in Malawi" (2008) 5 *East African Journal of Public Health* 103–, 104.

maternal deaths.[81] Maternal deaths were rare with TBAs, which could either indicate that TBAs are indeed referring high-risk cases to the hospitals, or that TBAs and community members do not report maternal deaths out of fear of repercussions. According to Bisika, as many as 200 women could be collectively referred to the hospital by TBAs in one community. Further, the same study notes that TBAs were aware of danger signs and complications such as haemorrhage, infections, obstructed labour, eclampsia and abortion. The main challenge was, however, referral logistics such as lack of transport and money.[82]

III.3 The providers of modern maternity care

In Malawi, the government is the main provider of health services, including maternity care. It provides 60 per cent of the available services that are supposed to be free of charge for users; however, the reality is that women are told to bring equipment such as a plastic cover with them to hospital. In addition, the medication required for treatment is often unavailable and patients have to purchase their medication from private pharmacies. The private sector, which provides the remaining 40 per cent of service delivery, is dominated by not-for-profit providers, mainly CHAM, and is particularly present in rural, hard-to-reach areas[83] and who charge a small fee from their clients. Because CHAM is subsidised by the government, this fee is low.[84]

The fact that TBAs have been popular among women is also to due to the severe shortage of maternity care professionals in Malawi.[85] A study from 2004 shows that 64 per cent of nurses and other health personnel posts in Malawi's public health system were not filled.[86] According to the baseline from 2010–2011, provided in the Malawi Health Sector Strategic Plan 2011–2016, only half of the health centres have the minimum staff levels needed to offer emergency health services.[87]

The National Organisation of Nurses and Midwives, a professional association, has grown in seven years from 50 to 9,000 members, which is indicative of the changes that maternity care is going through as a consequence of the hospitalisation of childbirth. However, not all of the nurses have studied, or have experience of, midwifery care. Since 1990, midwifery has not been compulsory on the Bachelor degree courses in nursing.[88]

---

[81]T Bisika, "The Effectiveness of the TBA Programme in Reducing Maternal Mortality and Morbidity in Malawi" (2008) 5 *East African Journal of Public Health* 103–.

[82]T Bisika, "The Effectiveness of the TBA Programme in Reducing Maternal Mortality and Morbidity in Malawi" (2008) 5 *East African Journal of Public Health* 103–, at 107–9.

[83]J James and T Collins, *Achieving Equity in Skilled Birth Attendance: Malawi* (Addressing Inequalities: The Heart of the Post-2015 Development Agenda and the Future We Want for All, 2012), 9.

[84]Meeting with CHAM (Lilongwe, 16 September 2013).

[85]A Nove, "Midwifery in Malawi: In-depth Country Analysis" (*State of the World's Midwifery 2011*) 3. Available at http://www.unfpa.org/sowmy/resources/docs/country_info/in_depth/Malawi_SoWMYIn DepthAnalysis.pdf (accessed 20 March 2014), 15.

[86]T Bisika, "The Effectiveness of the TBA Programme in Reducing Maternal Mortality and Morbidity in Malawi" (2008) 5 *East African Journal of Public Health* 103–, 104.

[87]Ministry of Health, *Malawi Health Sector Strategic Plan 2011–2016: Moving Towards Equity and Quality* (Government of Malawi, September 2011), 15.

[88]A Nove, "Midwifery in Malawi: In-depth Country Analysis" (*State of the World's Midwifery 2011*) 3. Available at http://www.unfpa.org/sowmy/resources/docs/country_info/in_depth/Malawi_SoWMYInDepth Analysis.pdf (accessed 20 March 2014), 6.

For those who choose to study midwifery as part of their nursing degree, there are two options: to become a registered midwife with a four-year training period leading to a degree, or enrol as a nurse midwife with a three-year period of training. The latter cadre are known as nurse midwives technicians. It is not possible to study midwifery separately from nursing.[89] Nurse midwives are trained to conduct all deliveries without a doctor,[90] including breech and twin births. They are also allowed to use instruments such as vacuum extractors. C-section operation is the only procedure relating to childbirth that they cannot do.[91] This puts the modern nurse midwife in a strong position as a provider of modern obstetric care. In contrast, in many parts of the world, medicalisation and hospitalisation of birth has been accompanied by the undermining of the role of the midwife. In the eighteenth century European regulations forbidding midwives from using instruments were strengthened, their role in gynaecology and minor surgery undermined and their competence confined to normal births, falling under the supervision of doctors.[92]

Although Malawi has started to train *community midwives* (18 months training) it is symptomatic that this new cadre of staff does not cooperate with the banned TBAs and is also prohibited from conducting deliveries and should instead refer mothers to a facility-based birth.[93] Their role seems to be similar to *health surveillance assistants* who are called "frontline workers" and act as community-based health workers employed by the government. Since the mid-2000s, the government has scaled up the employment of health surveillance assistants in hard-to-reach areas.[94] They are recruited in the communities and first receive 12 weeks of training and then an additional ten-week training period as their role has been extended to include maternal and child health. This training focuses on the importance of antenatal care, facility-based delivery, postnatal care, and danger signs during pregnancy, as well as community case management. It is believed that their input, supported by village chiefs, has played a key role in increasing "the demand for SBA".[95] Many of the women who accompany pregnant women to the nearest health facility to deliver are health surveillance assistants.[96] Their responsibilities include "home visits and inspections of sanitation facilities, collection of vital data and maintenance of the village register".[97] This strong focus on surveillance, inspections, registers and vital data concerning the health status of the population fits into the

---

[89]J James and T Collins, *Achieving Equity in Skilled Birth Attendance: Malawi* (Addressing Inequalities: The Heart of the Post-2015 Development Agenda and the Future We Want for All, 2012), 9 and 16.

[90]A Nove, "Midwifery in Malawi: In-depth Country Analysis" (*State of the World's Midwifery 2011*), 3. Available at http://www.unfpa.org/sowmy/resources/docs/country_info/in_depth/Malawi_SoWMYInDepthAnalysis.pdf (accessed 20 March 2014), 5.

[91]Meeting with perinatal nurse specialist (Blantyre, 13 September 2013).

[92]R DeVries, *A Pleasing Birth: Midwives and Maternity Care in the Netherlands* (Temple University Press, 2004), 62.

[93]J James and T Collins, *Achieving Equity in Skilled Birth Attendance: Malawi* (Addressing Inequalities: The Heart of the Post-2015 Development Agenda and the Future We Want for All, 2012), 15.

[94]F Bustero and P Hunt, *Women's and Children's Health: Evidence of Impact of Human Rights* (WHO, Geneva, 2013), 46.

[95]J James and T Collins, *Achieving Equity in Skilled Birth Attendance: Malawi* (Addressing Inequalities: The Heart of the Post-2015 Development Agenda and the Future We Want for All, 2012), 15.

[96]J James and T Collins, *Achieving Equity in Skilled Birth Attendance: Malawi* (Addressing Inequalities: The Heart of the Post-2015 Development Agenda and the Future We Want for All, 2012), at 16.

[97]F Bustero and P Hunt, *Women's and Children's Health: Evidence of Impact of Human Rights* (WHO, Geneva, 2013), 46.

biopolitical ideal of a "docile body that may be subjected, used, transformed and improved".[98] Training of community midwives and health surveillance assistants can be seen as an example of the subtle power given to local agents of behaviour change.

III.4 The position of childbearing women

The organisation and provision of maternity care is a mix of medical science, cultural ideas and structural forces. While other medical specialties have a high degree of technical uniformity that crosses national borders, this is not the case in birth care. According to DeVries, the influence of culture and society is not masked by uniformity in technology and practice. Ideas about sexuality, women and families are embedded in birth care.[99]

Malawi is a matrilineal and matrilocal society where women control the house, village and fields.[100] (One can hypothesise that as long as birth takes place in the house and with a TBA it is in the hands of women, but when birth moves to a public institution outside of the village power moves to men and public power holders.) The Chewa woman has traditionally been regarded as "the root of the linage". She was looked at as a "sacred vessel of life" and had high status as being responsible for the perpetuation of the linage and community.[101] In pre-colonial sub-Saharan Africa, women had unique roles because of the emphasis on kinship and reproduction. Reference can be found to royal queens and queen mothers, female rulers and priestesses in myths of both patrilineal and matrilineal groups.[102] This does not, of course, mean that it was an ideal society for women. The Chewa can be said to be both matrilineal and patriarchal as the most important person in a direct family line was the maternal uncle who had control over the woman and her offspring.[103] During colonialism, "civilising" missions sought to totally reconstruct African society and culture which also had an effect on the position of women.[104] Civilisation and Christianity went hand in hand to eradicate "superstitious beliefs in magic, spirits, ancestors, and witchcraft of the "primitive" people". The nineteenth and twentieth century western missionaries were also shaped by their worldview to place great value in science and reason, while retaining their faith in God. Schools and hospitals were therefore built in an effort to explain in neutral and scientific terms nature and diseases.[105] Women were primarily expected to be homemakers and mothers, and to be subordinate to their husbands, the church and societal customs and rules.[106] On the other hand, new legal options gave women some opportunities to air their

---

[98]Quoted in P Rabinow, "Introduction" in P Rabinow (ed), *The Foucault Reader* (Penguin Books, London, 1984), 3–29, at 17. Originally in M Foucault, *The History of Sexuality*, Vol. 1 (Pantheon Books, New York, 1978), 17. Originally from M Foucault, *Discipline and Punish* (1975; English translation Vintage Books, 1979), 198.

[99]R DeVries, *A Pleasing Birth: Midwives and Maternity Care in the Netherlands* (Temple University Press, 2004), 15.

[100]D Korpela, *The Nyau Masquerade: An Examination of HIV/AIDS, Power and Influence in Malawi* (Tampere University Press, Tampere, 2011), 32.

[101]M Longwe, *Growing up: A Chewa Girl's Initiation* (Kachere Series, Malawi, 2006), 19.

[102]NL Aniekwu, "Converging Constructions: A Historical Perspective on Sexuality and Feminism in Post-Colonial Africa", *Africa Sociological Review* 10 (2006), 143–60, at 146.

[103]M Longwe, *Growing up: A Chewa Girl's Initiation* (Kachere Series, Malawi, 2006), 20.

[104]Aniekwu (n 102 above) 146.

[105]M Longwe, *Growing up: A Chewa Girl's Initiation* (Kachere Series, Malawi, 2006), 27.

[106]M Longwe, *Growing up: A Chewa Girl's Initiation* (Kachere Series, Malawi, 2006), 34–35.

concerns against "cultural injustices", for example to object to extreme inequalities regarding traditional marriage and property rights.[107]

Arriving in post-colonial times, the feminist movement that has emerged in Africa can be described as heterosexual, prenatal and concerned with women's rights, political and economic issues. It differs from "western feminism" which largely advocates for sexual rights, female control over reproduction and choices within sexuality.[108] Symbolic gender distinctions and identities that "incorporate naturalist assumptions about what it means to be a man or a woman" tend to be accepted by a large group of African feminists while challenging the subordination of women.[109]

Childbirth is not separate from other major life transitions in women's lives. We know that initiation ceremonies for girls coming of age in Malawi (*chinamwali*) are changing as the old rituals have been condemned as "pagan" or unchristian. The traditional Chewa *chinamwali* ritual, which lasted over several days, has been replaced by a set of Christianised, written instructions and a short ceremony of a few hours. Girls are instructed on issues of puberty, marriage, first pregnancy and the birth of the first child by so called *alangizis*. Little emphasis is placed on ritual, symbols and the development of ceremonies.[110] A similar development is observable in childbirth: this transition is increasingly treated as a practical medical matter and less as a deeply personal and culturally significant rite of passage for a woman and her family that carries cultural, spiritual and social meaning and value.[111] (The weakening of initiation ceremonies for girls coming of age was also linked by many of the older women I met to the fact that girls as young as 11 years get pregnant.)[112] The custom of allowing a newly married young woman to attend a birth before it is her time to become a mother, in order for her to have confidence in the birthing process, is also disappearing as births are isolated into institutions.[113]

The women who took part in the group meeting for mothers were careful to let me know that they do prefer hospital but that often births are so fast that there is no time to relocate. What happens in most of the births that take place in the village, whether planned or accidental, is that the relocation to hospital is made after the baby is born. If the mother and child are doing well, the hospital staff will not ask many questions, but if there were complications the mother might get sanctioned. In cases of acute emergencies such as excessive bleeding, and subject to transportation options, the TBA or other birth assistant needs to first take the woman to the closest maternity ward. They may nevertheless be met with a lack of available drugs and equipment to assist. From here, they will receive a referral

---

[107]NL Aniekwu, "Converging Constructions: A Historical Perspective on Sexuality and Feminism in Post-Colonial Africa", *Africa Sociological Review* 10 (2006), 143–60, 147.

[108]NL Aniekwu, "Converging Constructions: A Historical Perspective on Sexuality and Feminism in Post-Colonial Africa", *Africa Sociological Review* 10 (2006), 143–60, 143

[109]NL Aniekwu, "Converging Constructions: A Historical Perspective on Sexuality and Feminism in Post-Colonial Africa", *Africa Sociological Review* 10 (2006), 143–60, 145.

[110]M Longwe, *Growing up: A Chewa Girl's Initiation* (Kachere Series, Malawi, 2006), 79–81.

[111]The White Ribbon Alliance for Safe Motherhood, 2013. Respectful Maternity Care - The Universal Rights of Childbearing Women, 2013. http://www.healthpolicyproject.com/pubs/46_FinalRespectful CareCharter.pdf (accessed 11 September 2014).

[112]Meeting with TBAs 2013; this was confirmed in other meetings.

[113]Meeting with group of mothers, southern district of Malawi, 14 September 2013.

to the hospital. Taking the bleeding woman straight to the hospital, they will be sent to the maternity ward for a written referral and lose valuable time.[114]

The reality in Malawian hospitals and clinics is that due to the limited number of staff and the increasing number of women coming from the villages to deliver as a result of the banned practice of TBAs, some women may end up giving birth to their baby without skilled attendance, despite waiting in a hospital shelter for the birth for an extended time. Women are encouraged to take a female guardian with them as they arrive at the shelter and sometimes this person is the one present when baby is born if the nurse is busy. In some instances, the guardian is chased away when labour starts due to limited space, thus some women end up giving birth alone, without any assistance.[115] Hospital cleaners also often assist at births in the absence of available nurses.[116] As a result of unassisted births, babies sometimes die in the hospitals. When women return to the village and share these stories with other women, they are discouraged from making the effort to go to hospital.[117]

Another factor that demotivates women is the sometimes harsh treatment by nurses.[118] The beating of pregnant women, rudeness, the performing of operations while inebriated, discrimination of poor women, delays in treating women and lack of privacy and confidentiality are issues mentioned in needs assessment studies.[119] I was told that women can be slapped by a nurse upon arrival at the hospital.[120] Yelling and inhibiting the presence of emotional and physical support from guardians seems to be common practice. Disrespectful and sometimes even abusive care by maternity ward nurses is a global problem and by no way unique to Malawi. New research shows that abuse and disrespect in facility-based childbirth is a major deterrent to skilled birth care utilisation in low-income countries. This deterrence has received less attention than other deterring factors such as geographic and financial obstacles.[121]

In Malawi, women who have negative experiences of public hospitals sometimes go to extreme efforts to raise money for private maternity and delivery care. Although I was told the care they receive in the private clinics is respectful and kind, there is another challenge in for-profit maternity care. The care-provider is more likely to find a reason to perform surgical birth and consequently send the client home with an expensive bill (and a surgical wound). Private hospitals do not provide the public with statistics revealing the percentage of

---

[114]Meeting with group of mothers, southern district of Malawi, 14 September 2014.

[115]See C Bowie and E Geubbels, *Epidemiology of Maternal Mortality in Malawi* (College of Medicine, Malawi, 2nd ed, 2013), 19.

[116]Meeting with perinatal nurse specialist (Blantyre, 13 September 2013) and Malawi Human Rights Commission (Lilongwe, 11 September 2013). Cleaners were also mentioned in group meetings with mothers and TBAs.

[117]This issue was taken up in all meetings both with nurse midwives, human rights activists, and ordinary mothers, and also in the group meeting with TBAs.

[118]The dissatisfaction with nurses' behaviour is raised also in newspapers, see E Shawa, "On Quality Nursing Care and Patients Needs" *The Nation* (Lilongwe, 9 September 2013).

[119]C Bowie and E Geubbels, *Epidemiology of Maternal Mortality in Malawi* (College of Medicine, Malawi, 2nd ed, 2013), 19.

[120]Meeting with pregnant woman and mother of two (Lilongwe, 10 September 2013).

[121]D Browser and K Hill, *Exploring Evidence for Disrespect and Abuse in Facility-Based Childbirth* (USAID-TRAction project, Harvard School of Public Health, 2010), 3. See also LP Freedman, "Human Rights, Constructive Accountability and Maternal Mortality in the Dominican Republic: A Commentary", (2003) 82 *Int J of Gynecology and Obstetrics* 111–14.

C-section births but according to anecdotal evidence it is high. I met a mother of five who had three C-sections and two vaginal births in a private hospital in Lilongwe. In one of the surgical births the baby died on the second day. The reason is unknown to the mother.[122]

Caesarean section is the most common major surgical operation in sub-Saharan Africa and most operative births are emergencies. C-sections have a much higher mortality rate for mother and baby in Africa compared with industrialised countries.[123] Despite the risks, there is a general trend among middleclass women to opt for a C-section without medical necessity and to normalise surgical births through highlighting that there is no difference between vaginal and surgical births.[124]

Women have the right to safe and humane treatment during pregnancy and birth, and abusive care is of course contrary to human rights standards, yet a discussion of this aspect of facility-based care is absent in Malawi, although the National Sexual and Reproductive Health and Rights Policy claims to apply a human rights-based approach.[125] There is no law protecting patients' rights and only one or two human rights activists have put women's experiences of negligence and sub-standard care into a human rights framework. The regulatory framework that exists – the Nurses and Midwives Council, the Medical Council of Malawi and the Pharmacies, Medicines and Poisons Board – remain passive and out of reach for most women.[126]

Childbearing women in Malawi may have little power over the institutionalised political order determining the preferred place of birth on their behalf, but they do have power to regulate their own inner state of being and behaviour. Ensuring that young women have seen uncomplicated, normal births is one strategy that gives them confidence and self-esteem. However, the impression I had from the two group meetings is that *social norms* concerning birth largely determine a *birthing woman's* behaviour. One example is of women in the discussion with mothers proudly telling me that the "delivery position" (their wording) is the same in the village as in the hospital, i.e., the lithotomy position in which woman lies on her back. According to the elders who dominated the discussions, the birthing woman is not free to choose another position. However, this question raised debate among the participants, some of whom had given birth unassisted and then assumed another position for the final stages of labour, which they found easier. This may indicate that the homogenising tendencies – that there is a standard way a modern woman should give birth – are equally strong regardless of the place of birth. The supine position is strongly associated with modern obstetric management. Women in "traditional societies" have, according to ethnologists and historians, adopted various birth positions, most often upright or crouching, squatting, kneeling, standing (supported by birth attendants), leaning and sitting but the recumbent position has been rare.[127]

---

[122]Meeting with mother of four, Lilongwe, September 2013.

[123]PM Fenton, "Caesarean Section in Malawi: Prospective Study of Early Maternal and Perinatal Mortality", (2003) *BMJ* 327–, at 587.

[124]P Mpaso, "Demystifying C-section Birth" (*Weekend Nation*, 7 September 2013).

[125]2009, 6.

[126]This was raised in meeting with a perinatal nurse specialist who has been actively involved in midwifery associations (Blantyre, 13 September 2013) and by Malawi Human Rights Commission (Lilongwe, 11 September 2013).

[127]J Balaskas, *Active Birth: The New Approach to Giving Birth Naturally* (Revised edition of 1992, first edition published in 1983, The Harvard Common Press), 11. Balaskas refers to Dr GJ Engelmann's famous book *Labour Among Primitive Peoples* from 1883.

In all settings, whether low-income or high-income, urban or rural, the biomedical model of caring for birth has become the norm. Birth has been taken out of its cultural context, doctors put into control (directly or indirectly) while the "patient" is to be passive. In this ideal, women are expected to abandon their instincts, emotions and intuitive knowing. Moreover, community and relationship is given low priority in this model of care where man is separated from the environment.[128] "Safety" is defined narrowly in terms of mortality and morbidity only – there is no place for long-term emotional, cultural and spiritual safety.

IV. Concluding Discussion

Although one can argue that making facility-based birth the only lawful option is a forceful intervention in women's choices, autonomy and self-determination, this is seldom the perspective offered. Rather, it is underlined that since women in higher wealth quintiles and urban areas tend to opt for professional care as opposed to their poor rural sisters this must mean that preference for TBA-services is more an issue of lack of choice for rural women than the contrasting view that TBAs possess positive attributes that "attract" women.[129] Just as liberalism has been built on the idea that the subject is decontextualised, ahistorical, and reasoning,[130] middle-class ideals are assumed to be rational and universal. To recognise this is not to advocate for TBA-care before SBA, but rather to call for a more nuanced analysis of birth politics, culture and society as complex and ever-changing.

In contemporary Malawi, there is a campaign to "demystify the cultural beliefs held against SBA",[131] so that women would seek skilled attendance and become acquainted with hospital protocol. The ban on TBAs seems to contribute to the social norms around childbirth and the *normalisation* of the practices of facility-based birth. According to Foucault, the development of biopower transforms the way the law operates so that it works as an *informal norm* where "the judicial institution is increasingly incorporated into a continuum of apparatuses (medical, administrative, and so on) the function of which are for the most part regulative".[132] Norms operate as if there were such a being as "the average man"; they refer to the characteristics of the population so normalised.[133] There are a number of social norms, both "modern" and "traditional", concerning how the "average woman" – the normalised childbearing population – is supposed to be and act.

Today's logic behind human rights and development interventions leads to increased regulation and homogenisation of what is the socially acceptable, safe and normal way to

---

[128]T Kopare, *Att rida stormen ut: Förlossningsberättelser i Finnmark and Sámpi* [Birthstories from Finnmark and Sámpi] (Akademisk avhandling, Göteborgs universitet, 1999), 18.

[129]A Kumar, *The Examination of Traditional Birth Attendant Practices and their Role in Maternal Health Services in Mwandama Village Cluster* (College of Medicine Master's Thesis in Public Health, Blantyre, Malawi, 2007), 1.

[130]R Kapur, *Erotic Justice: Law and the New Politics of Postcolonialism* (The Glass House Press, London, 2005), 26.

[131]Quote from J James and T Collins, *Achieving Equity in Skilled Birth Attendance: Malawi* (Addressing Inequalities: The Heart of the Post-2015 Development Agenda and the Future We Want for All, 2012), 18.

[132]M Foucault, *The History of Sexuality, Vol. 1: An Introduction* (Originally published in 1976; Vintage, 1990), 144.

[133]M Dean, *Governmentality: Power and Rule in Modern Society* (SAGE Publications, 1999), 118.

handle birth. As theorised by Foucault, biopolitical governance means directing people's conduct within the framework and using the instruments of, in this case, a post-colonial state that applies traditional legal mechanisms in order to change people's behaviour in the area of childbirth, thus increasing rational choices and the demand for SBA. (Women who opt for TBA-care are dismissed as crazy and ignorant of their own good.) To be free from excessive maternal mortality means to have a certain kind of modern state that is capable of taking care of its citizens.

The traditional birth culture in Malawi, embodied in TBAs, is portrayed as conservative, non-changeable, primitive and impossible to control and monitor, due to the oral tradition it is based on and the low literacy rate. In short, TBAs are a representation of "the Other". They are seen as unable to deal with the complications that sometimes cause maternal deaths. The homogenised delivery care offered by skilled attendants in safe hospitals is presented as the only solution. This care is the responsibility of the Foucauldian state and is, ideally, offered free of charge or at a subsidised price.

The ban of TBAs has contributed to a strong contradiction between SBAs and TBAs, creating a separation of the modern and the traditional. This dualistic thinking is characteristic of the modern political landscape.[134] Inherent in the dualistic view is also a separation of the mother and her child – between her and her baby's interests. The unborn is defined to be in need of protection against a potentially irrational mother who can make the wrong decisions. As stated by Ratna Kapur, "Protectionist responses continue to treat women as weak and vulnerable, incapable of taking decisions – in fact, inferior – while the state, in its *parens patriae* capacity (or even non-governmental actors) take actions on behalf of women".[135]

The discourse around the danger of TBA-supported birth outside medical control reflects and perpetuates a view in which women's bodies are flawed and in need of control and intervention. While women are socialised to believe that their inherent purpose of life is to bear children and reproduce society, they are also led to believe that their bodies are untrustworthy and dangerous to the potential life they carry.[136] TBAs and mothers opting for their services are challenging these views and, deemed irrational, can be seen a representation of the Other. Others are *spoken to* or *for* rather than listened to.[137]

However, moving birth from the villages and homes to clinics and hospital is a technical solution to a complex problem. Through banning the Other, it is pushed further away into the periphery. Complications leading to maternal mortality and morbidity will continue to take place regardless of the place of birth in a context of early childbearing, high fertility, unsafe abortions, anaemia, and HIV/AIDS. In addition, malaria and poor nutritional levels contribute to problems in pregnancy. The challenges of poor logistics and difficult transfers remain. Lack of equipment and a general lack of essential commodities for ensuring a clean

---

[134]V Plumwood, *Feminism and the Mastery of Nature* (Routledge, London, 1993), 3.

[135]R Kapur, *Erotic Justice: Law and the New Politics of Postcolonialism* (The Glass House Press, London, 2005), 43.

[136]JA Nall, "Mother Beware: Perilous Scholarly and News Media Discourse around Homebirth", 2 *Int J of Communication and Health* (2013), 46–.

[137]JA Nall, "Mother Beware: Perilous Scholarly and News Media Discourse around Homebirth", 2 *Int J of Communication and Health* (2013), 46–, 38.

delivery is a challenge not only for TBAs but also for health facilities. Sepsis is a major cause of in-hospital deaths. Overworked nurses have more pressing concerns than infection prevention.[138] These conditions contribute to the fact that postpartum infection, haemorrhage, obstructed labour, and pregnancy induced hypertension lead to maternal deaths.[139]

The problem of maternal mortality has many roots and its solution will require political, economic, social and cultural change. Raising standards of living, especially improved nutrition for mothers and their baby girls, the mothers of the future, is of key concern, and so is women's control of fertility. With improved maternal health and better control of fertility, many of the dangers of childbirth could be avoided, and resources could be saved for other complications.[140]

When a chief encourages his subjects to respect the ban of TBAs, and opt for modern antenatal care and to deliver with a skilled attendant as opposed to the unskilled TBA, he is participating in a political contract between central and local power. When a woman behaves according to the norm, i.e., she gives birth to her baby in a health facility, she is participating in a political contract – she is being an obedient, modern citizen. When she makes the choice, actively or passively, to stay at home until the birth starts and then fails to relocate, she is still an obedient citizen as long as she expresses that her preference is for an SBA. All of this contributes to the construction of the modern man, *homo economicus*, who is rational, objective, independent and universal (and whose worst nightmare is his own vulnerability).[141] Giving birth in a modern health facility is *the* rational thing to do. This is the only way to avoid the vulnerability and uncertainty (in terms of outcome) of the emotionally and sexually charged nature of childbirth. Following the thinking of Foucault, birth politics places the modern woman as a living being in question; being vulnerable is what makes us human. Modern birth politics reduces the birthing woman to a citizen giving birth to a new citizen.

Acknowledgements

Chisomo Kaufulu-Kumwenda's assistance before and during the research visit to Malawi was invaluable. Professor Jeremy Gould offered academic inspiration. This work was supported by the Academy of Finland through the research project "Integrating Human Rights and Development: Strategies, Impact and Emerging Issues" (2011–2013, grant number 131696).

---

[138]C Bowie and E Geubbels, *Epidemiology of Maternal Mortality in Malawi* (College of Medicine, Malawi, 2nd ed, 2013), 18.

[139]Ministry of Health, *National Sexual and Reproductive Health and Rights (SRHR) Policy* (August 2009) 9.

[140]M Tew, *Safer Childbirth? A Critical History of Maternity Care* (Chapman & Hall, London, 2nd ed, 1995), 307.

[141]See K Kielos, *Det enda könet* [The only sex] (Bonniers förlag, Stockholm, 2012).

Education in Pursuit of the Development Dream? Effects of Schooling on Indigenous Development and Rights in Bolivia

Tiina Saaresranta

PhD Candidate, Institute for Human Rights, Åbo Akademi University, Finland

Abstract: Education (formal education, schooling) is generally understood as a resource which enables development and leads to the enjoyment of other human rights. In this article, relationships between indigenous education, development and rights are explored. When development is defined as a human right, it aims at improving human rights in general and should not negatively impact them. However in practice, education may produce conflicts in the realisation of indigenous peoples' individual and collective rights, especially their linguistic and cultural rights, since cultural and linguistic assimilation are often the reported outcomes of indigenous education. This article uses Bolivia as a case study. Since 1994, indigenous peoples' languages and cultures have to some extent been recognised in the Bolivian education law. Despite this, the implementation of the law has been slow and discontinuous. Arguably, such implementation has not been consistent with indigenous peoples' cultural and linguistic rights; therefore indigenous peoples' right to education has not been fully implemented, neither has it produced the expected development or empowerment results.

I. Introduction

In this article, relationships between education (formal education, schooling), development and rights among indigenous peoples will be explored and problematised. Specifically, what happens with the assumption that education acts as a provider of development and rights when indigenous peoples gain access to education? This topic is dealt with mainly from the point of view of the effects of education on indigenous peoples' cultural and linguistic rights. For indigenous peoples' continued existence as distinct peoples and for the maintenance of the world's cultural and linguistic diversity, the vitality of indigenous languages and cultures is crucial. Since education is both a right as well as a duty,[1] the school plays a very significant role in the process of socialisation of indigenous young generations, and the cultural and linguistic reproduction of indigenousness.

First, a brief overview is given on the underlying assumption of education as a provider of development and other rights, which is then contrasted with a critical reading of the realities faced by indigenous peoples. Thereafter the article explores the situation in Bolivia where, first, indigenous peoples' experiences and expectations of education are presented and discussed. Secondly, the normative bases for indigenous peoples' cultural and linguistic rights

---

[1] On education as a duty and the compulsory nature of this right, see, e.g., M Mustaniemi-Laakso, "Core Content: Free and Compulsory Primary Education", in A Lundström Sarelin, *The Right to Education from a Developing Country Perspective*, KIOS Thematical Reports 2006:3 (Finnish NGO Foundation for Human Rights, Helsinki, 2006), 6–8.

are studied in the Bolivian legislation. Thirdly, the implementation of these norms is analysed. Finally, the article concludes by offering an overview on the effects of schooling on indigenous peoples' linguistic and cultural rights and development.

II. Exploring Interrelations of Education, Development and Rights

Development can be understood in different ways. As a concept, it started to flourish after World War II. The "development enterprise", as described by Rist, originated from western patriarchal thinking to "develop" the poor and to gain economic benefit and control over the countries of the South.[2] In the past few decades, different adjectives have been added to the word "development" in order to widen its meaning from a focus on economic growth towards such approaches as human, or sustainable development. In 1986, development was recognised as a human right.[3] The exercise of the right to development implies the full realisation of peoples' right to self-determination, with the sovereign use of natural resources.[4] Development is considered as a process, where both the outcomes of development as well as the ways in which they are produced are equally important and need to respect and advance all human rights and fundamental freedoms.[5] According to the former UN Independent Expert on the Right to Development:

> "… the realization of the right to development is the promotion or improvement in the realization of at least some human rights, whether civil, political, economic, social or cultural, while no other deteriorates. If any one right deteriorates, or is violated, then the right to development is violated."[6]

Education has an important status in the global development agenda. The achievement of universal primary education is one of the United Nations Millennium Development Goals, and education-related activities are also an important part of international development cooperation. In the Human Development Index system, managed by the United Nations Development Programme to measure and rank the level of development of the world's countries, education (calculated by years of schooling, and expected years of schooling) is one of the three main indicators for development, alongside life expectancy and gross national income per capita. Thus, the general assumption seems to be that education acts as a provider for development, even though there are also critical voices that question this assumption.[7]

---

[2]See G Rist, *The History of Development: From Western Origins to Global Faith* (Zed Books, London, 2002).

[3]United Nations Declaration on the Right to Development. UN General Assembly (4 December 1986) UN Doc A/RES/41/128.

[4]UN Declaration on the Right to Development: article 1(2).

[5]M Salomon and A Sengupta, *The Right to Development: Obligations of States and the Rights of Minorities and Indigenous Peoples*, Minority Rights Group, Issues Paper. (Minority Rights Group, London, 2003); and United Nations Declaration on the Right to Development. UN General Assembly (4 December 1986) UN Doc A/RES/41/128: articles 1 and 6.

[6]A Sengupta, "On the Theory and Practise of the Right to Development". (2002) 24 *Human Rights Quarterly*, at 869.

[7]T Kiilakoski, "Koululaitos ja toiveet kehityksestä", in T Kiilakoski, T Tomperi and M Vuorikoski (eds), *Kenen kasvatus? Kriittinen pedagogiikka ja toisinkasvatuksen mahdollisuus* (Vastapaino, Tampere, 2005), 139–65.

The human right to education is widely recognised in international law. It is characterised as an enabling right, which facilitates access to other rights, and leads to improved conditions in life, such as wealth, employment, health and gender equality.[8] International human rights law recognises specific rights of indigenous peoples in education, concerning the protection of their languages, cultures and participatory rights. The realisation of indigenous peoples' right to education requires positive measures by states to ensure that education is culturally appropriate, of good quality and in the best interests of indigenous peoples.[9] States shall provide indigenous individuals with education that prepares them with skills and knowledge that are useful both in their own community and in the national community. In addition, states have the responsibility to provide effective mechanisms in order to prevent or redress any action which has the aim or effect of depriving indigenous peoples of their integrity as distinct peoples, or of their cultural values or ethnic identities.[10] According to the UN Committee on the Rights of the Child, quality education contributes both to individual and community development among indigenous peoples, and acts as an essential means of achieving individual empowerment and self-determination of indigenous peoples.[11]

In practice, however, education is not always perceived and implemented from the human rights perspective. As pointed out by the former UN Special Rapporteur on the Right to Education, the increase in school enrolment rates does not necessarily improve access to or the exercise of the right to education. To move from "education" to the "right to education" requires a change in our vision of education.[12] A rights-based thinking of education moves beyond the traditional model of schooling, which has defined the aims of education very much from the government's perspective.[13] Also, in the implementation of the right to education, the indivisibility, interdependence and interrelatedness of rights apply:[14] "All rights of the child apply to education and in education. If they do not, human rights will not be achieved through education."[15]

---

[8] See UN Committee on Economic, Social and Cultural Rights "General Comment No 13: The Right to Education (article 13 of the covenant)", Implementation of the International Covenant on Economic, Social and Cultural Rights (8 December 1999) UN Doc E/C.12/1999/10.

[9] UN Committee on Economic, Social and Cultural Rights "General Comment No 13: The Right to Education (article 13 of the covenant)", Implementation of the International Covenant on Economic, Social and Cultural Rights (8 December 1999) UN Doc E/C.12/1999/10; and UN Human Rights Council "Expert Mechanism Advice No 1 (2009) on the Rights of Indigenous Peoples to Education"(31 August 2009) UN Doc A/HRC/12/33.

[10] ILO Convention No 169 Concerning Indigenous and Tribal Peoples in Independent Countries (27 June 1989): articles 26–31; and the UN Declaration on the Rights of Indigenous Peoples (2 October 2007) UN Doc A/RES/61/295: articles 8, 11, 13–15.

[11] Committee on the Rights of the Child, *General Comment No 11: Indigenous Children and their Rights under the Convention* (12 February 2009) CRC/C/GC/11, para 57.

[12] K Tomaševski *Removing Obstacles in the Way of the Right to Education*. Right to Education Primers No 1. (Raoul Wallenberg Institute of Human Rights and Humanitarian Law, and Sida, Gothenburg, 2001), 13.

[13] UNICEF and UNESCO, *A Human Rights-Based Approach to Education for All: A Framework for the Realization of Children's Right to Education and Rights within Education* (UNICEF and UNESCO, New York and Paris, 2007), 20.

[14] World Conference on Human Rights, "Vienna Declaration and Programme of Action" (25 June 1993) UN Doc A/CONF.157/24, para 5.

[15] K Tomaševski, *Removing Obstacles in the Way of the Right to Education*, Right to Education Primers No 1 (Raoul Wallenberg Institute of Human Rights and Humanitarian Law, and Sida, Gothenburg, 2001), 33.

III. The Two-Edged Sword of Indigenous Education

Different actors hold different interests and expectations of education. First, governments invest in education mainly in order to develop the economic workforce and to promote social cohesion, integration and a sense of national identity. Secondly, parents usually expect education to come with economic success, reinforcement of values and social standing for their children. Thirdly, children and young people that are being educated have their own aspirations.[16] In indigenous contexts, there is one more relevant actor: indigenous peoples and their organisations, which have their particular goals, where education is often part of a wider agenda of re-vindication of their rights.[17] These diverse or competing interests may create tensions in the educational agenda. In the following paragraphs, the generally held positive picture of education is problematised by presenting some of the negative impacts of education on indigenous peoples.

Educational efforts directed at indigenous peoples have largely focused on the access to education, and states have generally not devoted enough attention to their linguistic and cultural rights.[18] The former UN Special Rapporteur on the Situation of Human Rights and Fundamental Freedoms of Indigenous People has called education "a two-edged sword" for indigenous peoples; while the school system enables the acquisition of knowledge and skills, simultaneously it often *de facto* forcibly changes and in some cases destroys indigenous cultures.[19] According to the Special Rapporteur:

> It is clear that such education [assimilationist] has been largely successful, since over the years the dominant or hegemonic society succeeded in assimilating large segments of the indigenous population through public or missionary schools. At the same time, such education has served to accelerate the transformation and ultimate disappearance of indigenous cultures, and over time a great many indigenous languages have continued to vanish.[20]

---

[16]UNICEF and UNESCO, *A Human Rights-Based Approach to Education for All: A Framework for the Realization of Children's Right to Education and Rights within Education* (UNICEF and UNESCO, New York and Paris, 2007), 20–21.

[17]LE López, "'Del dicho al hecho …' Desfases crecientes entre políticas y practicas en la educación intercultural bilingüe en América Latina", (2013) 7 (9) *Página y signos. Revista de lingüística y literatura*, 54–55 (Cochabamba: Carrera de Lingüística Aplicada a la Enseñanza de Lenguas, Facultad de Humanidades y Ciencias de la Educación, Universidad Mayor de San Simón); and CONAMAQ, CSUTCB, CIDOB, APG, CSCB, FNMCB-BS, CEAM, CEPOG, CENAQ y CEA, *Por una Educación Indígena Originaria: Hacia la autodeterminación ideológica, política, territorial y sociocultural* (CONAMAQ et al, Santa Cruz, 2004).

[18]Even in this aspect, considerable problems still exist and educational services for indigenous peoples are in general far below the recommended minimum standards in their own countries. See UN Commission on Human Rights, "Report of the Special Rapporteur on the Situation of Human Rights and Fundamental Freedoms of Indigenous People, Rodolfo Stavenhagen" (6 January 2005) UN Doc E/CN.4/2005/88, para 27.

[19]UN Commission on Human Rights, "Report of the Special Rapporteur on the Situation of Human Rights and Fundamental Freedoms of Indigenous People, Rodolfo Stavenhagen" (6 January 2005) UN Doc E/CN.4/2005/88, para 15.

[20]UN Commission on Human Rights, "Report of the Special Rapporteur on the Situation of Human Rights and Fundamental Freedoms of Indigenous People, Rodolfo Stavenhagen" (6 January 2005) UN Doc E/CN.4/2005/88, para 42.

As expressed by a Maori researcher, the school system in fact educates indigenous children and youth away from their own families and cultures.[21] Many young people, who have gained access to education never returned to their home villages or organisations. One can say that a by-product of indigenous schooling is a more or less systematic "brain drain".

Education in a non-indigenous language affects indigenous peoples to the extent that the results of this type of education have been described as linguistic and/or cultural genocide or ethnocide. Children that have gone through non-indigenous monolingual schooling, or their children, are transferred to the dominant group linguistically and culturally. Research results also show that the length of mother tongue medium education is more important than any other factor, including a child's socioeconomic situation, in predicting educational success. Non-mother tongue medium schooling often hinders the development of children's capabilities, perpetuates poverty, and causes psychological problems. Such policies cause "social dislocation, psychological, cognitive, linguistic and educational harm and, partially through this, also economic, social and political marginalization."[22]

IV. Indigenous Peoples and Education in Bolivia

Bolivia is one of the few Latin American countries with a strong indigenous presence. Currently, approximately 36 indigenous peoples exist in Bolivia.[23] According to the population census of the year 2001, 62% of Bolivians defined themselves as indigenous.[24] However, the preliminary results of the latest population census from December 2012 show a drastic decrease in this figure, with only 41% of the population self-identified as indigenous.[25] Part of the explanation for this change is perhaps technical, i.e. how the census questions were formulated.[26] Another consideration is a real decrease in the transmission of cultural values and languages to younger generations, a tendency which has been statistically evident in the previous decades, especially among children. Sichra has concluded that

---

[21]LT Smith, *Decolonizing Methodologies: Research and Indigenous Peoples* (Zed Books, London and University of Otago Press, Dunedin, 2001).

[22]UN Permanent Forum on Indigenous Issues, "Forms of Education of Indigenous Children as Crimes against Humanity". Expert paper submitted by L-A Baer. Prepared in cooperation with O-H Magga, R Dunbar and T Skutnabb-Kangas (8 February 2008), UN Doc E/C.19/2008/7, paras 2–7, 25 and 34. See also UNESCO, *Mother Tongue Matters: Local Language as a Key to Effective Learning* (UNESCO, Paris, 2008); and LE López, *Reaching the Unreached: Indigenous Intercultural Bilingual Education in Latin America*. Paper commissioned for the EFA Global Monitoring Report 2010, Reaching the Marginalized, UNESCO, 2010/ED/EFA/MRT/PI/29, 38–40.

[23]This is the number of indigenous languages recognised as official languages in the 2009 Constitution. Public discourse in Bolivia has also held that the same number of indigenous peoples exist. The Constitution of Bolivia of 2009, article 5(I).

[24]Instituto Nacional de Estadísticas, 2001.

[25]Instituto Nacional de Estadística, Bolivia, "Características de población y vivienda. Censo Nacional de Población y Vivienda 2012". Available at http://www.censosbolivia.bo/ (accessed 23 October 2013), and Periódico Digital PIEB, "Reflexiones en torno a los resultados del censo", Programa de Investigación Estratégica en Bolivia, 8 August 2013. Available at http://www.pieb.com.bo (accessed 23 October 2013).

[26]See analysis concerning the formulations of the national census questions in 1992 and 2001 and the results of indigenous self-identification and languages spoken in Bolivia according to a survey "Barómetro de las Américas" made in Bolivia in 2012: D Moreno, "Los bolivianos y sus identidades" in Ciudadanía and LAPOP, *Cultura política de la democracia en Bolivia, 2012: Hacia la igualdad de oportunidades* (Ciudadanía and LAPOP, Cochabamba, 2012), 238–63.

intergenerational transmission of indigenous languages is low in Bolivia, since, according to the census results of 2001, 76.3% of elderly persons (65 years old or over) spoke an indigenous language, but only 25.1% of children up to four years old knew an indigenous language. Listed as reasons for this progressive loss of speakers of indigenous languages, she mentions indigenous migration from rural to urban areas; the assumption by parents that Spanish fluency will increase their children's social status and the higher and dominant status of Spanish generally in the society.[27]Sachdev, Arnold and Yapita suggest that the low transmission of indigenous languages is the consequence of national policies, especially in education, that systematically fail to give priority to indigenous identity. Although some efforts to uphold indigenous languages have been made in primary education, questions of identity through language and culture have been ignored at higher levels of education.[28]

In recent years, targeted measures taken by the government have improved the literacy and school enrolment rates significantly in Bolivia. As a result of the national literacy campaign "*Yo, sí puedo*",[29] 824,000 adults learned to read and write;[30] Bono Juancito Pinto, a grant given to school children in public schools, has aimed to decrease drop-out rates and to provide resources to buy school materials. In 2012, 95% of the Bolivian population (15 years old or older) declared that they could read and write, in comparison with the earlier results: 87% in 2001 and 80% in 1992. The current percentage of school attendance (individuals of 6 to 19 years old enrolled at school) is 84 per cent, compared with the previous census results (80% in 2001 and 72% in 1992). School enrolment at primary school is currently at 94 percent, whereas at secondary school it is 65 per cent.[31] Bolivia has the second highest public investment rate in education in the Latin American and Caribbean region, which is 8.7% of the GNP (after Cuba, with 12% of GNP).[32]

V. Education in Indigenous Visions and Experiences in Bolivia

As examples from other countries illustrate, indigenous peoples have judged education as necessary for the exercise of their rights, holding that schooling could facilitate the basic

---

[27]I Sichra, "Estado plurinacional – sociedad plurilingüe: ¿Solamente una ecuación simbólica?" (2013) 7 (9) *Página y signos. Revista de lingüística y literatura*, at 82–88 (Cochabamba: Carrera de Lingüística Aplicada a la Enseñanza de Lenguas, Facultad de Humanidades y Ciencias de la Educación, Universidad Mayor de San Simón).

[28]I Sachdev, D Arnold and J Yapita, "Indigenous Identity and Language: Some Considerations from Bolivia and Canada" (2006) 1 *Birkbeck Studies in Applied Linguistics* 108–11, based on an analysis made on the census results of the years 1976, 1992 and 2001 concerning the speakers of indigenous languages in Bolivia and self-identification as indigenous. They also conduct a critical analysis of the linguistic policy applied in the Education Reform during 1994–2004, and an empirical study of self-identification and languages spoken among Aymara population in Tiwanaku, Bolivia.

[29]"I certainly can do it."

[30]According to information provided by the Bolivian Ministry of Education available at http://www.minedu.gov.bo/minedu/pna/indice.html (accessed 9 June 2010). This literacy campaign was financed and designed by the Cuban state. It had an important impact by offering many Bolivians the opportunity to learn to read and write, but it was also criticised since the majority of persons who participated were taught in Spanish even though their mother tongues were indigenous languages.

[31]Instituto Nacional de Estadistica, Caracteristicas de poblacion y vivienda, *Censo Nacional de Poblacion y Vivienda 2012*, 11–15. Available at http://www.censosbolivia.bo/ (accessed 23 October 2013).

[32]"Día del Maestro: Morales destaca que se destina a la educación el 8.7% del PIB", *La Opinion* 7 June 2014, 5a.

information and skills needed to maintain relationships with the dominant non-indigenous society.[33]

In the history of Bolivia, indigenous peoples have considered schooling as an instrument to accede to, for example, land rights and political participation, bearing in mind that until 1952 only literate individuals had the right to vote and be elected in Bolivia. Already from the beginning of the 20th century, the first indigenous schools existed in the high lands of Bolivia, but often contrary to the will of landlords.[34] In the 1990s, in the Bolivian low lands, where entire communities of the Guarani people still lived in slavery-like conditions, literacy campaigns were organised in order to provide access to information and an awareness of their rights.[35]

Indigenous organisations have made great efforts over many decades in order to influence the governments of Bolivia in the planning and implementation of education related legislation and policies. In 2004, the national indigenous organisations drafted a document providing a critical analysis of education, and concluded that the function of education was to create a change in the power relations in society by respecting and strengthening indigenous peoples' rights. According to them, education should serve the development and expansion of indigenous languages, and the full exercise of indigenous practices and customs. The indigenous organisations proposed a new type of education that would be based in their territories and communities, and which would be plurilingual, pluricultural, participatory and productive.[36]

Whereas indigenous organisations in Bolivia see the political and indigenous rights dimensions of education at the grassroots level, for indigenous parents, the expectations are mixed. Parents who are aware of their rights and the benefits of intercultural and bilingual education in improved learning results, higher self-esteem etc. are in favour of an education that includes indigenous languages and cultures. Others expect schooling to facilitate their children in a more advantageous future in terms of access to the labour market and social mobility. Since they know from their own experience that speaking indigenous languages or adhering to traditional indigenous livelihoods does not promote this, they welcome the assimilating school model. When parents of rural indigenous families were asked what they expect from the schooling of their children, many answered: "that our children would not become like us". They envisioned education as a bridge out of poverty, a life influenced by racial, linguistic, and cultural discrimination; scarce access to land and other resources; and diminishing the sense of insecurity or insufficiency of not being able to provide for their children the living conditions expected in today's world.[37] Due to generations of discrimination and humiliation, even today many parents are not motivated to speak their

---

[33]J Hays, "Educational Rights for Indigenous Communities in Botswana and Namibia" (2011) 15 (1) *The International Journal of Human Rights*, at 128 and 137; and LE López, *Reaching the Unreached: Indigenous Intercultural Bilingual Education in Latin America*. Paper commissioned for the EFA Global Monitoring Report 2010, Reaching the Marginalized, UNESCO, 2010/ED/EFA/MRT/PI/29.

[34]R Choque Canqui and C Quispe Quispe, *Educación indígenal en Bolivia: Un siglo de ensayos educativos y resistencias patronales* (Unidad de Investigaciones Históricas UNIH-PAKAXA, La Paz, 2006).

[35]UNICEF, PROCESO, Teko Guaraní and APG. *Tataendi. El fuego que nunca se apaga: Campaña de alfabetización en guaraní* (UNICEF, PROCESO, Teko Guaraní and APG, Santa Cruz, 1994).

[36]CONAMAQ, CSUTCB, CIDOB, APG, CSCB, FNMCB-BS, CEAM, CEPOG, CENAQ y CEA, *Por una Educación Indígena Originaria: Hacia la autodeterminación ideológica, política, territorial y sociocultural* (CONAMAQ et al) Humanidades y Ciencias de la Educación, Universidad Mayor de San Simón, 2004), 7 and 50.

[37]T Saaresranta, *Educación indígena originaria campesina: perspectivas de la educación intracultural* (Fundación PIEB, La Paz, 2011).

indigenous mother tongue to their children, and they believe that it is the task of the school to teach Spanish to their children.[38] One can see these two currents of thought as either contradictory or complementary.

Indigenous families often make considerable sacrifices in order to gain access to schooling for their children; entire families leave their communities and migrate to cities in the hope of improved educational opportunities. In other cases, families may have to pay the teachers' salaries when the state fails to employ a sufficient number of teachers in their communities. Children may have to walk long distances every day in order to reach the school, under circumstances where different types of dangers may exist. Notwithstanding all the efforts the families make for the schooling of their children, they are often not satisfied with the learning results and the type of socialisation provided by the schools available to them. Schooling in general results in a phenomenon where younger generations leave their communities and find work elsewhere. This situation does not contribute to the well-being or development of the rural indigenous communities.[39]

VI. Normative Bases for Indigenous Rights in Bolivian Education

The recognition of indigenous languages and cultures in Bolivian school life took place as late as in 1994 when the Education Reform Law was approved, introducing the model of intercultural and bilingual education (IBE).[40] The Education Reform Law declared that the entire education system should be intercultural[41] and bilingual[42] – but at the same time the application of the law was delimited "mainly in those regions where the first language of the pupils is an indigenous language".[43] According to the bilingual modality of the Reform,

---

[38] See, e.g., LE López, "'Del dicho al hecho …' Desfases crecientes entre políticas y practicas en la educación intercultural bilingüe en América Latina" (2013) 7 (9) *Página y signos. Revista de lingüística y literatura*, 11–78 (Cochabamba: Carrera de Lingüística Aplicada a la Enseñanza de Lenguas, Facultad de Humanidades y Ciencias de la Educación, Universidad Mayor de San Simón); and T Saaresranta, and M Hinojosa Román, *Derechos de los pueblos indígena originarios campesinos de Cochabamba: Entre la ley y la realidad* (Componente de Transversalización de Derechos de los Pueblos Indígenas del Ministerio de la Presidencia and Fundación PIEB, La Paz, 2009).

[39] P Montellano and Z Ramos, *Luces y sombras de la educación secundaria rural: Estudio de un colegio en Chuquisaca* (Fundación PIEB, La Paz, 2011), 139–44; LE López, *Reaching the Unreached: Indigenous Intercultural Bilingual Education in Latin America*. Paper commissioned for the EFA Global Monitoring Report 2010, Reaching the Marginalized, UNESCO, 2010/ED/EFA/MRT/PI/29, 25–26; and T Saaresranta, *Educación indígena originaria campesina: perspectivas de la educación intracultural* (Fundación PIEB, La Paz, 2011), 67 and 95–96.

[40] Ley de Reforma Educativa, Ley No 1565 de 7 de julio de 1994.

[41] Even though these programmes have been labelled as "intercultural", the concept of interculturality as such goes beyond this recognition of diversity (multiculturalism). Interculturality questions the power relations between the dominant and non-dominant groups, and aims at transforming the society by constructing horizontal and inclusive forms and models for knowledge, education, group relations etc. See, e.g., C Walsh, "(De)colonialidad e interculturalidad epistémica: política, ciencia y sociedad de otro modo", in JL Saavedra (ed), *Educación superior, interculturalidad y descolonización* (Fundación PIEB and Comité Ejecutivo de la Universidad Boliviana, La Paz, 2007), 215–28. This type of interculturality has not been part of the so-called IBE models implemented as part of public policies in Latin America.

[42] Ley de Reforma Educativa, Ley No 1565 de 7 de julio de 1994: article 1(5).

[43] Decreto Supremo 23950 de Organización Curricular de la Reforma Educativa, 1 de febrero de 1995: articles 10–11. The law is rather general and declaratory in nature, and is therefore complemented by four supreme decrees which further regulate and specify its contents.

teaching was to be conducted mainly in the indigenous mother tongue during the first three grades of primary school, with the aim of gradually increasing the use of Spanish.[44] The intercultural approach of the Reform was to be applied by a curricular system that would allow regional variety by establishing a common "curricular trunk", with national applicability, and "complementary branches" to add local contents to education.[45]

As a consequence of the elections in 2005, which brought the victory of the political movement MAS (Movement towards Socialism), and with it significant indigenous participation, important legal reforms concerning the protection of indigenous peoples' rights took place in Bolivia.[46] In 2007, the full text of the UN Declaration on the Rights of Indigenous Peoples was adopted as domestic law[47] and in 2009 the new Constitution entered into force.[48] The Constitution established the new Plurinational State of Bolivia, acknowledging it as a state comprised of indigenous peoples and other ethnic groups, and it recognised the pre-colonial existence of indigenous peoples in the Bolivian territory and their right to self-determination. Many of the rights found in the UN Declaration on the Rights of Indigenous Peoples were also included in the Constitution.[49] In 2010, the Framework Law of Autonomies established the possibility for the creation of indigenous and other autonomies.[50] In 2010, a law penalising racial and other forms of discrimination was approved.[51] In December of the same year, the New Education Law "Avelino Siñani – Elizardo Pérez"[52] was adopted, and in 2012, the General Law of Linguistic Rights and Policies was approved.[53]

The current Constitution and Education Law establish the System of Plurinational Education. In this system, schooling is envisioned as a strategic priority for the construction of a new type of a society, where all Bolivian cultures would coexist in harmony, and where indigenous peoples' cultures and identities would be respected and protected. Decolonisation and observance of community values are mentioned among the principles of education. Social, community-based and parental participation in education is recognised, and shall be guaranteed through representative organisations at all levels of the state and within indigenous peoples. The education system has the task of developing knowledge produced by indigenous cultures, complementarily to "universal knowledge", in order to contribute to a holistic development and to construct an education based on Bolivian cultural identities. The school has the task of advancing harmonic coexistence between humanity and Mother

---

[44]Decreto Supremo 23950 de Organización Curricular de la Reforma Educativa, 1 de febrero de 1995: article 33.

[45]Ley de Reforma Educativa: article 8(4) and Decreto Supremo 23950: article 8.

[46]The President Evo Morales' party MAS gained the majority of votes in two consecutive elections, in 2005 and 2009.

[47]Adopted into domestic law in Bolivia by Ley No 3760 de 7 de noviembre de 2007.

[48]Constitución Política del Estado, entered into force 7 February 2009.

[49]Chapter four of the Constitution "The Rights of indigenous Peoples and Nations".

[50]Ley Marco de Autonomías y Descentralización Andrés Ibáñez, Ley No 031 de 19 de julio de 2010.

[51]Ley Contra el Racismo y Toda Forma de Discriminación, Ley No 045 de 8 de octubre 2010.

[52]Ley de la Educación "Avelino Siñani – Elizardo Pérez", Ley No 070 de 20 de diciembre de 2010. This law carries the names of two Bolivian pioneers of indigenous schooling, who in the 1930s created the first indigenous teacher training center.

[53]Ley General de Derechos y Políticas Lingüísticas, Ley No 269, 2 August 2012.

Earth. The law establishes the need to elaborate new indicators and parameters based on the sociocultural and linguistic diversity of Bolivia to evaluate the quality of education.[54]

According to the law, intraculturality, interculturality, and plurilinguism are key issues which should be applied to the education system overall. Intraculturality is defined as the recovering, strengthening and development of indigenous cultures and identities. It has a political function, since it is defined as a condition for the construction of the Plurinational state. Intraculturality in education means that indigenous wisdom and knowledge will be incorporated in the curriculum. Interculturality, on the other hand, is defined as the interrelation and interaction of knowledge, wisdom, science, and technologies between indigenous and other cultures, with the aim of strengthening the identities and the conditions for equal interaction of all Bolivian cultures with those of the rest of the world.[55] The curricular planning of the Plurinational Education System is constituted in intra- and interculturality in a way that the national curricular basis follows the principle of interculturality, and the regional curricula, which complement the national one, follow the principle of intraculturality and diversity.[56]

According to the Education Law, schooling shall begin in the pupil's mother tongue. In those populations where the indigenous languages are mainly spoken, the first language of instruction shall be an indigenous language and Spanish will be used as the second language. In areas where Spanish is the main language, it should be the first language of teaching and an indigenous language will be taught as the second language. The studying of a foreign language is also compulsory for all.[57] Notably, the principle of plurilinguism shall be applied to the entire school system – not only in rural indigenous areas during the first years of schooling, as applied by the previous school legislation.

The General Law of Linguistic Rights and Policies establishes some general standards for plurilinguism in education.[58] As defined in the Education Law, it reiterates that all Bolivians have the right to receive education in their mother tongue and in their second language and, moreover, specifies that it is also the duty of Spanish speakers to study an indigenous language as a second language.[59] Students have the right to express themselves in their mother tongue and according to their culture in different spaces related to education, and they should not be discriminated against when doing so.[60] Indigenous students in higher education have the right to use their languages in both written and spoken forms in their studies; however, the implementation of this right will be introduced progressively.[61] Further, endangered indigenous languages shall be prioritised through public measures concerning linguistic planning, intracultural, intercultural and plurilingual education as well as research and publications.[62] The education system is given the task of conducting research and linguistic standardisation and promoting the use of indigenous languages in different

---

[54]Articles 78(II), 79, 89(II) and 83 of the Constitution; and articles 1–5 of the Education Law Avelino Siñani – Elizardo Pérez.

[55]Education Law Avelino Siñani – Elizardo Pérez: article 6(I–II).

[56]Education Law Avelino Siñani – Elizardo Pérez: article 69.

[57]Education Law Avelino Siñani – Elizardo Pérez: article 7.

[58]Chapter Four: Languages in the Plurinational Education System.

[59]General Law of Linguistic Rights and Policies: articles 6(1) and 12.

[60]General Law of Linguistic Rights and Policies: article 12(II).

[61]General Law of Linguistic Rights and Policies: article 12(III).

[62]General Law of Linguistic Rights and Policies: article 9.

areas of the Bolivian society.[63] The application of the General Law of Linguistic Rights and Policies is to be specified with a regulation.[64]

The Education Law defines as a long-term goal of education the transformation of the Bolivian society towards "live well".[65] "Live well" is a new development paradigm which was established as the guiding principle of the national development plan in 2006.[66] Live well (in Spanish: *vivir bien*) is a rough translation of the concepts that exist in some of the Bolivian indigenous languages to describe what is considered as a desirable and correct mode of life.[67] According to the Bolivian government: "The 'Live Well' philosophy basically rests on the complementary nature of access to and enjoyment of material goods, on the one hand, and emotional, subjective and spiritual fulfilment, on the other, in harmony with nature and in a community of human beings".[68]

The System of Plurinational Education represents a significant change in relation to norms and public policies that had previously been regulated in Bolivian education. It intends to introduce the intracultural, intercultural and plurilingual focus throughout the education system and also given the fact that it declares as the long-term goal the establishment of a society of live well. The spirit and the principles of this law are progressive and generally in accordance with indigenous rights. The intent of the new law is to change the education system into an education inclusive of indigenous knowledge and cultures.

VII. Implementation of Indigenous Peoples' Linguistic and Cultural Rights in Bolivian Education

In Bolivian schools, the implementation of indigenous peoples' cultural and linguistic rights has been slow and discontinuous. The implementation of the IBE modality as designed in the Education Reform Law started in 1996 among Aymara, Quechua, and Guaraní indigenous peoples.[69] Its implementation remained at the primary school level.[70] According to statistical information available from 2002, 27% of primary schools in rural areas declared that they were implementing the IBE modality. If these schools had implemented IBE in all grades and by all teachers, the IBE at that time would have covered 11% of all primary

---

[63] General Law of Linguistic Rights and Policies, article 10(II).

[64] General Law of Linguistic Rights and Policies, first transitory provision.

[65] Education Law Avelino Siñani – Elizardo Pérez: article 4.

[66] Ministerio de Planificación del Desarrollo, *Plan Nacional de Desarrollo: Bolivia Digna, Soberana, Productiva y Democrática para Vivir Bien. Lineamientos Estratégicos 2006*. The implementation of the National Development Plan was extended until 2014.

[67] For example in Y Farah and L. Vasapollo (eds), *Vivir bien; ¿Paradigma no capitalista?* (CIDES-UMSA, La Paz, 2011); and F Huanacuni Mamani, *Vivir Bien/Buen Vivir: Filosofía, políticas, estrátegias y experiencias regionales*, 4th edn (Instituto Internacional de Integración III-CAB, La Paz, 2010).

[68] Annual Ministerial Review of the Economic and Social Council, "Fulfilment of the Millennium Development Goals: National Voluntary Presentation of the Report of Bolivia" (15 June 2009) UN Doc E/2009/96 at 4.

[69] Aymara, Quechua and Guaraní are the three most widely spoken indigenous languages in Bolivia.

[70] CONAMAQ, CSUTCB, CIDOB, APG, CSCB, FNMCB-BS, CEAM, CEPOG, CENAQ y CEA, *Por una Educación Indígena Originaria: Hacia la autodeterminación ideológica, política, territorial y sociocultural* (CONAMAQ et al, Santa Cruz, 2004), 21.

school pupils.[71] Through the Reform, educational materials in indigenous languages were created and distributed to the IBE schools. Teachers were trained in the new pedagogical approaches and the use of indigenous languages in teaching. The intercultural dimension of the Education Reform remained very weak; the intended introduction of indigenous knowledge or local content through the system of curricular branches was never implemented as such. Only some aspects of indigenous cultures, such as dances or local foods were taken to the schools on specific occasions. In the majority of cases, the participation of indigenous communities through the school boards remained limited to the control of administrative issues.[72]

In general, the implementation of the Education Reform faced serious challenges. In the beginning, the teachers' unions in particular opposed it strongly. Developing appropriate education materials and training teachers was complex, given the IBE's progressive approach in comparison to the previous model of monocultural and monolingual education. Pedagogical advisors of the Reform played a central role in IBE's implementation, since they brought the new ideas to the local school level. The system of pedagogical advisors, however, was closed down in April 2003 due to the lack of political will to continue with the Reform, pressure by the teachers' unions and when the external funding for the salaries of the advisors ended.[73] According to World Bank evaluators:

> The reform efforts needed teachers capable of incorporating an intercultural approach to their practice, competent in teaching in both languages, and knowledgeable in how to organize the interaction of both languages. Pedagogical advisors could not transfer these skills unless they were trained in a significantly different manner than that contemplated at the time. This did not occur, and it turned out to be one of the reform's major downfalls.[74]

In 2003, political instability increased in Bolivia, with several changes of government and presidents until January 2006 when president Evo Morales commenced his governing period. During these years of instability, the government did not offer continuity for IBE education, and gradually its implementation in schools was abandoned and teachers went back to the

---

[71]N Nucinkis, "La EIB en Bolivia", in LE López and C Rojas (eds), *La EIB en América Latina bajo examen* (Banco Mundial, GTZ and Plural Editores, La Paz, 2006), 30–40. The real percentage of the implementation of the EIB was however much lower, since a significant percentage of teachers working at these schools did not speak the local indigenous language, nor had the training to teach in these languages.

[72]Several studies confirm this, e.g. N Nucinkis, "La EIB en Bolivia", in LE López and C Rojas (eds), *La EIB en América Latina bajo examen* (Banco Mundial, GTZ and Plural Editores, La Paz, 2006), pp. 25–110. CONAMAQ, CSUTCB, CIDOB, APG, CSCB, FNMCB-BS, CEAM, CEPOG, CENAQ y CEA, *Por una Educación Indígena Originaria: Hacia la autodeterminación ideológica, política, territorial y sociocultural* (CONAMAQ et al, Santa Cruz, 2004); M Contreras and ML Talavera Simoni, *The Bolivian Education Reform 1992–2002: Case Studies in Large Scale Education Reform.* Country Studies Education Reform and Management Publication Series, vol II, No 2 (The World Bank, Washington DC, 2003),.

[73]See in N Nucinkis, "La EIB en Bolivia", in LE López and C Rojas (eds), *La EIB en América Latina bajo examen* (Banco Mundial, GTZ and Plural Editores, La Paz, 2006), 51–53.

[74]M Contreras and ML Talavera Simoni, *The Bolivian Education Reform 1992–2002: Case Studies in Large Scale Education Reform.* Country Studies Education Reform and Management Publication Series, vol II, No 2 (The World Bank, Washington DC, 2003),, at 38.

old modality of teaching only in Spanish and working with the pedagogic materials used prior to the Education Reform.[75] Consequently, in 2009, the UN Committee on the Rights of the Child remarked on Bolivia's "failure to adapt the national education system to the traditional indigenous cultures".[76]

The implementation of the new System of Plurinational Education in Bolivia will be progressive. Although supreme decrees to regulate the law's application have yet to be approved, until such time, the previous regulations from the era of the Education Reform remain valid.[77] The Ministry of Education has developed a new curriculum that reflects the philosophy and aims of the current educational legislation. The foundations of the curriculum are a response to a holistic, interdisciplinary way of thinking and learning, inspired by, *inter alia*, indigenous thinkers and critical pedagogy. The curricular structure is based on three main categories: (a) fields of wisdom and knowledge, (b) areas of wisdom and knowledge, and (c) articulating themes. The fields of wisdom consist of: land and territory; technology and productivity; community and society; and cosmos and thinking. The areas, however, are almost equivalent to the traditional, fragmentary subjects taught in Bolivian schools such as mathematics, languages, biology, geography, etc. The articulated themes mentioned are intraculturality, interculturality and plurilinguism; education for production; sociocommunitarian values; and living together with nature and community based health. These themes are intended as threads to create coherence between the contents expressed in the fields and the areas in which the specific identity of the new model of Bolivian education can be obtained. The subjects or areas should be implemented through four different dimensions of the human person (to be, to know, to do, and to decide) that together would lead to a holistic education.[78] These four dimensions reflect the worldview of indigenous peoples, especially the Aymaras and Quechuas, the idea being that when the four different dimensions of life are taken into account, equilibrium and well-being can be reached.[79]

This model of education was implemented into schools as of February 2013[80] when the application of the new curriculum began in the first grades of primary school (grade 1) and

[75]Y Gutierrez and M Fernández, *Niñas (des)educadas: Entre la escuela rural y los saberes del ayllu* (Fundación PIEB, La Paz, 2011); T Saaresranta, *Educación indígena originaria campesina: perspectivas de la educación intracultural* (Fundación PIEB, La Paz, 2011); and interview with Noemi Ramirez (teacher, Cochabamba, 11 May 2010).

[76]UN Committee on the Rights of the Child, "Concluding Observations: The Plurinational State of Bolivia". Consideration of Reports Submitted by States parties under Article 44 of the Convention (2 October 2009) UN Doc CRC/C/BOL/CO/4, para 85.

[77]Education Law Avelino Siñani – Elizardo Pérez: Disposición abrogatoria and Disposiciones finales: Primera. By June 2014, three and a half years after the approval of the Education Law, the new Supreme Decrees to regulate the implementation of the law had not been passed, mainly because of the opposition of some sectors of the teachers unions which have strong influence in the Ministry of Education.

[78]Ministerio de Educación. *Curriculo Base del Sistema Educativo Plurinacional: Curriculo Subsistema de Educación Regular.* Serie currículo, documento de trabajo (Ministerio de Educación, La Paz, 2012).

[79]See, e.g., Centro de Culturas Originarias Kawsay, *Methodology with Indigenous Identity: Education that Makes a Difference* (Centro de Culturas Originarias Kawsay, Cochabamba, 2006).

[80]The school year in Bolivia starts in February and ends in November.

secondary school (grade 7).[81] Since the school year of 2014, it should be implemented in all grades of basic education.[82] According to norms established by the Ministry of Education, all schools (public and private) should guarantee an intracultural and intercultural education. As an outcome of intracultural and intercultural education, the Ministry has established that pupils ought to have: (1) the capacity of self-identification as a person belonging to a specific culture and world view; (2) the capacity to recognise and accept the existence of different cultures in the Bolivian territory with their own world views, traditions and customs; (3) the commitment to contribute to a non-discriminative society; (4) the ability to contribute to an intercultural dialogue in Bolivia; and (5) an understanding of the importance and development of indigenous peoples' knowledge for the construction of a pluricultural society.[83] These outcomes suppose attitudinal changes and reflect the need to change the current situation of discrimination, racism and lack of knowledge among Bolivian cultures. However, what is surprising about these expected outcomes is that they mainly focus on education for non-discrimination and tolerance, though establish no competences or skills in relation to the use and study of/in indigenous knowledge systems.

It remains unclear how plurilinguism will be applied in practice, given the Education Law's general nature. According to curricular documents provided by the Ministry of Education, pupils should simultaneously develop bilinguism, i.e. learning at the same time both Spanish and an indigenous language.[84] This appears to be the focus at least at the beginning of primary education; however, in secondary education only two hours a week are designated for the study of an indigenous language.[85] The general norms of the Ministry of Education for the 2014 school year establish that when education is conducted in both the mother tongue and in a second language, both languages shall be used in their written and oral forms. According to the Ministry, indigenous languages shall be used in educational processes as instruments of communication and knowledge production. Teachers are to implement methods that are suitable for the plurilinguistic modality of education, and plan specific times for the learning, revitalisation and development of these languages. Each school district shall conduct a sociolinguistic survey amongst the main actors concerned to establish consensus regarding the use of indigenous languages.[86]

Many unresolved challenges remain in the implementation of the current norms. In general, great legal advancements have been accomplished during the past few years in Bolivia, but their implementation has not been a simple task. The traditional elites who have sought to do away

---

[81]Ministerio de Educación, Resolución Ministerial No 001/2013 Normas Generales para la Gestión Educativa 2013: article 31(f).

[82]Ministerio de Educación, Resolución Ministerial No 001/2014 Normas Generales para la Gestión Educativa 2014: article 29.

[83]Ministerio de Educación, Resolución Ministerial No 001/2014 Normas Generales para la Gestión Educativa 2014: article 107.

[84]Ministerio de Educación, *Sistema Educativo Plurinacional: Educación Primaria Comunitaria Vocacional. Programa de Estudio: Primer Año*. Serie currículo, documento de trabajo (Ministerio de Educación, La Paz, 2012), 15.

[85]Ministerio de Educación. *Curriculo base del Sistema Educativo Plurinacional: Curriculo Subsistema de Educación Regular*. Serie currículo, documento de trabajo. (Ministerio de Educación, La Paz, 2012), 58.

[86]Ministerio de Educación, Resolución Ministerial No 001/2014 Normas Generales para la Gestión Educativa 2014: articles 45, 109, 110, 114 and 115.

with the "indigenous problem" during the centuries have found it difficult to accept two consequent electoral victories of a political party with significant indigenous participation. Consequently, the opposition has put considerable effort into trying to hamper the reforms proposed by the government. In addition, internal contradictions within the governing party have made the process of implementation of the norms slower. In a comparative review made of the linguistic and cultural education policies in Bolivia, Guatemala and Peru, a growing gap was found between legal norms and their application in schools.[87]

One of the weaknesses of the Education Reform was that, although indigenous languages were introduced into schools, there was otherwise no public status or use for them. In order to promote indigenous peoples' rights efficiently, the implementation of the new education law needs to be linked to linguistic and cultural policies. The Bolivian government has taken the first steps in this direction and they have come to fruition in recent years in the form of initial changes in prejudices regarding indigenous cultures and languages.

Another concrete challenge in the implementation of the education law is attitudinal. In the society in general, the contents of the law are not fully accepted and understood, nor does there exist a debate or dialogue on indigenous peoples' rights in education. In some sectors of the Bolivian society, the inclusion of intracultural, intercultural and plurilingual education is regarded as a backward development or as an attack against the universal knowledge and schooling as a means to civilise. The new curriculum now features the indigenous respect of the notion that nature, in all its forms, comes from life. A teachers' union leader in opposition to the curriculum held that: "Their [the Bolivian government's] point of departure is that everything possesses life … and that is a conception of reality which is totally reactionary and pre-scientific."[88]

The success or failure in the implementation of culturally and linguistically relevant education depends much on the competence level and attitudes of teachers. With respect to the latter, it is clear that Bolivian schools today still disseminate attitudes and ideals that picture non-indigenous and/or urban life as a better, easier and more desirous life than that of indigenous traditions.[89] According to the Union of Urban Teachers, the new curriculum will lower the quality of education, and they have gone on strike in various departments of Bolivia to express their discontentment.[90] Yet another issue is the cultural and linguistic competence of the teachers. The state has started with teacher training in the new modality of education, however there is no clear plan on how to guarantee their required linguistic competences. Many teachers speak an indigenous language (mainly Aymara or Quechua), though it is possible that they do not know how to write it or manage methods to teach it. Finally, a notable problem is also the system of

---

[87]LE López, "'Del dicho al hecho …' Desfases crecientes entre políticas y practicas en la educación intercultural bilingüe en América Latina" (2013) 7 (9) *Página y signos. Revista de lingüística y literatura*, 62–68 (Cochabamba: Carrera de Lingüística Aplicada a la Enseñanza de Lenguas, Facultad de Humanidades y Ciencias de la Educación, Universidad Mayor de San Simón).

[88]Interview of Miguel Llora, General Secretary of the Federation of Urban Teachers of Cochabamba. In the newspaper *Opinión*, "Brecha entre colegio y universidad será mayor", 2 May 2014, 8a (author's translation).

[89]T Saaresranta, *Educación indígena originaria campesina: perspectivas de la educación intracultural* (Fundación PIEB, La Paz, 2011), 56–60; and A Zambrana Balladares, *Papawan Khuska Wiñaspa. Socialización de niños quechuas en torno a la producción de papa* (UMSS, Plural Editores and PROEIB Andes, La Paz, 2008), 28–29.

[90]In the newspaper *Los Tiempos*, "En contra de la ley 070: Maestros salieron a mercados", 11 May 2014, A7.

assigning teachers to schools, which does not necessarily foresee that a teacher speaking an indigenous language is placed in a region where the same language is spoken.[91]

VIII. Effects of Schooling

The point of departure in this article was to review critically the assumption that education enables the development and rights of indigenous peoples. When development is seen in terms of improved material conditions, a general observation is that schooling among indigenous peoples, whether in rural or urban areas, is often of such low quality that the dream of progress by means of education does not fully materialise. According to information provided by the World Bank, the impact of schooling on the economic well-being (years of schooling in relation to the personal income level) is less among the indigenous than the non-indigenous population in Bolivia.[92]

One effect of the schools in Bolivia has been the indigenous migration from rural to urban areas. There are different reasons why indigenous families migrate, such as employment, but one is the search for educational opportunities. In many rural areas, education is still available only for the first years of primary school. To receive secondary education, the pupil or the whole family needs to uproot to where the school is located, provided that they have the economic resources. Moreover, in many cases, the quality of teaching and pedagogic materials are very low in the rural areas. Another factor is that schools ostensibly still promote the idea that indigenousness and/or rural life do not give any hope for the future. For these reasons, many families opt to move. It is, however, common that families who migrate find themselves in marginalised suburbs, where the schools are overcrowded, without an appropriate infrastructure and with the same level of pedagogic resources as in their home villages.[93] This therefore leads to a demographic situation where an increasing number of indigenous families live in urban areas.

An interesting perspective in the current education legislation in Bolivia is the definition that education aims towards "live well" as the expected long-term impact of schooling. Some elements of live well thinking are present in the new curriculum, such as the intended holistic education. Furthermore, in contrast to the previous humanistic model of education, productive education is now being included, a development which could possibly create the capacity to contribute to new alternatives of livelihoods and development.

The new Education Law establishes 14 years of compulsory education. Early childhood education consists of two years of schooling, the duration of primary school is six years and

---

[91]LE López, "'Del dicho al hecho …'. Desfases crecientes entre políticas y practicas en la educación intercultural bilingüe en América Latina" (2013) 7 (9) *Página y signos. Revista de lingüística y literatura*, 19, 58–59 (Cochabamba: Carrera de Lingüística Aplicada a la Enseñanza de Lenguas, Facultad de Humanidades y Ciencias de la Educación, Universidad Mayor de San Simón).

[92]UN Human Rights Council "Report of the Special Rapporteur on the Situation of Human Rights and Fundamental Freedoms of Indigenous People, Rodolfo Stavenhagen: Mission to Bolivia", Promotion and Protection of All Human Rights, Civil, Political, Economic, Social and Cultural Rights, Including the Right to Development (18 February 2009) UN Doc A/HRC/11/11, para 62.

[93]T Saaresranta, "Jaihuayco (zona sur de Cochabamba) Transiciones del Vivir Bien: migraciones y tejidos urbano – rurales", in R Mamani Pacasi, W Molina Argandoña, F Chirino Ortiz and T Saaresranta (eds), *Vivir Bien significados y representaciones desde la vida cotidiana. Cuatro Miradas: Jesús de Machaca (La Paz), San Ignacio de Mojos (Beni), La Guardia (Santa Cruz) y zona sur Cochabamba* (Fundación PIEB, La Paz, 2012), at 172.

that of secondary school is also six years.[94] If the law is to be implemented as such,[95] it means that indigenous children and young people will be partially separated from their families, family-based education and the cultural and linguistic environment from early childhood (4 years old) until they are adult. The establishment of compulsory pre-school education can be viewed as contrary to indigenous organisations as, according to the latter, pre-school education should be managed by indigenous families and communities.[96] Rather, it is likely that the extended length of schooling will provide an even more rapid and deeper assimilation of indigenous peoples into the non-indigenous society of Bolivia.

From a human rights perspective, this article has looked at indigenous peoples' cultural and linguistic rights in Bolivian education. Different models of education with reference to how they approach indigenous languages and cultures have been implemented in Bolivia. The linguistic policies applied in education have responded to models of submersion; transition; maintenance and development; (maintenance and development is one model, plurilinguism is another one) and plurilinguism. The status of indigenous cultures in education has oscillated between the non-recognition of indigenous cultures, interculturalism and intra- and intercultural education. In the model of submersion, indigenous languages and cultures are seen as a threat to the national development and unity, the objective of this model is therefore assimilation and a monolingual and monocultural society. Here, the role of indigenous languages in education is none, or is used by the teacher to give simple instructions to facilitate pupils' understanding. The model of transition pursues similar objectives, and uses indigenous languages in teaching during the first years of schooling with the purpose of efficient learning of the dominant language. In these first two models, indigenous peoples' cultures and knowledge are not recognised. The model of maintenance and development aims at high level bilingualism and multi- or intercultural society, here the indigenous mother tongue is used as the first language in teaching, and the dominant language as the second. The model of intracultural, intercultural and plurilingual education aims at achieving bilinguism (indigenous and non-indigenous language) and the affirmation and positioning of indigenous languages and cultures in the society in general.[97] Table 1 sets out a synthesis of the implementation of linguistic and cultural policies in education in Bolivia:

Interestingly, what the table reveals is that while indigenous peoples' linguistic and cultural rights were incorporated in Bolivia's educational legislation 20 years ago, the actual implementation of these rights in schools has only – to an extent – been achieved for a total

---

[94]Education Law Avelino Siñani – Elizardo Pérez: articles 9–14.

[95]At the moment the implementation of 14 years of compulsory education is not possible, since the school network (especially pre-school and secondary education) does not cover the whole country.

[96]CONAMAQ, CSUTCB, CIDOB, APG, CSCB, FNMCB-BS, CEAM, CEPOG, CENAQ y CEA, *Por una Educación Indígena Originaria: Hacia la autodeterminación ideológica, política, territorial y sociocultural* (CONAMAQ et al, Santa Cruz, 2004), 54–56.

[97]See the definitions concerning the different models in T Skutnabb-Kangas, and T McCarty, "Key Concepts in Bilingual Education: Ideological, Historical, Epistemological, and Empirical Foundations", in J Cummins and N Hornberger (eds), *Bilingual Education, Encyclopedia of Language and Education*, vol 5, 2nd edn (Springer, New York, 2008), 3–17; and the interpretations of these models in Latin-America in LE López, "'Del dicho al hecho …' Desfases crecientes entre políticas y practicas en la educación intercultural bilingüe en América Latina" (2013) 7 (9) *Página y signos. Revista de lingüística y literatura*, 26–28 (Cochabamba: Carrera de Lingüística Aplicada a la Enseñanza de Lenguas, Facultad de Humanidades y Ciencias de la Educación, Universidad Mayor de San Simón).

Table 1. Education models implemented in Bolivia with reference to the status of indigenous languages and cultures in education

Time frame	−1996[a]	1996–2003[b]	2004–2012[c]	2013[d]	2014[e]
Linguistic model applied in education[f]	*Submersion*	(a) *Submersion*: Schools that did not implement bilingual education at all, or where indigenous languages were taught only as a subject. (b) *Maintenance and development*: Rural schools which implemented IBE. According to the Reform, the policy was of maintenance and development; in practice, the bilingual education was truncated after the primary school, therefore the implementation could be labelled also as *transitional*.[g]	Mainly *submersion*, at some schools *transition*.	*Plurilingual*: The law declares all education to be plurilingual, however, there is insufficient clarity as to how to implement it. Schools started teaching indigenous languages as a subject in grades 1 and 7. Indigenous languages are still treated as subjects, and not as medium of instruction, the implementation does not yet respond to bi/plurilingual education.	*Plurilingual*: The law declares all education to be plurilingual, however, there is insufficient clarity as to how to implement it. Schools started teaching indigenous languages mainly as a subject in basic education. The implementation does not yet respond to bi/plurilingual education.
Education policy concerning the status of indigenous cultures in education	*Non-recognition*: Education policy does not take into account the existence of indigenous cultures in practice.	*Interculturality*: The law declared education to be intercultural, but very few substantial curricular changes in practice.	A period of lack of clarity in the implementation of education policies, the inclusion of indigenous cultural characteristics (mainly folkloric) in education depended on the initiative by each teacher/school.	*Intra- and interculturality*: The law declares all education to be intra- and intercultural. A new curriculum is created, however it is not yet clear how to apply it in the classroom.	*Intra- and interculturality*: The law declares all education to be intra- and intercultural. The norms of the Ministry of Education focus on attitudinal changes, but establish no competences in relation to the study of/in indigenous knowledge systems.

Table 1 (*Continued*)

Time frame	−1996[a]	1996–2003[b]	2004–2012[c]	2013[d]	2014–[e]
Underlying objectives, or effects of education to indigenous languages and cultures[h]	Assimilation, monolingual and monocultural society.	(a) Assimilation, monolingual and monocultural society. (b) Preservation and development of indigenous languages and cultures. Multicultural society.	Assimilation, monolingual and monocultural society. Subtractive language learning.	The ideal of society projected by this model is plurinational, decolonial and of live well. In practice the status of indigenous languages and cultures at schools is still unclear and reflects the practices of the previous decades.	The ideal of society projected by this model is plurinational, decolonial and of live well. In practice the status of indigenous languages and cultures at schools is still unclear and reflects the practices of the previous decades.

Notes:

[a] The period prior to the implementation of the Law of Education Reform (the Reform).

[b] The period of implementation of the Reform.

[c] Implementation of the Reform faded away and schools returned to old practices prior to the Reform.

[d] Implementation of Education Law Avelino Siñani – Elizardo Pérez was started in the first and seventh grade of basic education.

[e] Implementation of Education Law Avelino Siñani – Elizardo Pérez was started in all grades of basic education (with the limitations mentioned earlier in this article).

[f] See on the definitions of the different linguistic models in T Skutnabb-Kangas and T McCarry, "Key Concepts in Bilingual Education: Ideological, Historical, Epistemological, and Empirical Foundations", in J Cummins and N Hornberger (eds), *Bilingual Education, Encyclopedia of Language and Education*, vol 5, 2nd edn (Springer, New York, 2008), 3–17.

[g] See, e.g., I Sachdev, D Arnold and J Yapita, "Indigenous Identity and Language: Some Considerations from Bolivia and Canada" (2006) 1 *Birkbeck Studies in Applied Linguistics* 107–128.

[h] T Skutnabb-Kangas and T McCarry, "Key Concepts in Bilingual Education: Ideological, Historical, Epistemological, and Empirical Foundations", in J Cummins and N Hornberger (eds), *Bilingual Education, Encyclopedia of Language and Education*, vol 5, 2nd edn (Springer, New York, 2008), 3–17; and LE López, "'Del dicho al hecho …' Desfases crecientes entre políticas y practicas en la educación intercultural bilingüe en América Latina" (2013) 7 (9) *Página y signos. Revista de lingüística y literatura*, 11–78 (Cochabamba: Carrera de Lingüística Aplicada a la Enseñanza de Lenguas, Facultad de Humanidades y Ciencias de la Educación, Universidad Mayor de San Simón).

of less than ten years. Moreover, during this period, at its peak, implementation only reached 11% of primary school pupils. When looking at the underlying objectives and effects these education models produce, the predominant tendency has been assimilation, monolingualism and monoculturalism. The above presented statistical information concerning indigenous self-identification and languages spoken reaches a similar conclusion.

IX. Final Remarks

In this complex scenario, one can conclude that indigenous children and young people should be entitled to the right to learn, but not under conditions where the price paid for education is their conversion to non-indigenous persons. Indigenousness in a modern world can take many different forms and can be based on diverse and multiple identities; it is possible to be indigenous in various ways, though, even in this context, indigenous cultural values, practices and languages are important. According to the education law in force in Bolivia, parents have the right to choose the type of education best suitable for their children.[98] However, there is a problem, as none of the currently existing options are suitable when measured in terms of the protection of indigenous peoples' cultural and linguistic rights.

Notwithstanding the existence of international and national legal corpus for the protection of indigenous rights, education continues producing adverse effects to the linguistic and cultural reproduction of indigenousness. The type of education currently available to indigenous peoples in Bolivia is far from the full implementation of their right to education. A full implementation of the right to education entails the observance of the indivisibility, interdependence and interrelatedness of human rights. For indigenous peoples this means that their cultural, linguistic and other rights need to be fulfilled in education. The fully implemented right to education has been said to be a precondition to the exercise of indigenous peoples' right to self-determination and development; the problem is that this very seldom exists and, consequently, its absence is an important factor contributing to indigenous marginalisation, poverty and dispossession – or non-development.[99] When development is defined as a human right, it aims to improve of human rights and freedoms. When indigenous peoples' linguistic and cultural rights in education are violated, so too are their rights to education and development. Continuing this type of education cannot be in the best interests of indigenous peoples.

---

[98]Education Law Avelino Siñani – Elizardo Pérez: article 2(V). It reads: "The rights of mothers and fathers: The right of mothers and fathers to choose the best suitable education for their children is respected" (author's translation from Spanish).

[99]The negative effects of the lack of quality education is affirmed for example in: UN Human Rights Council "Expert Mechanism Advice No 1 (2009) on the Rights of Indigenous Peoples to Education"(31 August 2009) UN Doc A/HRC/12/33.

Mainstreaming Human Rights in Development Programmes and Projects: Experience from the Work of a United Nations Agency

Sisay Alemahu Yeshanew

Post-doctoral Researcher, Institute for Human Rights, Åbo Akademi University, Finland

Since the 1990s, mainstreaming has become a word of fashion. It generally stands for methods of integrating ideals considered disparate or bringing some value from the periphery to the centre. Many development organisations have been working on mainstreaming human rights into their activities. With a focus on the work of the Food and Agriculture Organisation of the United Nations (FAO), the present article analyses the progress made and challenges faced in human rights mainstreaming. It suggests ways of strengthening the work on mainstreaming the right to adequate food at FAO. Based on practical knowledge from working with the organisation, the author argues for streamlining the mainstreaming work currently done within FAO and the development of a corporate strategy that has stronger organisational support.

I. Introduction

Human rights are values of human dignity that aim at protecting and advancing the liberty, equality and well-being of human beings. They project corresponding duties on states to abstain and protect from interference with the enjoyment of rights, and to proactively facilitate and sometimes ensure the fulfillment of these rights. Mainstreaming, however, is concerned with the conscious, systematic and concrete integration of certain values and standards into policies, plans, programmes, priorities, processes and results of the work of an organisation. Human rights mainstreaming refers to the deliberate infusion of human rights standards into the work of organisations in areas such as development, emergencies and peace and security. It is a result of a general endeavour to develop approaches that promote the integrated application of interdependent values. Hence, it seems to avoid or at least minimise parallel and disparate functioning in areas that are essentially interrelated. Human rights mainstreaming at FAO is therefore about the integration of human rights perspectives into the organisation's work in the achievement of food security for all.

Human rights mainstreaming is considered part of the human rights-based approach, which is a conceptual framework for the process of human development. It is normatively based on international human rights standards and operationally directed towards promoting and protecting human rights. Under this approach, human rights become part of the overall objective of development, humanitarian and other interventions that aim at strengthening the capacity of duty-bearers to meet their obligations and rights-holders to claim their rights. The human rights and good governance principles of participation, accountability, non-discrimination, transparency and empowerment guide the process of delivery of development, humanitarian and other objectives. By placing focus on the governance dimensions of developmental and humanitarian problems and the power dynamics that cause and reinforce exclusion and discrimination, the approach, and hence human rights mainstreaming, helps to ensure the efficiency and effectiveness of programmes/projects and the sustainability of their outcomes. It aims to ensure the free, active and meaningful participation of individuals in decisions that affect themselves and to analyse the roles, responsibilities and capacity gaps of relevant state and non-state actors.

Mainstreaming should, however, be understood as only one among many other ways of implementing human rights. It is different from the direct promotion, enforcement of or advocacy for the realisation of human rights; it requires another area of work, such as development, in which human rights are to be infused. Furthermore, the body that mainstreams human rights should have authority over or play a role in a process. A development or humanitarian organisation may, for example, mainstream human rights in its own plans, programmes and activities. However, it may only advocate for the integration of human rights in related policies of states through capacity development, information provision and partnership. For example, FAO may apply the right to food standards in the design, implementation and monitoring of programmes and projects that it implements on its own or together with other partners, whereas it may only advocate for the integration of the right to food standards in the food security policies of states.

Established in 1945, FAO is a specialised United Nations (UN) agency with 194 member nations, two associate members and one member organisation: the European Union. It has the triple goals of eradicating hunger, food insecurity and malnutrition; the elimination of poverty and driving forward economic and social progress for all; and the sustainable management and utilisation of natural resources.[1] It is one of the intergovernmental organisations which has recognised the relevance of human rights to their work relatively early. After laying down a broader framework within which human rights mainstreaming within FAO may be looked at, this article demonstrates why it is important to mainstream human rights in the work of the organisation and then assesses the state of affairs. By laying focus on the human right to adequate food, it examines the mainstreaming work at FAO based on an analytical framework with institutional, instrumental and resource-related components.

The article aims to document the relevant work of FAO and to provide specific recommendations towards the effectiveness of its efforts in human rights mainstreaming, based on a review of pertinent literature and the practical exposure of the author to the work of the organisation. The next two sections briefly present the human rights mainstreaming work at the UN in general and at FAO in particular. Section four makes a relatively in-depth examination of the work of FAO based on selected criteria for effective human rights mainstreaming. The last section closes with remarks on how to strengthen the organisation's mainstreaming work.

II. Mainstreaming within the UN in Brief

As the UN Charter and the specialised instruments adopted under it clearly show, the promotion and protection of human rights has been one of the main objectives of the organisation.[2] Nevertheless, human rights were for long considered to be the *domaine exclusif*

---

[1] See FAO (2014), "About FAO", available at http://www.fao.org/about/en/ (accessed 9 July 2014).

[2] UN Charter, arts 1(3), 55 and 56. See also the International Bill of Rights constituted of the Universal Declaration of Human Rights, the International Covenant on Civil and Political Rights and the International Covenant on Economic, Social and Cultural Rights (ICESCR), and other human rights treaties adopted within the UN. All the human rights instruments are available at http://www.ohchr.org/EN/ProfessionalInterest/Pages/InternationalLaw.aspx (accessed 9 July 2014).

of some relatively isolated set of bodies, especially the Commission on Human Rights (now the Human Rights Council) and treaty monitoring bodies.[3] With the understanding of development as a multidimensional increase in people's capability to lead the lives they value, human rights has been associated with another issue of focus for the UN, namely, development.[4] In his report on UN reform in 1997, the UN Secretary-General (UNSG) designated human rights as a crosscutting issue for the whole of the UN system, stating that they should be mainstreamed into the programmes, policies and activities of all UN specialised agencies, programmes and funds.[5] Human rights were later designated as one of the three interlinked pillars of the UN system – alongside development and peace and security.[6] The repeated reaffirmation of this interrelationship, including in the Millennium Declaration of 2000 and the UNSG's milestone report "In Larger Freedom" of 2005, reinforced the idea of integrating human rights in the other areas of work of the UN.

The designation of human rights as a crosscutting issue of the UN system ushered in policy and programming shifts within the UN agencies, programmes and funds, which have been exerting separate and common efforts in the integration of human rights in their work. Following the confirmation of the fundamental importance of human rights in the UNSG's report on "further change" in 2002, Action 2 of the plan of actions for reform was devoted, *inter alia*, to the integration of human rights throughout the UN system in humanitarian, development and peacekeeping work and to apply a human rights approach to programming in UN actions at the country level.[7] The Office of the High Commissioner for Human Rights (OHCHR) has been entrusted with the overall responsibility of driving the policy of human rights mainstreaming forward.[8] This was boosted by the invitation of the High Commissioner to the executive committees of the UN.[9]

UN agencies, programmes and funds have been mainstreaming human rights in their work to differing degrees. Organisations such as the United Nations Children's Fund (UNICEF) and the United Nations Development Programme (UNDP) have had relatively wider experience based on specific mainstreaming policies on integrating human rights, especially in development and humanitarian work. Having made the Convention on the Rights of the Child its frame of reference in 1996, UNICEF made the actualisation

---

[3]See Z Kedzia, "Mainstreaming Human Rights in the United Nations", in G Alfredson et al (eds), *International Human Rights Monitoring Mechanisms* (2nd rev ed, Martinus Nijhoff, Leiden, 2009), 231.

[4]For example, see Vienna Declaration and Program of Action, art 8, World Conference on Human Rights 1993.

[5]*Renewing the United Nations: A Program for Reform*, Report of the Secretary General, (A/51/1950), 14 July 1997.

[6]The World Summit in 2005 and the 2007 General Assembly resolution on Triennial Comprehensive Policy Review.

[7]*Strengthening of the United Nations: An Agenda for Further Change*, report of the UN Secretary-General, 2002, para 45. Action 2 was a capacity-building program that is no longer operational, but it exhibited an increased interest in human rights mainstreaming in the work of the UN and its training materials are still in use.

[8]See G Oberleitner, *Global Human Rights Institutions: Between Remedy and Ritual* (Polity Press, Cambridge, 2007), 104.

[9]See Z Kedzia, "Mainstreaming Human Rights in the United Nations", in G Alfredson et al (eds), *International Human Rights Monitoring Mechanisms* (2nd rev ed, Martinus Nijhoff, Leiden, 2009), 233.

of the rights of women and children part of its foundation strategies and has been providing assistance to strengthening national and local capacities in human rights-based programming.[10] UNDP established mainstreaming human rights in development programming as one of the strategic areas of its work at least since 2005.[11] Although they do not have overarching human rights mainstreaming policies, organisations such as the World Health Organisation (WHO), the World Food Programme (WFP) and FAO have normative, policy and/or institutional frameworks that exhibit human rights-based approaches (HRBA). The WHO launched a mainstreaming process that brings together gender, equity and human rights under a team mandated to stimulate actions from the corporate to national levels and with national counterparts; WFP integrated human rights and gender issues in its humanitarian protection policy; and the FAO has normative documents and guiding tools on the right to food and HRBA.[12] Institutions such as OHCHR and the United Nations Population Fund (UNFPA) have also developed detailed manuals to help their staff and partners operationalise an HRBA in their work.[13] All these and other UN bodies are further engaged at the country level in the Common Country Assessment and the UN Development Assistance Framework, which use gender equality and HRBA as their programming principles.[14]

The 32 member UN Development Group (UNDG), which was established in 1997 with the purpose of designing system-wide guidance to coordinate, harmonise and align UN development activities, has served as a common platform for the promotion of human rights mainstreaming. In 2003, it adopted the Common Understanding on HRBA to Development Cooperation and Programming which consists of furthering the realisation of human rights, being guided by human rights standards and principles, and developing the capacities of rights-holders and duty-bearers. The different UN agencies, funds and programmes showed diversified levels of interest in terms of giving human rights more prominence in practice than referring to them in policy documents.[15] In the 2005 World Summit, the UNSG reported that although the concept of "mainstreaming" human rights had gained greater attention, it was not adequately reflected in key policy and resource decisions.[16] Participating states resolved "to support the further mainstreaming of human rights through the UN system".[17] The UNDG human rights mainstreaming mechanism (HRM) was established in 2009 to further strengthen system-wide coherence, collaboration

---

[10]UNICEF, *Global Evaluation of the Application of the Human Rights-Based Approach to UNICEF Programming* (Final Report – Volume I, New York 2012), 29–35.

[11]UNDP, *Mainstreaming Human Rights in Development Policies and Programming: UNDP Experience* (2012), 3.

[12]World Bank and Organization for Economic Cooperation and Development (OECD), *Integrating Human Rights into Development: Donor approaches, experiences and challenges* (2nd ed, 2013), 14.

[13]OHCHR, *Frequently Asked Questions on A Human Rights-Based Approach to Development Cooperation* (Geneva, 2006); and UNFPA and Harvard School of Public Health, *A Human Rights-Based Approach to Programming: Practical Implementation Manual and Training Materials* (2010).

[14]UN Development Group, Guidance Note: Application of the Programming Principles to the UNDAF (January 2010), available at http://www.ilo.org/public/english/bureau/program/dwcp/download/undafnote.pdf (accessed 1 April 2014).

[15]See Z Kedzia, "Mainstreaming Human Rights in the United Nations", in G Alfredson et al (eds), *International Human Rights Monitoring Mechanisms* (2nd rev ed, Martinus Nijhoff, Leiden, 2009), 233.

[16]In larger freedom: towards development, security and human rights for all, "Report of the Secretary-General", A/59/2005, para 144.

[17]2005 "World Summit Outcome" A/RES/60/1.

and support for UN Resident Coordinators, Country Team and member states. As an active member of the UNDG and also as a specialised organ with the mandate to "ensuring humanity's freedom from hunger",[18] FAO has been working towards mainstreaming human rights in general and the right to food in particular at the normative, analytical and operational levels.

It should finally be noted that the increasing interest of UN agencies in HRBA and human rights mainstreaming also faces some operational challenges. First, it falls prey to the general aversion to conditionalities imposed by donors on cooperating partners in the South. It is seen as yet another form of conditionality that attaches the delivery of aid to the fulfilment of preset human rights standards at the domestic level. Secondly, the Aid Effectiveness principles of *ownership* by "recipient" states and *alignment* of donor interventions with the states' strategies and existing systems of governance pose another challenge to the imperatives of human rights mainstreaming as the international standards may not necessarily be honoured in domestic policies and practices. Nevertheless, these challenges do not disprove the importance of infusing internationally agreed upon human rights standards in the programmes and projects of the UN bodies. They rather suggest that mainstreaming should be context-sensitive and non-confrontational – issues addressed towards the end of this article.

III. Human Rights Mainstreaming at FAO

Freedom from hunger is at the core of FAO's mandate. The substantive work of FAO has human rights dimensions relating mainly to food security and nutrition, gender, livelihood and decent work and indigenous peoples. These issues relate to the human right to adequate food, the right to work, the right to equality, women's rights and indigenous people's rights. Human rights mainstreaming in the various areas of FAO's work, including agriculture, food security, nutrition, emergencies and investment, should, therefore, take these interrelated values into account. The present article focuses on mainstreaming the human right to adequate food, which is a right to feed oneself in dignity by producing or procuring food items. This right does not impose an obligation on governments to hand out food for free, but it requires the state to put in place safety nets for those who are unable to feed themselves.

With specific reference to the right to food, FAO has a relatively long history. It played an instrumental role in normative developments relating to the human right to adequate food at the international level. It initiated and facilitated discussion on the implementation and realisation of the right to food in the 1996 World Food Summit, which requested the clarification and full implementation of the right to adequate food and freedom from hunger.[19] FAO provided technical support in the elaboration of General Comment No 12 on the right to adequate food that was issued by the UN Committee on Economic, Social and Cultural Rights (CESCR) in 1999.[20] When the UN Commission on Human Rights established the Special Rapporteur mandate on the right to food in 2000, it requested the

---

[18] *Constitution of the Food and Agriculture Organization of the United Nations* (1945), preamble in Basic Texts, Volumes I and II, 2013 ed, available at http://www.fao.org/docrep/meeting/022/k8024e.pdf (accessed 1 April 2014).

[19] Rome Declaration on World Food Security, para 1 and the Summit Plan of Action, objective 7.4.

[20] General Comment No 12, *The Right to Adequate Food (Article 11)*, (12 May 1999), E/C.12/1999/5.

mandate holder to work in cooperation with FAO.[21] Following the identification of the need to provide states with practical guidance on the progressive realisation of the right to adequate food in the 2002 World Food Summit, the FAO Council established the Intergovernmental Working Group to elaborate such guidelines.[22] After two years of negotiations, the Voluntary Guidelines to Support the Progressive Realization of the Right to Adequate Food in the Context of National Food Security (Right to Food Guidelines) were adopted by consensus at the FAO Council meeting in 2004.[23] This instrument provides practical guidance for the implementation of the right to food by, *inter alia*, creating an enabling environment, building institutional and resource capacity, advocacy and monitoring, and covers such areas as development cooperation, trade, disasters and food aid. It lays down an elaborate foundation for mainstreaming the right to food in the different areas of work of FAO and its partners and for advocacy on its integration in the relevant policies of states.

Human rights and HRBA have also received increasing attention in the normative and programming framework documents of FAO. The Voluntary Guidelines on the Responsible Governance of Tenure of Land, Fisheries and Forests in the Context of National Food Security (VGGT), which was endorsed by the Committee on World Food Security (CFS) in May 2012, has the purpose of supporting the progressive realisation of the right to adequate food.[24] It also enshrined other relevant human rights provisions (including indigenous people's rights) as well as human rights principles (human dignity, non-discrimination, gender equality, consultation and participation, rule of law, transparency and accountability). The HRBA is also identified as one of the country programming principles in the FAO's Country Programming Framework,[25] although the programming guidelines do not provide guidance on the operational requirements of the right to food.[26] It is similarly enshrined in FAO's Project Cycle Guide, which provides some guidance on the application of the right to food and other human rights standards within a project cycle.[27] The right to food has further been part of the FAO's corporate commitments.[28] Under the reviewed strategic framework of the organisation (2010–2019), the development and implementation of frameworks and mechanisms for the realisation of the right to adequate food is one of the main outputs under Strategic Objective 1 on contributing to the eradication of hunger, food

---

[21]Commission on Human Rights resolution 2000/10, the right to food, 52nd meeting, 17 April 2000, para 11(b).

[22]*Declaration of the World Food Summit: Five Years Later* (2002), para 10.

[23]FAO, "Voluntary Guidelines to Support the Progressive Realization of the Right to Adequate Food in the Context of National Food Security" (Rome, 2005), available at http://www.fao.org/docrep/009/y7937e/y7937e00.htm (accessed 10 July 2014).

[24]FAO, "Voluntary Guidelines on the Responsible Governance of Tenure of Land, Fisheries and Forests in the Context of National Food Security" (Rome, 2012), available at http://www.fao.org/nr/tenure/voluntary-guidelines/en/ (accessed 15 May 2014).

[25]FAO, *Country Programming Guidelines: Principles and Policy*. Paper prepared for the 108th session of the FAO Programme Committee, 10–14 October 2011, Rome, Italy, available at http://www.fao.org/docrep/meeting/023/mc218e.pdf (accessed 1 April 2014).

[26]See FAO, *Guide to the formulation of the Country Programming Framework* (Rome, 2012), 18.

[27]FAO, *Guide to the Project Cycle: Quality for results*, version 8 November 2013, Rome, available at http://www.fao.org/docrep/016/ap105e/ap105e.pdf (accessed 1 April 2014).

[28]Under FAO's Strategic Framework that was adopted in 2009, the right to food was a key component of the Organizational Result H2 that contributes to achieving Strategic Objective H – Improved Food Security and Better Nutrition.

insecurity and malnutrition.[29] The right to food and the principles of participation, equality, transparency, accountability further underpin the other four strategic objectives of FAO and the two crosscutting themes of gender and governance.[30]

Despite the existence of normative and programming framework documents, it should be emphasised that human rights mainstreaming in the work of FAO is not a matter over which there is political consensus. At the time of the adoption of the Right to Food Guidelines, for example, a number of countries asked FAO to mainstream the right to food into its work, while some countries did not.[31] Of course, FAO's role can only be one of providing technical support to states in the implementation of the Guidelines and its mainstreaming work cannot extend to areas that require the negotiation and decision of states. In this sense, objections to mainstreaming by FAO may relate less to mainstreaming the right to food in its programmes and activities than to advocating for its infusion in states policies relating to food and agriculture. The latter may also be regarded as a way of implementing states' commitment under the Right to Food Guidelines to adopt national human rights-based strategies for food security and poverty reduction.[32] However, the differences on FAO's mandate to mainstream the right to food in themselves indicate that mainstreaming strategies should target not only the programme and practical level, but also the political level. That is, states need to be convinced of the benefits of mainstreaming the right to food in the work of FAO as well as in their own policies.

Infusing or integrating the human right to adequate food in the work of FAO is important for various reasons. In the first place, it facilitates the execution of the human rights mandate, which emanates from the UN Charter and other internationally agreed upon standards and its designation as one of the three pillars of the UN system, in an area most relevant to the mandate of FAO as a specialised organ. It helps frame development cooperation and assistance relating to food security in terms of entitlements, responsibilities and obligations rather than discretionary charity initiatives. Mainstreaming the right to food in the availability, access, stability of supply and utilisation dimensions of food security helps address critical governance dimensions in the fight against hunger and malnutrition.[33] It strengthens the participation and coordination of relevant public institutions, including civil society organisations, independent human rights commissions and parliamentarians in the development and implementation of food security programmes. At a more general level, human rights mainstreaming contributes to ensuring the sustainability of outcomes through the empowerment of rights-holders to participate in decision-making and to claim

---

[29]FAO Conference, "Reviewed Strategic Framework", 38th Session, 15–22 June 2013, Rome, Italy, C 2013/7; and "The Director-General's Medium Term Plan 2014–17" and "Program of Work and Budget 2014–15", C 2013/3.

[30]FAO Conference, "Reviewed Strategic Framework", 38th Session, 15–22 June 2013, Rome, Italy, C 2013/7; and "The Director-General's Medium Term Plan 2014–17" and "Program of Work and Budget 2014–15", C 2013/3.

[31]Report of the Council of FAO, 127th Session, Rome 22–27 November 2004, CL/127/REP, para 26.

[32]FAO, "Voluntary Guidelines to Support the Progressive Realization of the Right to Adequate Food in the Context of National Food Security" (Rome, 2005), available at http://www.fao.org/docrep/009/y7937e/y7937e00.htm, Guideline 3 (accessed 1 April 2014).

[33]FAO, "Right to Food. Making it Happen: Progress and lessons learned through Implementation" (2011) 6–7.

their rights, and building the capacity of duty-bearers to meet their obligations.[34] It can also increase coherence among measures taken in different areas.

It should be emphasised, however, that mainstreaming the right to food does not replace existing development efforts towards hunger eradication. It may not also lead to radical changes in or the replacement of existing approaches and methods of work. Rather, it brings new dimensions to or complements traditional approaches to fight hunger, food insecurity and malnutrition in various contexts. With a view to increasing the effectiveness of FAO's work and the sustainability of the results, the right to food mainstreaming can help bring the much needed focus on activities "that have the highest impact on food-insecure people".[35]

The implementation of HRBA as well as human rights mainstreaming require moving beyond referring to human rights in policy instruments. Mainstreaming for an effect should happen at the operational level. As described in its website on the right to food, FAO's efforts to mainstream the right to food at the programme level are exerted based on the following three central criteria:[36]

- The realisation of the right to food as an overall objective or guiding framework;
- Ensuring that the process (design, implementation, monitoring and evaluation of programmes) respects the principles of participation, accountability, non-discrimination, transparency, human dignity, empowerment and rule of law (known at FAO by the acronym PANTHER) to improve the efficiency and quality of outcomes; and
- Promoting rights, obligations, responsibilities and accountability mechanisms by focusing on empowerment and capacity development, of duty bearers to meet their obligations and of right holders to claim their rights.

While evidence on the application of these criteria and their effects are generally scarce, it can be said that the practical implementation of the approach will go a long way in terms of increasing the effectiveness of the work of the organisation and the sustainability of the results.

IV. Seeing the Work at FAO against the Requisites of Mainstreaming

The work of mainstreaming a certain value in an organisational setting presupposes the existence of agency or authority to mainstream, a normative or policy instrument on the crosscutting value and a mandated area of work or a programme in which the value is mainstreamed. For example, FAO does not mainstream the right to food in the food and nutrition security programme of a given state. Rather it may advocate or provide technical support for the integration of the right in such an instrument. It is up to the concerned state to mainstream human rights in its policy and programme instruments. This shows that the organisational mandate and the resulting method of work affect the approach to mainstreaming. Furthermore, "mainstreaming" in an organisational context may be seen in contradistinction with "targeting". Targeting refers to the direct implementation of a policy by

---

[34]UNDP, *Mainstreaming Human Rights in Development Policies and Programming: UNDP Experience* (2012).

[35]FAO, "Evaluation of FAO's Role and Work in Food and Agriculture Policy" (2012), para. 337, Recommendation 1.2.

[36]See http://www.fao.org/righttofood/our-work/mainstreaming/en/ (accessed 1 April 2014).

a specialised organ, whereas mainstreaming is about the implementation of a certain policy through the instrumentality of all branches of an organisation. Comparatively, mainstreaming is an ambitious approach that requires more resources and continuous staff attention, whereas targeting is more focused and often limited in terms of scope, size and time.[37] Moreover, mainstreaming may be slow in producing results but has better prospect of long-term sustainability, whereas targeted interventions tend to be disparate and short-term, and hence score lower in terms of sustainability.[38] It should nonetheless be emphasised that the two approaches are complementary. One may diagrammatically present targeting and mainstreaming in relation to a human rights policy as follows:[39]

Targeting: human rights policy → specialist unit/specialised organisation → implementation

Mainstreaming: human rights policy → specialist unit → the entire organisation → implementation

Mainstreaming the right to adequate food at FAO, therefore, means that the right will be integrated in the work of the various departments, programmes and projects of the organisation (from headquarters to regional and country levels) to which it is pertinent. As indicated earlier, mainstreaming is not only about policy level integration. It should be exhibited in the development of knowledge and skills in the normative and practical aspects of the right to food as well as its conscious and concrete application in the relevant activities of concerned staff. A reasonable effort at mainstreaming basically requires a specialist unit, clear and feasible policy and tools of implementation, capable and dedicated staff and organisational support. The following sub-sections assess these elements with specific reference to mainstreaming the rights to adequate food at FAO.

IV.1. Specialist unit

When the FAO Council adopted the Right to Food Guidelines in November 2004, many member states requested the FAO Secretariat to ensure adequate follow-up to the Guidelines through mainstreaming and the preparation of information, communication and training materials, and to strengthen its capacity to assist members in their implementation.[40] The Right to Food Team was founded in 2007 within the Agricultural Development Economics Division (ESAD) of FAO to support the implementation of the right to food. The multidisciplinary team works with the Development Law Service of the Legal Office of FAO, which provides legal advice to states in relation to normative frameworks for the right to food, with the Office for Partnerships, Advocacy and Capacity Development (OPC), which is involved, among others, in advocacy for the right to food, and with the Governance and Policy Team under the Economic and Social Development Department that leads the work on the cross-cutting issue of governance under the Revised Strategic Framework of FAO. The division of labour among these units is not fully clear and may cause tension or duplication if

---

[37]A Tostensen, H Stokke and S Trygged, "Means, Modes and Methods: Donor Support Strategies for Child Rights in Kenya", in P Gready and W Vandenhole, *Towards a Theory of Change: Human Rights and Development in the New Millennium* (Routlege, Oxon, 2014), 84–85.

[38]A Tostensen, H Stokke and S Trygged, "Means, Modes and Methods: Donor Support Strategies for Child Rights in Kenya", in P Gready and W Vandenhole, *Towards a Theory of Change: Human Rights and Development in the New Millennium* (Routlege, Oxon, 2014).

[39]See F Uggla, *Mainstreaming at Sida: A Synthesis Report* (Sida Studies in Evaluation 2007:05), 10.

[40]Report of the Council of FAO, 127th Session, Rome 22–27 November 2004, CL/127/REP, para 26.

aspects of their right to food mandate are not delineated specifically and properly. While multidisciplinarity is important to address the relevant issues from different perspectives, the difference in the disciplinary background of those who are engaged in right to food work as well as those targeted by the mainstreaming agenda may also pose challenges. The Right to Food Team does a good job in trying to make effective use of the disciplinary diversity of its (small and mainly temporary) staff and partners in other divisions, but more has to be done to build the acceptance of the importance of the right to food among the economists in the ESAD itself and other staff within the organisation.

Nevertheless, the Right to Food Team has cooperated well with the legal office in its work of supporting legal processes, capacity development, mainstreaming, partnering with civil society and assessment and monitoring in relation to the right to food.[41] In relation to mainstreaming, the Team has been implementing projects on integrating the right to food and good governance into global and regional food security initiatives, into national policies, legislation and institutions, and into sub-national plans and strategies.[42]

Together with its above-mentioned partners, the Right to Food Team at FAO forms a specialised unit for mainstreaming the right to food in the normative, analytical and operational work of the organisation. At the normative level, it works towards the inclusion of appropriate human rights language in standard setting and outcome documents of major norm-development and policy-making processes through the provision of information and technical advice. The integration of appropriate human rights language in the VGGT and the designation of HRBA as one of the programming principles of the Country Programming Framework are two good examples. The team does analytical work by conducting studies on how the right to food relates to such other areas of work as food security, land tenure and nutrition and by contributing to broader international reports. For example, it conducts studies on how the right to food can help guide the implementation of the VGGT and the Global Strategic Framework on Food Security and Nutrition and makes contributions to the right to food aspects of UN reports (e.g., to the Africa Human Development Report 2012). At the time of writing, the team was carrying out a ten-year review of the progress and challenges in the implementation of the Right to Food Guidelines by conducting a series of studies (in collaboration with its partners), which feed into a synthesis report to be presented at the CFS in October 2014.[43] The team and its partner units further develop practical tools and inform the various operational or technical areas of FAO's work with the right to food standards. These include the collaborative projects on the development of the methodological toolbox, which includes guides to legislating on and monitoring and assessment of the right to food, and the preparation of a guidance note on integrating the right to food into food and nutrition security programmes.[44]

The Right to Food team has been operating mainly based on project funding. The reliance on trust funds and short-term professional staff has an adverse effect on the sustainability of the team's work and its impact. Effective mainstreaming requires dedicated support staff, and even focal persons in other divisions if possible, that are engaged in the

---

[41]For the details of the work of the team, see http://www.fao.org/righttofood/our-work/en/ (accessed 9 July 2014).

[42]http://www.fao.org/righttofood/our-work/en/ (accessed 9 July 2014).

[43]See the thematic studies at http://www.fao.org/righttofood/news-and-events/2014-right-to-food-guidelines10/thematic-studies/en/ (accesses 9 July 2014).

[44]Available at http://www.fao.org/righttofood/publications/en/ (accessed 9 July 2014).

right to food work on a more sustainable basis than extra-budgetary support that leaves it to the will of donors.[45] The generally low level of internal support it receives threatens even the very existence of the Right to Food Team in the structures of the organisation.

IV.2. Mainstreaming strategy and tools of implementation

Mainstreaming often suffers from receiving mere lip service or from being considered a "feel good" rhetorical agenda. It is often framed as a desirable objective without a clear strategy and concrete mechanisms of implementation. There is a need to ensure that the value being mainstreamed, the right to adequate food in this case, is clearly articulated and does not disappear in an overarching objective or an agenda "more prominent" in the views of the executing departments or staff. The detailed standards in the Right to Food Guidelines, the integration of the right to food and other human rights principles in the objectives and crosscutting issues of the Revised Strategic Framework, the identification of the HRBA as one of the principles of the Country Programming Framework and the progressive human rights provisions in more specific instruments such as the VGGT serve as foundations and entry points for mainstreaming the right to food in the work of FAO. The publications of the organisation, such as the Right to Food Methodological Toolbox, the Monitoring Framework for the Right to Adequate Food, the Right to Food Making it Happen (progress and lessons learned through implementation), and the Guidance Note on how to integrate the right to food into food and nutrition security programme[46] provide practice-orientated tools that can be used in mainstreaming the right to food in the work of FAO at the normative, analytical and operational levels.

The above-mentioned normative instruments and implementation guides are being put to use to differing degrees in the various projects and contexts. These strategic tools can be strengthened by an operational mainstreaming strategy that FAO does not have at present.[47] A comprehensive right to food mainstreaming strategy that clearly sets out the policy and concrete mechanisms of implementation helps create coherence among relevant activities and increase the effectiveness of related interventions by ensuring that mainstreamed values do not disappear into other overarching agendas. In tandem with the mainstreaming activities it presently pursues, FAO may consider experiences in such agencies as UNICEF in developing a corporate strategy that helps it carry out the work in a more coordinated and structured manner at various levels. Such a strategy could define goals and objectives, guiding principles, the means to achieve the goals (including resources and institutional set-up), core activities from the global to the national levels, tools of implementation and provisions for evaluation and monitoring. The strategy will build on completed and ongoing interdepartmental work in which the Right to Food team and its partners are involved.

The development of a corporate or organisational strategy on mainstreaming should take into account the other human rights-related values or issues that fall within the mandate and work of FAO. One of the main criticisms against mainstreaming has been that there are

---

[45] Report of the Special Rapporteur on the right to food, Olivier De Schutter, "Mission to the Food and Agriculture Organization of the United Nations", Human Rights Council 22nd Session, 14 January 2013, para 39.

[46] All available at http://www.fao.org/righttofood/publications/en/ (accessed 9 July 2014).

[47] See World Bank and Organization for Economic Cooperation and Development (OECD), *Integrating Human Rights into Development: Donor approaches, experiences and challenges* (2nd ed, 2013), 14.

increasingly too many values that have formed part of the main themes of the mainstreaming approach, including gender equality, human rights, governance, environmental sustainability and HIV/AIDS. In response to this, a broader mainstreaming strategy may lay down a comprehensive framework for the integration of various interrelated values in the different areas of work of the organisation. It could identify the values to be mainstreamed (including gender, governance, nutrition, the right to food, employment, indigenous people's rights) and the thematic areas of mainstreaming (emergencies, forestry, natural resources, socio-economic development etc.). Such an initiative could depart from an assessment of the state of the art and build on relevant on-going activities within the organisation and may draw lessons from experiences in other UN and development agencies. Lessons learned from the mainstreaming framework and practice in the areas of gender and nutrition in FAO are surely important inputs. In this connection, the collaborative work of the Right to Food team with FAO divisions in charge of gender, nutrition and emergencies on a joint organisational output on mainstreaming gender, nutrition and the right to food in emergencies could be taken into account for the purposes of a broader corporate strategy.[48]

IV.3. Staff capacity

Effective mainstreaming requires that professionals from a variety of disciplines work together, understand each other's terminologies and draw on each other's perspectives and experiences.[49] The involvement of an entire organisation or staff (rather than a specific specialised group) in the implementation of a right to food mainstreaming policy portends difficulties in its operationalisation. First, it obviously requires resources for capacity development. Secondly, it demands the commitment of staff who will have to add the right to food and other related considerations on top of other tasks to which they are primarily devoted. These factors may combine to make mainstreaming a relatively challenging process.[50] Nevertheless, building the capacity and willingness of diverse staff to effectively mainstream the right to food in the work of FAO is a worthwhile undertaking that will pay in the long run.

Staff training could have the objective of creating understanding on the practical implications of the human rights to food in various areas and places of work. Expertise in human rights standards and practices should be developed in the context of designing, implementing, monitoring and evaluating programmes. In this connection, particular attention should be given to building the capacity of programme and project review staff so that they consider such issues as participation, marginalisation and grievance mechanisms during project appraisal.[51] Training does not introduce an alien subject, but requires framing or looking at already existing activities in terms of the right to food, governance and HRBA by providing concrete examples or evidence on the positive impacts of human rights

[48]FAO, *The Right to Adequate Food in Emergency Programmes* (forthcoming, 2014).

[49]UNDP, *Mainstreaming Human Rights in Development Policies and Programming: UNDP Experience* (2012).

[50]See A Tostensen, H Stokke and S Trygged, "Means, Modes and Methods: Donor Support Strategies for Child Rights in Kenya", in P Gready and W Vandenhole, *Towards a Theory of Change: Human Rights and Development in the New Millennium* (Routlege, Oxon, 2014).

[51]Report of the Special Rapporteur on the right to food, Olivier De Schutter, "Mission to the Food and Agriculture Organization of the United Nations", Human Rights Council 22nd Session, 14 January 2013Report of the Special Rapporteur.

mainstreaming. For training, the Right to Food Team and its partners at FAO may cooperate with the UN System Staff College, which has accumulated experience from training the diverse staff of the UN on such subjects as HRBA. In the context of a broader mainstreaming strategy, the staff training should also be conducted in a way that aims to infuse the interrelated issues of gender, governance, nutrition, indigenous people's rights etc. together with the right to food. Capacity building for mainstreaming does not end with staff training; there should be follow-up and monitoring to make sure that the right to food and related values are integrated in the actual work of concerned staff. It should be noted however that there is much to be desired in terms of equipping the FAO staff with the normative and practical aspects of HRBA in general and the right to food in particular.

Those with the right to food mandate at FAO should work on raising the resources required for staff training and follow-up by showing to decision-makers the benefits of mainstreaming the right to food in the work of FAO. This may build, for example, on the recommendation for capacity development on programming principles including HRBA in a Strategic Evaluation of FAO country programming in 2010[52] and the Learning Programme that is launched as a result.[53] An even stronger case may be made based on FAO's partnership with other UN bodies and intergovernmental agencies, for example, within the framework of the UNDG on human rights mainstreaming. Capacity building and resource allocation generally require organisational support, which is a very important factor in mainstreaming.

IV.4. Organisational support

As mentioned above, mainstreaming is much more than a rhetorical exercise as it has significant practical implications. Implementing a mainstreaming strategy may affect the way an organisation works in terms of internal structure and bureaucratic practices.[54] As mentioned previously, the orientation of UNICEF's work changed with its adoption of the Convention on the Rights of the Child as its frame of reference, whereas the WHO created a new structure with the decision to launch its recent mainstreaming process.[55] Of course, the degree of change or accommodation that mainstreaming a certain value requires depends also on whether an organisation has been carrying out work related to the issue. It may, for example, entail the adoption of specific programmes or projects on human rights or the reorientation of existing programmes to human rights. Organisational culture in relation to integrating new ideals or standards and institutional openness to such developments will have significant impact on the extent to which a mainstreaming policy may succeed. In this regard, FAO stands a comparative advantage as the right to food, good governance and HRBA have formed part of its normative and practical work. The mainstreaming of these and related

---

[52]FAO Programme Committee, Strategic Evaluation of FAO Country Programming, 2010, PC 104/4.

[53]At the time of writing, an e-learning course targeting the FAO programming and technical staff was under preparation on three of the five UN Common Country Programming Principles, i.e., gender equality, human rights-based approach and capacity development. The Right to Food Team prepared the part on HRBA.

[54]G Oberleitner, *Global Human Rights Institutions: Between Remedy and Ritual* (Polity Press, Cambridge, 2007), 105–6.

[55]UNICEF, *Global Evaluation of the Application of the Human Rights-Based Approach to UNICEF Programming* (Final Report – Volume I, New York 2012); World Bank and Organization for Economic Cooperation and Development (OECD), *Integrating Human Rights into Development: Donor approaches, experiences and challenges* (2nd ed, 2013).

values at a broader level needs to be carried out through the strengthening of existing inter-departmental collaborations and the creation of new ones. What may be required in some cases is infusing relevant aspects of the right to food in already existing programmes and activities.

Gaining the support of the management and decision-making levels to the right to food mainstreaming, which requires in-house advocacy, is important for three basic reasons. First, the right to food becomes an important part of the organisational strategic objectives and plan of work. Secondly, a supportive tone from above will build staff commitment and catalyse the integration of the right to food and related values in their work. Thirdly, it will have implications for the allocation of sufficient resources for the implementation of a mainstreaming strategy. The political support of the decision-making level and its effect in terms of human and financial resource commitment will be invaluable to the development and implementation of mainstreaming strategy. They will facilitate the work of the specialist unit in mainstreaming. Support at the higher level should also mean that activities relating to right to food mainstreaming are supported by the regular budget than depending solely on extra-budgetary support or the will of donors. The right to food work at FAO clearly needs more organisational support, for example, through the establishment of regular budget posts for the work.

V. Concluding Remarks

Human rights mainstreaming is about the infusion of internationally agreed upon standards in the work of an organisation internally as well as with its partners. It is important for the purposes of addressing critical governance matters in development, humanitarian and other interventions, and to improve targeting, effectiveness and sustainability of such interventions. There is no one best way to mainstream any value or issue in the work of organisations operating in different areas in various parts of the world. This means that mainstreaming work should be contextualised or adapted to the circumstances in which it is implemented. Strategies to mainstreaming any value should take into account, *inter alia*, the mandate and nature of work of the organisation, organisational culture, institutional and staff capacity and the receptiveness of the partners at operational level. FAO has important bases for mainstreaming the right to food and related human rights and governance principles. It has undertaken related activities. This may be strengthened with more organisational support to such activities, the elaboration of a corporate human rights mainstreaming strategy and the development of staff capacity on the right to food and related principles.

If the work of mainstreaming the right to food in the organisation's operational activities or advocacy for its integration in a sectoral policy is, for example, undertaken in or with a state whose government is sensitive to human rights, one may focus more on the substantive contents or principles of the right to food rather than framing the intervention or cooperation in the human rights terminology. In this regard, the human rights principles, including participation, accountability, non-discrimination and empowerment, may be more useful in that they may be articulated in a way that does not require highlighting the human rights language. The technical nature of some values may also require "vernacularisation", i.e., making use of language that relevant officials may easily understand or feel comfortable with. Relating the right to food to some work which is already being undertaken in the area of food security in a particular state may, for example, provide a way to using a language which creates both comfort and understanding in some cases. However, human rights standards should not be watered down under the pretext of their circumstantial technicality or sensitivity as they are after all based on internationally agreed instruments some of which are adopted by the consensus of states. Last but not least, in advocating for the mainstreaming of a certain value in states' policies, the approach of an organisation like FAO can be one of offering a menu of possible useful measures so that the countries decide what is best for them.

Evidence in Demand: An Overview of Evidence and Methods in Assessing Impact of Economic and Social Rights

Hans-Otto Sano

Senior Researcher, Danish Institute for Human Rights, Copenhagen

The article examines evidence and methods in the recent human rights literature which reports on the impact of economic and social rights. The article is structured according to the four main analytical entry points under which distinct methods of social rights impact assessment are used: social rights litigation (evidence through analysis of legal texts and mainly qualitative evidence), the results of ratifications and constitutionalisation (evidence through comparative quantitative data analysis), the results of human rights policy reforms (evidence through the use of quantitative data and qualitative interpretation) and the results of civil society advocacy and human rights-based approaches (predominantly qualitative evidence). The paper concludes that positive changes are documented with respect to all methods examined, but the causal linkages between the social rights analysed and the results on the ground are not always well-established, or they provide conflicting interpretations, demonstrating that this field of research is still relatively young.

I. Introduction

Human rights and development discourses have been an important feature of human rights scholarship since the late 1990s. This feature has been accompanied by studies on the challenges of implementing human rights-based approaches (HRBA) as this volume makes clear, and also by an interest in evidence on the effectiveness and impact of integrating human rights into development. Impact discussions may, however, tend to be narrow in the way effectiveness and impact are addressed: qualitative scholarship and documentary evidence analysis tend to ignore the quantitative discussions, while quantitative approaches are often characterised by a unilateral focus on regression analysis. Exceptions to these observations exist, however. There are studies which seek to pull together the different methodological approaches. One example is Landman and Carvalho's book *Measuring Human Rights*, another is Hafner-Burton's and Ron's article "Human Rights Impact through Qualitative and Quantitative Eyes". Fons Coomans, Fred Grünfeld and Menno T Kamminga's book *Methods of Human Rights Research* also makes timely and relevant reflections on the state of methodology in human rights research.[1]

---

[1] T Landman and E Carvalho, *Measuring Human Rights* (Routledge, London, 2010). EM Hafner-Burton and J Ron, "Seeing Double: Human Rights Impact through Qualitative and Quantitative Eyes" (2009) 61(2) *WorldPolitics*, 360. See also EM Hafner-Burton, "A Social Science of Human Rights" (2014) *J of Peace Research* 51(2), 273. F Coomans, F Grünfeld and MT Kamminga (eds), *Methods of Human Rights Research* (Intersentia, Antwerp, 2009).

This article focuses on the kind of data used in assessing human rights impact[2] with respect to economic and social rights (short form: social rights).The focus is on global comparative studies and studies in developing countries. The questions undertaken here are: what are the methods used in establishing causal linkages between ratifications, policies, advocacy and rights-based engagement and evidence of change? And secondly, what data are used in producing evidence, and how well do the methods using the data produce convincing evidence with respect to economic and social rights impact?

The concept "evidence" is often associated with quantitative data in social science research. In human rights research, evidence has rarely been used to refer to qualitative data documenting or verifying a hypothesis, an explanation or an interpretation of legal or social factors.[3] In human rights studies, multiple data sources are used, but the explication of methods is not often explicit, and critical discussions on the nature of data used tend to be limited. Quantitative human rights approaches tend to ignore other types of evidence, and qualitative approaches have a similar inclination not to acknowledge the existence of quantitative data. Another characteristic of methodology discussions in human rights research is the tendency of implicitly classifying legal texts as qualitative evidence. Yet, this type of data may have a fundamentally different character compared with data produced by a semi-structured interview. Furthermore, the fact that official administrative data are often used in human rights analyses is insufficiently recognised.[4] It is argued here that judicial texts and administrative records should be treated as documentary research evidence rather than being pooled into a box labelled qualitative evidence.[5] The origin of the source as, for example, an official document may be just as important in a methodological assessment as its use in a qualitative interpretative context or in a research context where administrative evidence is coded for use in quantitative comparative analysis.

Finally, issues of levels of analysis deserve attention. Quantitative analyses will often be comparative and will approach the subject of social rights at the level of cross-country comparison; qualitative approaches are very often applied in case studies. Studies using

---

[2]No distinction is made in this article between outcomes and impact. In programme implementation and evaluation, outcomes are associated with the nature of positive change produced by the programme (programme effectiveness), whereas impact relates to the longer-term intended or unintended negative or positive changes that are attributable to the programme. See EA Andersen and H-O Sano, *Human Rights Indicators and the Program and Project Level* (Danish Institute for Human Rights, Copenhagen, 2006). However, outside the specific programme frames, outcomes and impact are often blurred. UNHCHR, *Human Rights Indicators, A Guide to Measurement and Implementation* (UNHCHR, Geneva, 2012) classifies one set of indicators as "Outcome indicators" without making distinctions between outcomes and impact.

[3]See H-O Sano and H Thelle, "The Need for Evidence-Based Human Rights Research", in F Coomans, F Grünfeld and MT Kamminga (eds), *Methods of Human Rights Research* (Intersentia, Antwerp, 2009).

[4]Landman and Carvalho treat administrative data in their discussions on sources used in events-based analysis and thus link such data to human rights violations. See T Landman and E Carvalho, *Measuring Human Rights* (Routledge, London, 2010), 36–39 and 51–53). However, administrative records may also be policy documents from governments and are therefore not only used in event-based analyses.

[5]Documentary evidence could be government publications and legislation; non-government institutional sources such as UN documents or documents produced by NGOs; academic publications; printed media and visual documentation. Reed et al label this methodological entry "Document Review". See K Reed and A Padskocimaite, *The Right Toolkit. Applying Research Methods in the Service of Human Rights*" (Human Rights Center, University of California, Berkeley, 2012), 12–14.

judicial or administrative data will often focus on the individual country level or, more rarely, local government data.

Human rights research methodology is an emerging discipline, also so in development studies where human rights are appearing as increasingly important. Often, studies of human rights impact will focus on state compliance with treaty obligations, while the present article seeks to measure impact in terms of how human rights integration in development processes and programmes will have effects on social relations and distribution of resources.[6]

The purpose of this article is mainly methodological but, given the vastness of the subject, it is far from exhaustive. Apart from demonstrating the nature of positive or negative human rights impact, its aim is to reflect on the variety of methods used in establishing causal linkages between policies, court rulings, ratifications, advocacy and social change. In order to achieve this, the article reviews a selection of illustrative studies. The studies reviewed were selected on the basis of their relatively recent publications and their different research designs in an effort to demonstrate methodological diversity. A number of qualifications are warranted.

First, implementation of social rights through social policies will often operate in conjunction with other public policies and activities. For this reason, their separate attributable impact can often be difficult to identify. It therefore begs the question: to what extent, and at what level of analysis, can attributable change be verified?

Secondly, how are normative human rights obligations integrated into state policies and social actions? Are they constitutionally embedded, or are they the result of ratification of "external" human rights treaties? Further, does social rights reinforcement take place irrespective of law and "legal reflexes",[7] and is thus the result of the merger between human rights and development goals – so-called rights talk[8] – and collective action? It may be argued that human rights impact is affected by the respective pathways leading to change. Litigation may grow out of domestic constitutional development, but civil society actors may also respond to ratification in advocacy efforts and campaigns. Donors and civil society actors may influence social rights policies through human rights-based programmes.

Micro-change, for instance reducing poverty, may occur without traceable change at the macro-level in the short-term.[9] Human rights activists and scholars may often run into this paradox as they work at the micro-level. Macro-economists, political scientists and lawyers using methods of randomised control samples or who examine departure in

---

[6]For a predominant focus on compliance, see special issue of *Nordic Journal of Human Rights* 2012, vol 3, edited by M Langford and S Fukuda-Parr.

[7]The term of "legal reflex" was used by P Gready and J Ensor in their Introduction to *Reinventing Development? Translating Rights-Based Approaches from Theory into Practice* (Zed Books, London 2005). They described legal reflexes as the automatic and unconsidered recourse to legal instruments to ensure protection and promotion of human rights (9).

[8]This is the broad concept used by authors such as S Engle Merry, "Rights Talk and the Experience of Law. Implementing Women's Human Rights to Protection from Violence" (2003) 25(2) *Human Rights Quarterly*, 324. See also V Gauri and S Gloppen, "Human Rights-Based Approaches to Development: Concepts, Evidence, and Policy" (2012) 44 *Polity* 496, 502.

[9]A Sen identified the paradox of micro-successes and macro-failures in poverty reduction in *Development as Freedom* (Alfred A. Knopf, New York, 1999). See also International Council on Human Rights Policy, "No Perfect Measure: Rethinking Evaluation and Assessment of Human Rights Work. Report of a Workshop" (2012, Geneva, Switzerland). Available at http://www.ichrp.org/files/reports/68/181_evaluating_hr_work_report.pdf (accessed 3 February 2014).

ratifications and constitutional orders are often at a distance from the micro-situation. They may tend to arrive at conclusions which seem less credible to micro-analysts because the conclusions run counter to acquired knowledge obtained from observations at the micro-level. Part of this discrepancy between macro- and micro-level observations is discussed under the heading of decoupling: the fact that organisations operating at the macro level derive their core features and interpretations from the institutional environments in which they are imbedded rather than from internal conditions and practices.[10] However, macro-analysts and scholars may also have their concerns. Hafner-Burton and Ron argue that those working in the more established case study tradition tend to be more optimistic to the possibility of positive human rights impact, while those working in the quantitative genre are more sceptical.[11] This may, unconsciously, lead to a bias in methodological choice. According to a recent survey on research methods conducted with a limited number of human rights scholars chosen non-randomly, the case study was one of the most popular methods among human rights professionals and scholars.[12]

Thirdly, the answer to the question about impact is vexed by lack of data. Social rights evaluation and research is a relatively recent discipline which has gained importance over the last 20 years. There are continuous calls for indicators. Indicators are held up as indispensable instruments, but their use and utility depend on purpose and method, and their reliability on the primary data. Progress has been made in defining indicators,[13] but the challenges remain concerning the legitimacy of the indicators and the underpinning data. Anecdotal and qualitative data are often easier to locate than data that can be used in quantitative and comparative analyses. Paradoxically, the data now being discussed on ESCR impact may have greater reliability than the standard based data used when assessing civil and political rights.[14]

In other words, the task of assessing the impact of strategies or methods of social rights advocacy is complex. The following will seek to explicitly address this complexity in discussing each point of the methods identified for discussion.

I shall go through four impact assessment approaches:

---

[10]For an example of this, see WM Cole and FO Ramirez' discussion on the impact of national human rights institutions: "Conditional Decoupling: Assessing the Impact of National Human Rights Institutions, 1981to 2004" (2013) 78(4) *Am Soc Rev*, 702. Cole and Ramirez report on a particular dimension of decoupling with departure in what Keck Sikkink has termed the information paradox: the fact that human rights observers on the ground expose perceptions of deteriorating human rights practices even when objective practices remain constant due to the fact that changing conditions, for instance newly established national human rights institutions exposing information on hitherto unknown human rights violations (708).

[11]EM Hafner-Burton and J Ron, "Seeing Double: Human Rights Impact through Qualitative and Quantitative Eyes" (2009) 61(2) *WorldPolitics*, 363.

[12]K Reed and A Padskocimaite, *The Right Toolkit. Applying Research Methods in the Service of Human Rights*" (Human Rights Center, University of California, Berkeley, 2012), 9.

[13]UNHCHR, *Human Rights Indicators, A Guide to Measurement and Implementation* (UNHCHR, Geneva, 2012). Available at http://www.ohchr.org/EN/Issues/Indicators/Pages/HRIndicatorsIndex.aspx (accessed 6 January 2014); S Mcinerney-Lankford and H-O Sano, *Human Rights Indicators in Development. An Introduction* (World Bank, Washington DC 2010).

[14]T Landman uses the term standard-based data from the coded country level information about (mostly) civil and political rights on a standardised scale that typically is both ordinal and limited in range. Examples are the CIRI Human Rights Data Project, the Freedom House Civil and Political Liberties scale or the Political Terror Scale. See T Landman and E Carvalho, *Measuring Human Rights* (Routledge, London, 2010), 64.

- the impact of social rights litigation;
- the impact of treaty ratification on social human rights protection;
- the impact of policy reforms; and
- the impact of advocacy and human rights-based approaches.

For each area, the article will discuss the data used, the broader methodological category, and the way in which causality is established in the research under review.

II. The Impact of Social Rights Litigation

According to Langford, constitutionally based legal mobilisation for social rights before domestic courts has increased in frequency and scope over the last two decades in many parts of the developing world.[15] It has become the focus of considerable attention – from activists and scholars – as an avenue for bringing social and economic rights to bear in national politics and law. In a situation where many countries have adopted new constitutions and strengthened their judiciaries, social rights litigation represents an alternative means to advocacy-based approaches for holding duty-bearers at the different levels to account for their legal obligations.[16] According to Gauri and Gloppen,[17] the more notable cases are litigation on the right to food in India, court cases from South Africa, Brazil, Costa Rica and elsewhere that have sought to provide antiretroviral drugs to people living with HIV/AIDS, and a Colombian case that sought to equalise access to health services.

Many of the prominent cases relate to health rights, but cases on the right to education also prevail in Indonesia (on resource allocation for education) and in India on schools' effectiveness in increasing enrolment and permissible school fees.[18]

In *Courting Social Justice*, the authors argue that the poor are at least as likely to benefit from social rights litigation as the more wealthy groups. Even in Brazil, where HIV/AIDS litigation was spearheaded by the relatively wealthy, innovations introduced by the judiciary were quickly incorporated and spread to many others who had never brought a legal claim. In Indonesia, interventions in education by the Constitutional Court sought to increase funding for public education throughout the country, in principle benefiting all school-age children.[19] In a more recent study, Gauri and Brinks conduct new analyses of the extent to which social rights court cases are likely to benefit the underprivileged. They conclude that even though it might be commonsensical to expect litigation to be an elite game, the evidence does not support a finding

---

[15]M Langford, "Social Rights Jurisprudence: Emerging Trends in International Comparative Law" (Cambridge University Press, Cambridge, 2008).

[16]V Gauri and S Gloppen, "Human Rights-Based Approaches to Development: Concepts, Evidence, and Policy" (2012) 44 *Polity* 496–, 496–502.

[17]V Gauri and S Gloppen, "Human Rights-Based Approaches to Development: Concepts, Evidence, and Policy" (2012) 44 *Polity* 496–, 497.

[18]Gauri and Brinks reviewed court cases in Nigeria on the right to education and health and noted a timidity of courts in Nigeria concerning social rights unlike the situation in Brazil, India and Indonesia. In Nigeria the courts were more concerned with the rights *in* education compared with the rights *to* education, Brinks and Gauri, "Introduction: The Elements of Legalization and the Triangular Shape of Social and Economic Rights" in V Gauri and DM Brinks (eds), Courting Social Justice (Cambridge University Press, Cambridge, 2008, 8–9).

[19]DM Brinks and V Gauri, "A New Policy Landscape: Legalizing Social and Economic Rights in the Developing World" in V Gauri and DM Brinks (eds), Courting Social Justice (Cambridge University Press, Cambridge, 2008), 334–351.

that only the better-off benefit. In fact, in many cases, the primary beneficiaries of the cases were the underprivileged. Examining the socio-demographic characteristics of those who benefitted, revealed the cases that alleviate the poor tend to encompass a vast number of beneficiaries. According to the authors, a rough overview of cases with the greatest impact suggests that the poor are at least as likely to benefit as the middle classes or the elite.[20]

The data used for this analysis are interpretations of court case material. However, the data employed also relate to assessment and interpretation on how larger groups than litigants and direct beneficiaries may benefit indirectly from court decisions and their impact. There are direct effects on non-litigants, indirect effects internal to the legal system, i.e. higher level court decisions that may affect court decisions at the lower level. Finally, there are indirect effects external to the legal system, i.e. for instance resulting in political claims as a consequence of litigation.[21] In terms of the methods applied, legal interpretation is coupled with qualitative methods (for instance interviews with the judiciaries), but also involves quantitative data and methods (sampling of court cases, transformation into logarithmic scales to facilitate comparison from one country to the next). The causal linkages established between a court decision and the proportion of the population who benefit from it are therefore formed on the basis of legal, quantitative and qualitative approaches.[22]

III. Relating Social Outcomes to Ratifications and Changing Human Rights Structures[23]

In reviewing the quantitative literature on human rights impact, the majority of studies focus on civil and political rather than economic and social rights.[24] The latter studies have mainly been added during the last 15 years. As noted by Cole (quoting Hertel) economic rights in particular "have remained the poor step-sister to other types of human rights research, scholarship and advocacy".[25] Another characteristic of this type of quantitative

---

[20]DM Brinks and V Gauri, "A New Policy Landscape: Legalizing Social and Economic Rights in the Developing World" in V Gauri and DM Brinks (eds), Courting Social Justice (Cambridge University Press, Cambridge, 2008), 340–341.

[21]See V Gauri and DM Brinks, "Introduction: The Elements of Legalization and the Triangular Shape of Social and Economic Rights" in V Gauri and DM Brinks (eds), Courting Social Justice (Cambridge University Press, Cambridge, 2008, 22–25.

[22]In estimating the number of people benefitting directly and indirectly from two collective court cases on antiretroviral treatment medicine in India, Gauri and Brinks used a formula that involves estimates by Indian researchers based on qualitative research on the proportion of benefits that actually reached the intended recipients. For the details, see V Gauri and DM Brinks, Courting Social Justice (Cambridge University Press, Cambridge, 2008), 226–27.

[23]In the following section, I use "Changing Human Rights Structures" to denote changes in the acceptance, commitment and intent to undertake measures in keeping with human rights obligations. This also involves the incorporation of human rights law into domestic law. See UNHCHR, *Human Rights Indicators, A Guide to Measurement and Implementation* (UNHCHR, Geneva, 2012), 34.

[24]These studies had either negative conclusions on the effect of treaty ratifications (O Hathaway, "Do Human Rights Treaties Make a Difference?" (2002) 111 *Yale Law Rev J* 1935–2042) or they provided very nuanced or negative conclusions, for instance E Neumayer, "Do International Human Rights Treaties Improve Respect for Human Rights?" (2005) 49 (6) *J of Conflict Resolution*, 925–53.

[25]W Cole, "Strong Walk and Cheap Talk: The Effect of the International Covenant on Economic, Social and Cultural Rights" (2013) 92 (1) *Social Forces* 167.

research is that it tends to be Anglo-American based.[26] In the review below, the primary aim is to elucidate the nature of conflicting conclusions on, respectively, positive and negative impact, and to report on data and method use, including the interpretation of causality.

In a recent article, Cole examines whether ICESCR (International Covenant on Economic, Social and Cultural Rights) membership promotes and protects collective labour rights, contributing to their *de jure* enactment and their *de facto* protection. The data used in the analysis is a weighted index of time series data on collective labour rights comprising six categories of rights: freedom of association, the right to form and join trade unions, rights to other union activities, the right to bargain collectively, the right to strike, and the rights of workers in export processing zones. The index can be disaggregated into scores measuring the status of these rights in law as well as in practice.[27] Wade Cole controls for economic development (proxied by GDP/capita logged), and economic growth (annual percentage GDP growth). He also controls for trade openness (proxied by total trade as a percentage of GDP) foreign direct investments, and democracy (measured by the polity IV index). Two dummies are also included, one for the presence of leftist (non-communist) government and one for communist government (175). Cole then regresses the disaggregated index on labour right practices on ICESCR membership. He finds, first, that ICESCR membership reduced the *de jure* scores, i.e. ratifications reduced the propensity to enact labour rights *laws*. In terms of labour rights *practices*, however, higher levels of economic development were associated with improved labour right practices. ICESCR ratifications also imply a significant positive effect on labour rights practices. Hence, despite the fact that the ratifications of ICESCR tended to associate with weaker legal protection of labour rights, membership of ICESCR tended to improve practices irrespective of the domestic legal provisions of labour rights. Despite this positive impact, the data also revealed that the countries ratifying ICESCR had systematically lower scores on the labour rights practice index, i.e. starting from a low level of the labour rights practice index. This could indicate that countries ratified for legitimation purposes.[28]

Has CEDAW (Convention on the Elimination of All Forms of Discrimination against Women) improved the rights of women around the world? This question is raised by Simmons after having reviewed the impact of ratifications of civil and political rights.[29] Concerning the ICCPR (the International Covenant on Civil and Political Rights),

---

[26]In fact, US scholarship dominates this quantitative line of research focusing on regression analyses. Exceptions are E Neumayer's "Do International Human Rights Treaties Improve Respect for Human Rights?" (2005) 49 (6) *J of Conflict Resolution*. Also C Bjørnskov and J Mchangama, *Do Social Rights Affect Social Outcomes?* (Social Science Research Network, Copenhagen, September 2013) is available at the network. Neither of these studies are reviewed here, given that the former dates back some time, and the latter has not been published in a peer-reviewed journal.

[27]See W Cole, "Strong Walk and Cheap Talk: The Effect of the International Covenant on Economic, Social and Cultural Rights" (2013) 92 (1) *Social Forces* 167, 171–72.

[28]W Cole, "Strong Walk and Cheap Talk: The Effect of the International Covenant on Economic, Social and Cultural Rights" (2013) 92 (1) *Social Forces* 167, 180 and 187.

[29]B Simmons, *Mobilizing for Human Rights. International Law in Domestic Politics* (Cambridge University Press, Cambridge, 2009), 159–255.

Simmons found the strongest impact in *transitional countries*, i.e. not in stable democracies or stable autocracies.[30] In her analysis of CEDAW, Simmons assessed ratifications with respect to the girl and boy ratio in primary and secondary education. The assessment of positive results occurred while Simmons controlled for a time trend (prior to the ratification itself), fixed effects making the country a natural candidate for improvement in education of girls, and a lagged baseline departure from which to measure improvements.[31] Simmons found that ratification of CEDAW had a positive and significant effect on girls' enrolment in primary and secondary schools, especially in transitional countries.[32]

With respect to the impact on health, Palmer et al ask whether the ratification of human rights treaties has effects on population health.[33] The data used in the regression analyses were data for 170 countries that had ratified at least one major human rights treaty (65% of the countries in the analysis had ratified all six treaties under review), a population size of more than 100,000 people, were sovereign states before 2006, and had available data for at least two of 11 health and social well-being indicators. These indicators concerned HIV prevalence, maternal mortality, infant mortality rates, life expectancy, under five mortality rates, human development index, child labour, gender gaps, corruption, political rights and civil liberties. The data for these indicators derived from WHO (World Health Organisation), UNICEF (United Nations International Children's Emergency Fund), World Economic Forum, Freedom House and Transparency International (1987–1988). Stratifying countries by global burdens of disease region, they did not find significant, positive relations between country groupings, ratifications and the health and social development indicators. Comparing countries before and after ratification did not reveal positive results in health status (1989). However, they also concluded that the *findings should not be interpreted* to mean that human rights treaties have no effect on important health issues. In putting forward this argument, they stress that the right to health enshrined in several constitutions or in international treaties has been effectively used to reduce child labour, increase access to antiretroviral care, promote care for the elderly and mentally ill, and improve the quality of public spaces. However, these observations derive from other types of documentation separate from the large-scale comparative and quantitative analyses.

Scruggs et al examine the impact of ratifying the ICESCR on an index, summarising different *social security laws*.[34] The data used in the analysis are coded data from a US-based

---

[30]B Simmons, *Mobilizing for Human Rights. International Law in Domestic Politics* (Cambridge University Press, Cambridge, 2009), 200–2.

[31]B Simmons, *Mobilizing for Human Rights. International Law in Domestic Politics* (Cambridge University Press, Cambridge, 2009), 215.

[32]B Simmons, *Mobilizing for Human Rights. International Law in Domestic Politics* (Cambridge University Press, Cambridge, 2009), 217. It should be noted that Simmons, among those who have analysed empirically the influence of treaty ratification, is deemed "probably the most optimistic". See V Gauri and S Gloppen, "Human Rights-Based Approaches to Development: Concepts, Evidence, and Policy" (2012) 44 *Polity* 496–, 491.

[33]A Palmer, J Tomkinson, C Phung, N Ford, M Joffres, KA Fenandes, L Zeng, V Lima, JSG Montaner, GH Guyatt and EJ Mills, "Does Ratification Of Human Rights Treaties Have Effects On Population Health?" (2009) 373(9679) *The Lancet* 1987–92.

[34]L Scruggs, C Zimmermann and C Jeffords, "Implementation of the Human Right to Social Security Around the World: A Preliminary Analysis of National Social Protection Laws", in L Minkler (ed), *The State of Economic And Social Human Rights. A Global Overview* (Cambridge University Press, Cambridge, 2013), 117–134.

official programme summarising *Social Security around the World*. Explanatory variables apart from the ratification of the covenant were income, democracy, civil law systems, socialist law systems and ethnic divisions. The research controlled for all explanatory variables including a random effects estimator and for the effects of all variables at the same time (fixed effects). Being a party to the covenant increases the number of social security laws by about 0.3. However, the causality may run both ways, i.e. the existence of social security laws may also lead to ratifications of the covenant. Some of the positive association may be due to the fact that countries with more social protection laws are more likely to become parties to the covenant.[35] This interpretation, despite its emphasis on laws and practices, is not entirely consistent with Cole's finding indicated above that countries with the worst record on labour rights practices were most apt to ratify the ICESCR. The relatively modest but still positive assessment of the importance of the covenant's ratification is, however, qualified by the fact that the national standard of living is likely the most important determinant of the presence of social security laws, followed by the presence of a civil legal system.[36]

These analyses indicate nuanced, positive, modestly positive, contradictory and negative conclusions on the effect of treaty ratifications on labour, women's rights, social security legislation, and health rights. No firm conclusions on the impact of ratification of treaties can be derived from the studies reviewed. Rather, it seems that the specific methods employed and the data used play a decisive role in determining whether conclusions are positive or negative concerning the impact of ratifications. Apart from treaty information, the data used is derived from survey data, perception survey data (corruption), standard-based data (Freedom House), coded official overview records, and from WHO and UNICEF health statistics. The methods employed are quantitative. The causality is established via complex regression analyses displaying different methods of controls in use, and different techniques (logistical regression in one case). However, one of the studies (Palmer et al) uses qualitative and legal evidence to qualify its causal arguments. Interestingly, the majority of recent studies express more positive conclusions on the effect of ratification than earlier studies focusing on civil and political rights. Palmer et al's study reviewed here is an exception which is then qualified by non-quantitative evidence. Overall, however, these studies make clear that the discussion on the specific methods of undertaking the regression analyses could be more elaborate and more interactive. The type of controls and the matter of fixed effects tend to diverge although there seems to be consensus between Cole's and Simmon's studies.

---

[35] Apart from the estimated importance of ratifying the covenant, Scruggs, Zimmermann, and Jeffords conclude that country income levels play a role together with socialist legal traditions. Uncertain explanatory variables are democracy and ethnic heterogeneity. See L Scruggs, C Zimmermann and C Jeffords, "Implementation of the Human Right to Social Security Around the World: A Preliminary Analysis of National Social Protection Laws", in L Minkler (ed), *The State of Economic And Social Human Rights. A Global Overview* (Cambridge University Press, Cambridge, 2013), 131.

[36] L Scruggs, C Zimmermann and C Jeffords, "Implementation of the Human Right to Social Security Around the World: A Preliminary Analysis of National Social Protection Laws", in L Minkler (ed), *The State Of Economic And Social Human Rights. A Global Overview* (Cambridge University Press, Cambridge, 2013), 132.

IV. The Impact of Policy Reforms

One study object that is weakly developed in human rights research is how actors within governments and international organisations translate human rights rhetoric and commitment into practical policy.[37] Especially rare are studies on state policies and their respective ministries and actors within ministries. Human rights research on non-state actors is better represented than human rights research on state actors, excepting studies on violation of human rights law, i.e. the rationale behind the positive, but varying human rights implementation by duty-bearers is an understudied subject. More informed studies on donors than on state duty-bearers are available.[38]

This deficiency also means that impact studies are difficult to make because the processes and details of policy reforms are vague. Are positive outcomes in education, health and social security a result of rights-induced measures of specific policy instruments in individual countries or are they more likely tied to reforms where rights components form just one part? Can a demonstrable impact be verified and made plausible between specific policy reforms and rights related outcomes? Answering such questions requires analysis at the level of individual states and their local governments. Comparative country case studies of e.g. health, education or social ministries and their specific integration of human rights policies would be relevant.

One of the most interesting impact studies recently in the human rights field is Flavia Bustreo and Paul Hunt's recent study undertaken for WHO, *Women's and Children's Health: Evidence of Impact of Human Rights*.[39] This study focuses on the detailed programmes of the various governments, though not from an insider's point of view in the health ministries. However, it addresses the issue of impact systematically. Not only is the study interesting given its case study selection (Nepal, Brazil, Malawi and Italy), but also because of the methodology applied. Inspired by Habicht et al in health science,[40] Bustreo and Hunt distinguish between adequacy, plausibility and probability. These are method designs intended for evaluations of public health sector interventions.

Adequacy refers to assessment of whether the predefined goals were reached. Causal mechanisms are generally not established.

Plausibility refers to assessment which renders it likely that a project's internal mechanisms explain the outcomes, i.e. a statement is plausible if it is an "apparently true

[37]Vandenhole and Gready point this out in the present volume. J Oestrech has conducted three case studies on how international organisations (WHO, UNICEF, and the World Bank) incorporate and deal with human rights. See J Oestrech, *Power and Principle. Human Rights Programming in International Organizations* (Georgetown University Press, Washington DC, 2007).

[38]OECD and World Bank, *Integrating Human Rights into Development. Donor Approaches, Experiences, and Challenges*, 2nd edn (OECD and the World Bank, Washington DC, 2013). See also D D'Hollander, A Marx and J Wouters, "Integrating Human Rights in Development Policy. Mapping Donor Strategies and Practices" (Leuven Centre for Global Governance Studies, Leuven, 2013), Paper #4.

[39]F Bustreo and P Hunt, "Women's and Children's Health: Evidence of Impact on Human Rights" (World Health Organization, 2013). Available at http://apps.who.int/iris/bitstream/10665/84203/1/9789241505420_eng.pdf (accessed 3 February 2014).

[40]JP Habicht, CG Victoria and JP Vaughan, "Evaluation Designs for Adequacy, Plausibility and Probability of Public Health Programme Performance and Impact" (1999) 28(1) *Int J of Epidemiology*.

or reasonable, winning assent".[41] Plausibility assessment attempts to control for the influence of external factors by choosing control groups before an evaluation is done, or afterwards during the analysis of data. There are alternatives to the choice of control groups, but the final choice is selected by taking best advantage of the existing situation.[42]

Probability assessment seeks to establish that only a small known probability, due to chance or bias, exists in the difference between programme and control areas.[43] This method requires randomisation and control groups. Statistical tests are required to establish confidence levels.

Bustreo and Hunt base themselves largely on plausibility arguments. However, at times when reading the report, readers may feel that they are closer to adequacy than plausibility assessments. This is in part because the authors do not always make specific causal linkages between policies and outcomes, and also because control groups are implicit. That said, in Nepal there are clear improvements in immunisations, under five mortality rates, maternal mortality rates, and pregnant women receiving more than four ante-natal visits. Moreover, especially after 2007, policies concerning reproductive health were clearly human rights-inspired. However, the reader wonders whether the results achieved are due to a focus on the Millennium Development Goals (MDGs) rather than human rights, or a combination of the two.[44] In Nepal, the National Policy of Skilled Birth Attendance was not based explicitly on a human rights-based approach. It is stated in the report that the programme did incorporate equity, access and availability concerns. However, these programme instruments could equally be inspired by the World Bank as human rights, especially when it becomes clear that the programme is based on conditional cash transfer, a typical World Bank employed tool.

In Brazil, the report points to the narrowing of gaps between wealth quintiles between 1996 and 2006/07. This goes for contraceptive use, skilled birth attendance and antenatal care. These are important developments, yet the report itself acknowledges that the changes may be due to *Bolsa Familia*, a conditional cash programme outside the health sector.[45] In the Malawi study, the report provides data on under-five mortality rates and on the reduction in respiratory infections in children. The incidence of diarrhoea has also been substantially decreased. However, the Malawi section of the study fails to establish causal links between these positive trends and human rights-inspired health policies.[46] In the general conclusion,

---

[41]JP Habicht, CG Victoria and JP Vaughan, "Evaluation Designs for Adequacy, Plausibility and Probability of Public Health Programme Performance and Impact" (1999) 28(1) *Int J of Epidemiology*, 13, Bustreo and Hunt 88-89.

[42]Distinctions are made between historical control groups (same target institutions or population, Internal control groups (individuals or groups who should have received the intervention, but did not), and External control groups. See JP Habicht, CG Victoria and JP Vaughan, "Evaluation Designs for Adequacy, Plausibility and Probability of Public Health Programme Performance and Impact" (1999) 28(1) *Int J of Epidemiology*, 11–15.

[43]JP Habicht, CG Victoria and JP Vaughan, "Evaluation Designs for Adequacy, Plausibility and Probability of Public Health Programme Performance and Impact" (1999) 28(1) *Int J of Epidemiology*, 14.

[44]It can be argued that too little is done to falsify the thesis of positive human rights impact.

[45]JP Habicht, CG Victoria and JP Vaughan, "Evaluation Designs for Adequacy, Plausibility and Probability of Public Health Programme Performance and Impact" (1999) 28(1) *Int J of Epidemiology*, 40.

[46]JP Habicht, CG Victoria and JP Vaughan, "Evaluation Designs for Adequacy, Plausibility and Probability of Public Health Programme Performance and Impact" (1999) 28(1) *Int J of Epidemiology*, 43–47.

the study states that the country experiences of Nepal, Brazil, Malawi and Italy demonstrate a plausible level of evidence that a human rights-based approach has contributed to health gains for women and children. "In summary, applying human rights to women's and children health policies, programmes and other interventions not only helps governments comply with their binding national and international obligations, but also contributes to improving the health of women and children."[47] However, the question remains as to what degree human rights have contributed *fundamentally and positively* to the implementation of health improvements.

In sum, it becomes evident from this report that human rights contributed to the formulation of health policies and programmes in Nepal, Brazil and Malawi. What remains somewhat less clear is how this was achieved exactly, and how the outcomes of health policy reform related specifically to human rights instruments.

The data used in this pioneering analysis are MDG data and quantitative data on health service utilisation. The method is qualitative, though could have been more quantitative inasmuch as the original arguments around plausibility presupposed the use of control groups. The interpretation of causal linkages between specific human rights measures and results is therefore less convincing.

V. The Impact of Advocacy and HRBA

While some donors and policy-makers have been influenced by human rights-based approaches, organisations working at the local level in developing countries, whether international or domestic based NGOs, are more fundamentally influenced by HRBA methods in their programming and actions. International NGOs like Oxfam-Novib, CARE, Save the Children, Action Aid and Plan International have all sought to promote and implement human rights rights-based approaches. Local NGOs have in many cases been involved in the domestication of HRBA at the local level.[48] A cascade of rights-based development thinking, advocacy and empowerment is becoming more important in the field.[49] While human rights-based approaches have influenced NGO programming significantly, their impact remains difficult to ascertain nationally.[50] This, particularly if the concept of HRBA is understood to imply a specific method of instituting development programmes which involves the application of human rights principles of accountability, participation, and non-discrimination and the mobilisation of vulnerable groups to claim their rights.[51] There are well-known cases in India where collective action and social

---

[47]JP Habicht, CG Victoria and JP Vaughan, "Evaluation Designs for Adequacy, Plausibility and Probability of Public Health Programme Performance and Impact" (1999) 28(1) *Int J of Epidemiology*, 97.

[48]See H-O Sano, "The Drivers of Human Rights Change in Development", in P Gready and W Vandenhole (eds), *Human Rights and Development in the New Millennium. Towards a Theory of Change* (Routledge, Oxon, 2014), 37.

[49]See D D'Hollander, A Marx and J Wouters, "Integrating Human Rights in Development Policy. Mapping Donor Strategies and Practices" (Leuven Centre for Global Governance Studies, Leuven, 2013), Paper #4, 33, quoting Kindornay.

[50]For national importance in Kenya, see BA Andreassen, "Legal Empowerment of the Poor – a Strategy for Social Change", in in P Gready and W Vandenhole (eds), *Human Rights and Development in the New Millennium. Towards a Theory of Change* (Routledge, Oxon, 2014), 101–2.

[51]V Gauri and S Gloppen, "Human Rights-Based Approaches to Development: Concepts, Evidence, and Policy" (2012) 44 *Polity* 496–, 486–87 use a broader concept of HRBA as "targeted interventions on part of governments, donors and civil society actors".

and civil society movements have succeeded in creating landmark legislation such as the Right to Information Act and the National Rural Employment Guarantee Act. Moreover, campaigns on the right to food from the early 2000s were instrumental in laying the groundwork for the Supreme Court Orders of food rights in the mid-2000s.[52]

However, the documentation on how HRBA and advocacy contribute to the improvement of peoples' lives *locally* remains disparate and anecdotal. The NGOs involved rarely reflect on the broader impact on the ground apart from ad hoc references, and to many donors HRBA is a new strategy where results have not yet been gauged.[53] Below are some of the more recent examples of insights on the effectiveness of HRBA.

In her chapter, "Social Movements and Economic and Social Rights", Young emphasises that social movements are galvanised by and, in turn, galvanise demands for social rights. Such movements play an important role in effecting change in formal law as in the Indian cases above, but no less important is the impact that these movements have on the intersection of law and social reality. Together these collective actions bring law and legal consciousness together by effecting both law and cultural change. In Ghana, a new meaning and legal application of the right to health was generated by the contestation of a small community. The Legal Resource Centre in Ghana contested that a Mr Zakari was obliged to pay user fees for his treatment in hospital. As he was poor and unable to pay, he was detained on the hospital grounds without food or bed. He was only allowed outside the hospital in order to buy food with funds donated to him by the family and the community. However, before a court case could begin, anonymous benefactors paid Mr Zakari's fees, benefactors who, according to Young, were most likely to be "certain officials" who recognised that trouble was brewing and sought to end it.[54]

In Kenya, Bård Anders Andreassen examines a case concerning legal empowerment and collective advocacy action that reached national authorities. The Lake Naivasha Basin Stakeholders Forum, composed of farmers' organisations, animal welfare groups, pastoralists, consumer networks, CSOs, traders and individual inhabitants, tabled a memorandum opposing implementation of the management plan for the lake and the riparian land before the parliamentary Committee on Agriculture, Land and Natural Resources. The plan had been gazetted by the Ministry for Environment and Natural resources in 2004. The protesting forum of stakeholders denounced the plan on the grounds that it did not address the needs of the community, and the locals had not been consulted during the drafting stages. In particular, the forum claimed that the plan had neglected issues of local people's access to water, pollution of the lake and destruction of the riparian vegetation cover to pave the way for investment in flower industries. After a fact-finding mission, the Parliamentary Committee not only ruled that the government order flower farms, ranchers, tourist companies and other land owners to unblock entry points to the lake, provide the local community access and even made the access points wider.[55]

---

[52]R Mutatkar, "State, Civil Society And Justice: The Case of India", in M Albrow and H Seckinelgin (eds), *Global Civil Society 2011. Globality and the Absence of Justice* (Palgrave Macmillan, Houndmills, 2011).

[53]The excellent paper by D D'Hollander, A Marx and J Wouters, "Integrating Human Rights in Development Policy. Mapping Donor Strategies and Practices" (Leuven Centre for Global Governance Studies, Leuven, 2013), Paper #4 does not address local level impact in detail.

[54]K Young, *Constituting Economic and Social Rights* (Oxford University Press, Oxford, 2012), 223, 232.

[55]BA Andreassen, "Legal Empowerment of the Poor – a Strategy for Social Change", in in P Gready and W Vandenhole (eds), *Human Rights and Development in the New Millennium. Towards a Theory of Change* (Routledge, Oxon, 2014), 100.

In her balanced analysis of the transformative potential of human rights-based approaches in rural districts in Malawi, Sarelin argues that community members were empowered by awareness-raising efforts that "I have a right". Empowerment was in this case a process that led people to perceive themselves as able and entitled to make claims and demand accountability (192). However, as a platform for making demands, human rights entered at a political level, not a legal one. It was assumed that outcomes from development interventions were, or should be, *de facto* rights for people. It was the act of identifying duty-bearers and rights-holders that was key. Accountability was in this context about a political process where citizens put pressure on the government to deliver certain services, and these services were understood to be part of a rights agenda. Accountability was linked to obligations, although without making explicit linkage to legal provisions. In the final conclusion of her study, the author asserts that it was difficult to "prove" that the rights language had changed the mind-set of actors involved in the food security programme.[56]

In a study from rural Bangladesh, Kabeer et al documented how rights and empowerment mobilisation contributed to a tangible improvement of livelihoods for the poorest groups. The strategy employed by Nijera Kori, a local NGO, emphasised the importance of social mobilisation of the poorest groups. Mobilisation of the poorest around injustices, advocacy, conscientisation and training and rights awareness were among the tools employed. The quantitatively documented outcomes (comparison with control groups) were improved access to land, better nutrition, better knowledge of government policies and better female mobility. While rights-thinking was inspiring the research strategy, no reference is made to HRBA in the research.[57]

However, while rights-based strategies are employed in various localities globally with results for individuals and marginalised groups in some localities, similar strategies are also employed in so-called social accountability efforts without explicitly applying the language of rights, but institutionalising empowerment with significant results for communities. In Uganda, Björkman and Svensson conducted a study of health services, detailing 25 health dispensaries where report cards (monitoring through score cards) were used and also 25 dispensaries where no report cards were used. The dispensaries monitored exhibited 19% less nurse absenteeism, 7–10% higher immunisation rates, 16% higher facilitation utilisation, and 33% drop in infant mortality.[58] Of 15 programmes where social accountability instruments were included in the design, Ringold et al found that 10 programs had significant positive impact.[59] Human rights-based approaches and rights-based advocacy may therefore be one tool of empowerment among others that can be employed in mobilisation of marginalised communities.

---

[56]A Sarelin, *Exploring the Role and Transformative Potential of Human Rights in Development Practice and Food Security. A Case Study from Malawi* (Åbo Akademi University Press, Åbo, 2012).

[57]N Kabeer, A Haq Kabir and T Yasmi Huq, "Quantifying the Impact of Social Mobilisation in Rural Bangladesh: Donors, Civil Society and the 'Road not Taken'", IDS Working Paper 333 (2009). Available at http://www.ids.ac.uk/files/dmfile/Rs3331.pdf (accessed 3 February 2014).

[58]M Björkman and J Svensson, "Power to the People: Evidence from a Randomized Field Experiment of a Community-Based Monitoring Project" (2008) 124(2) *QuarterlyJ of Economics* 735–, 769. See also M McNeil and C Malena (eds), *Demanding Good Governance. Lessons from Social Accountability Initiatives in Africa* (World Bank, Washington, DC, 2010).

[59]D Ringold, A Holla, M Koziol and S Srinivasan, *Citizens and Service Delivery. Assessing the Use of Social Accountability Approaches in Human Development* (World Bank, Washington, DC, 2012).

VI. Conclusions

This article has discussed the various pathways to social rights reinforcement in developing and global contexts. It reported outcomes resulting from social litigation, social rights ratifications, policy reforms influenced by rights norms and obligations, and collective action remedies by local actors employing human rights-based approaches or resorting to legal and social empowerment methods.

It is reassuring to see that multiple data sources are used in these studies. However, resorting to quantitative methods is mainly reserved for a very specialised group of human rights scholars. When qualitative methods are employed, scholars tend to only make casual reference to their methods, indicating sometimes scant attention to methodology. It is also reassuring to note that a pioneering study has been undertaken concerning the tools of establishing causal linkages via plausibility assessment as done by Bustreo and Hunt. This can lead to greater awareness about causal relations in human rights research. Otherwise, outside the domain of specialised quantitative research, the attention paid to causality tends to be implicit and modest. The narrative account and its logic is perhaps so congruent with the results that further explicitation is not warranted. Table 1 below summarises the studies reviewed and the data, methods and causal links employed in the studies.

With respect to outcomes reported in the studies, positive change is evident according to all entries in Table 1. In other words, commitment and effort to implement social rights can be demonstrated to have positive results across these entries of litigation, ratifications, policy reforms and HRBA from below. However, the evidence may be contradictory as in the case of ratifications, and in some cases it can only be demonstrated that actions seeking to affect laws, or specific plans or measures can be effective like in the Kenya and Ghana cases, while actions that seek to bring relief and empowerment to marginalised communities depend strongly on models of implementation as indicated by the Bangladesh and Malawi cases. In the former instance, no reference was made to a human rights-based approach.

Court cases on social rights are increasingly important. The evidence suggests that even poorer groups may benefit from such cases, but litigation is mostly based on domestic law or constitutions. This does not make them less important, but it demonstrates that causal flows between the social rights covenant and results are not always straightforward. Context matters as the relatively weak importance of social rights litigation demonstrates in African countries.

Policy reforms may be based on human rights, for instance with respect to the right to health, but the specific measures which are effective in creating change on the ground may or may not be rights-based. Studies on how human rights are integrated in policy reforms are very rare, especially when it comes to state reforms in development. Human rights may do well to use plausibility evidence as explained by Bustreo and Hunt, but the rigor by which evidence is linked to policy instruments is crucial.

The quantitative evidence on the effects of human rights ratification and social results is mixed. Scholars and analysts use different data, research questions, and departure years. While statistical analysis cannot be argued to be uniformly negative in cross-national analyses of effects of rights of education, health and social security, they cannot be argued to be uniformly positive either. This is an emerging field where various methods make it hard for the non-statistical human rights expert to assess the evidence.

Lastly, the evidence on the importance of advocacy and empowerment is strong, though scholars would also argue that the positive evidence on empowerment is context dependent. There is positive evidence from South Asia as well as from Latin America, and South Africa.

Table 1 Overview of studies reviewed, their data sources, the classification of methods used, and the causality

Studies reviewed	Data sources	Method	Causality
The impact of litigation a. Gauri and Brinks	a. Legal documents and qualitative and quantitative evidence and secondary literature	a. Legal, qualitative and quantitative. Interpretation of court rulings and quantification of social implications of court decisions	a. Using a mix of data sources, estimating direct and indirect beneficiaries of court decisions on social rights in South Africa, India, Brazil, Nigeria, and Indonesia
The impact of HR structure change b. Cole (labor rights) c. Simmons (CEDAW) d. Palmer et al (health) e. Scruggs et al (social security)	b. Index on collective labor rights *de jure* and *de facto* c. Ratio of boys to girls in primary and secondary schools d. Health, human development, child labor, and political and civil liberties indicators e. Coded data on social security programs and legislation	b. Quantitative estimating probabilities of positive impact c. Quantitative estimating probabilities of positive impact d. Quantitative, estimating probabilities of positive impact e. Quantitative, estimating probabilities of positive impact	b. Regression analysis, regressing collective labor rights on ICESRC membership c. Gender ratios in primary and secondary schools regressed on CEDAW ratifications d. Regression analysis – regressing the health and other indicators on ratifications of six core treaties e. Regression analysis -regressing the coded legislation data on ratification of ESCR
The impact of policy reforms f. Hunt and Bustreo	f. Quantitative data on maternal mortality ratios and on service utilisation	f. Qualitative assessment of plausibility	f. Interpretation of plausible links between quantitative evidence and policies
The impact of advocacy and HRBA g. Young h. Andreassen i. Sarelin j. Kabeer	g. Qualitative data and legal documents h. Stakeholder interviews, administrative records i. Data from semi-structured individual and group interviews j. Quantitative survey data in each of the two areas where the organisation worked	g. Qualitative and documentary h. Qualitative and documentary i. Qualitative, based mainly on semi-structured interviews with local inhabitants and government officials j. Quantitative	g. Interpretation of events-based data. h. Interpretation of events-based and administrative data i. Interpretation of recorded interviews j. Measuring results by use of control groups

Note: Beth Simmon's book contains examples of ratification effect regressions other than that on CEDAW.

However, positive evidence from most of Africa, including North Africa and the Middle East is scant. The question of the positive impact of social rights in development, therefore, should be handled with some care, and with an open mind to context and methods.

Index

Abahlali base 'Mjondolo Movement of South Africa v Premier of the Province of KwaZulu-Natal 40, 41
abusive nursing care 61, 62
accountability 8, 114; mutual 18; social 114
ActionAid 21–3
adaptation 13–17, 25
adequacy 110–11
adjudication, participatory model of 2, 26–44
administrative data 102–3
advocacy 105, 112–14, 115–16
African feminism 60
aid effectiveness principles 90
Andreassen, B.A. 113
Arnold, D. 71
assimilation 69, 72, 84
attitudinal change 80–1

'bad buildings' 36–9
Banda, J. 52
Bangladesh 114
bargaining inequalities 43
bilingualism 73–4, 79
biopolitics 49–50
biopower 50, 63
birth positions 62
Bisika, T. 57
Björkman, M. 114
Bolivia 2, 70–85; Constitution 74; education policy reforms 73–81
Bolsa Familia programme 111
bottom-up approaches 9, 10
'brain drain' 70
Brand, D. 31
Brazil 105, 111, 112
Brinks, D.M. 105–6
Bustreo, F. 110–12

Caesarean sections (C-sections) 61–2
Campaign for Accelerated Reduction of Maternal Mortality (CARMMA) 45
Campolina Soares, A. 21–2
capacity-building 18–19, 20, 24, 97–8

Carvalho, E. 101
causal chain theories 11
causal linkages 103, 115–16
CHAM 57
Chapman, J. 21–2, 23
Chewa society 59–60
childbirth: global birth politics 48–51; hospitalisation of 45–7, 48–51, 60–5; modernisation of maternity care in Malawi 2, 45–65; position of childbearing women in Malawi 59–63; positions for 62
children's rights 13, 20–1, 88
Christian missionaries 59
civil and political rights 28
Cole, W. 106, 107, 109
collective labour rights 107
colonialism 59–60
coming-of-age rituals 60
Common Country Assessment (CCA) 17, 89
community midwives 58–9
complex approach to change 11
compulsory education 81–2
confrontation 9, 13, 19, 23, 24–5
Convention on the Elimination of All Forms of Discrimination against Women (CEDAW) 107–8
Convention on the Rights of the Child (CRC) 13, 20–1, 88
Coomans, F. 101
corporate strategy 96–7
cultural rights 2, 66–85
curriculum 78
customary legal mechanisms 53

Dahl, R. 30
Dean, M. 50
Declaration on the Rights of Indigenous Peoples 74
decoupling 104
degree of application of human rights principles 16
deliberation 33
democratic deficit 30
development: education, rights and 67–8; human rights-based approaches to 1, 5–25;

mainstreaming human rights in development programmes and projects 2, 86–100; right to 5
developmental state 29
DeVries, R. 59
dialogic models of adjudication 32
dialogue 19, 20
donor states 20–1
drivers of change 12, 25; ActionAid 22; donor states 21; UNDG 17–19; UNICEF 13–14, 17

economic rights: adjudication of socio-economic rights 2, 26–44; impact assessment 2–3, 101–16
education: development, rights and 67–8; indigenous peoples and 2, 66–85
empowerment 8, 10; impact assessment 105, 112–14, 115–16
Ensor, J. 8
entry points to change 9–10
evictions law 2, 34–43
evidence 102
evidence-based approach 24
experimentalist models of adjudication 33
expert bodies 8

feminism, African 60
fertility, control of 65
Finland 50–1
food, right to 2, 90–100
Food and Agriculture Organisation (FAO) 2, 86–100
Foucault, M. 49, 50, 52, 63, 64

Gauri, V. 105–6
gender equality 97
Ghana 113
global birth politics 48–51
Global Evaluation of the Application of the Human Rights-Based Approach to UNICEF Programming 15–16
Global Strategic Framework on Food Security and Nutrition 95
Gloppen, S. 105
governmentality 48–51
Gready, P. 8, 9, 22, 23
Grünfeld, F. 101

Hafner-Burton, E.M. 101, 104
health: maternity care in Malawi 2, 45–65; population health 108; public health policy reforms 110–12; services in Uganda 114
health surveillance assistants 58
HIV/AIDS 52
home births, illegalisation of 49
hospital fees 113
hospitalisation of childbirth 45–7, 48–51, 60–5

housing: evictions law in South Africa 2, 34–43; rights 34, 42
Human Development Index 67
human rights-based approaches to development (HRBADs) 1, 5–25; and organisational change 1, 6–7, 12–25; role of law and legal institutions 7–8
human rights-based approaches' impact assessment 105, 112–14, 115–16
human rights mainstreaming 2, 86–100
human rights principles 8, 93; degree of application of 16
human rights structures 106–9, 115, 116
human rights theory, transformative potential of 8–12
Hunt, P. 110–12

identity narrative 23
illiteracy of TBAs 54–7
impact: assessment 2–3, 101–16; of education on indigenous peoples 69–70, 81–5
implementation: education policy in Bolivia 76–81; tools for mainstreaming 96–7
India 112–13
indicators 104
indigenous organisations 72
indigenous peoples 2, 66–85; and education in Bolivia 2, 70–85; impact of education 69–70, 81–5
Indonesia 105
initiation ceremonies 60
intercultural and bilingual education (IBE) 73–4; implementation 76–8
interculturality 75, 79, 83–4
international collaborations 9
International Covenant on Civil and Political Rights (ICCPR) 107–8
International Covenant on Economic, Social and Cultural Rights (ICESCR) 107, 108–9
international NGOs 112
intraculturality 75, 79, 83–4
Italy 112

Joe Slovo I case 39–40, 42
Johannesburg 36–9; Inner City Regeneration Strategy 36

Kabeer, N. 114
Kamminga, M.T. 101
Kapur, R. 64
Kenya 113
Korpela, D. 52
KwaZulu-Natal Elimination and Prevention of Re-emergence of Slums Act 40

labour rights, collective 107
Lake Naivasha Basin Stakeholders Forum 113

Landman, T. 101

Langford, M. 105

languages: bilingualism 73–4, 79; indigenous peoples' linguistic rights 2, 66–85; plurilinguism 75–6, 82, 83–4

law: education laws in Bolivia 73–7; HRBADs and the role of 7–8; liberal nature of 10; role in development 9–10; South African evictions law 2, 34–43

leadership 13, 14, 17, 18, 24

legal institutions 7–8

legal instrumentalism 10

legitimacy 33

legitimising anchors 11, 24

liberalism 50

linguistic rights 2, 66–85

linkage to human rights norms 8; *see also* normativity, norms

literacy campaigns 71, 72

'live well' philosophy 76, 81

localism 9, 10

macro-level 103–4

mainstreaming human rights 2, 86–100

maintenance and development model of education 82, 83

Malawi 111–12, 114; Health Sector Strategy Plan 53; modernisation of maternity care 2, 45–65; National Sexual and Reproductive Health and Rights (SRHR) policy 52, 63; Road Map for Accelerating the Reduction of Maternal and Neonatal Mortality 53

maternal mortality 46–7, 53–4, 56–7, 64–5

maternity care 2, 45–65

matrilineal and matrilocal society 59–60

meaningful engagement 2, 32–3, 34–44

micro-level 103–4

midwives 57–9; *see also* skilled birth attendants (SBAs), traditional birth attendants (TBAs)

migration 81

Millennium Development Goals (MDGs) 111

Miller, V. 21–2

minimalist interpretation 31

misalignment-realignment cycles 22–3, 25

models of education 82–5

modernisation of maternity care 2, 45–65

monitoring 8, 43

multiple and complex methods 9

Munro, L.T. 15

National Building Regulations and Building Standards Act (NBRSA) 36–9

National Organisation of Nurses and Midwives 57

Nepal 111, 112

Nijera Kori 114

non-discrimination 8

non-governmental organisations (NGOs): impact assessment 112–14, 115–16; organisational change 21–3

normativity 8, 16, 24

norms: around childbirth 63–5; normative bases for indigenous rights in Bolivian education 73–6

NORAD 20–1

Norway 20–1

nurse midwives 58

nurses, abuse by 61, 62

nutrition 97

Occupiers of 51 Olivia Road v City of Johannesburg (*Olivia Road* case) 36–9, 41, 42, 43

Oestreich, J.E. 7, 13, 14

Office of the High Commissioner for Human Rights (OHCHR) 7, 19, 88, 89

organisational change 1, 6–7, 12–25

organisational support 98–9

Ouagadougou Declaration on Primacy Health Care (PHC) and Health Systems in Africa 46

Palmer, A. 108, 109

PANEL/PANEN 8

PANTHER 93

participation 8, 10

participatory democracy 30, 32

participatory model of adjudication 2, 26–44

Pateman, C. 49–50

peace and security 88

plausibility 110–11

plurilinguism 75–6, 82, 83–4

plurinational education system 74–6; implementation 78–81

policy reforms: education in Bolivia 73–81; impact of 105, 110–12, 115, 116; implementation 76–81; modernisation of maternity care in Malawi 51–4

political rights 28

polical work vs confrontation 9, 24–5

population health 108

Port Elizabeth Municipality v Various Occupiers (*PE Municipality* case) 35–6

poverty 105–6

Pretoria 40–1

Prevention of Illegal Eviction from and Unlawful Occupation of Land Act (PIE) 35

private maternity care 61–2

probability 110–11

programming cycle 16

promotion-protection dichotomy 19–20

public health policy reforms 110–12

qualitative research 102, 115–16

quantitative research 102, 115–16

ratifications 103, 105, 106–9, 115, 116
reasonableness 31–2, 37–8
regulatory regimes around birth 52
representative democracy 32
Resident Coordinators (RCs) 18, 19, 20
Residents of Joe Slovo Community v Thubelisha Homes & Others (Joe Slovo I case) 39–40, 42
result-based approach 11
result-based management (RBM) 1, 11–12, 17, 23, 24
Right to Food Guidelines 91, 92, 94, 95
Right to Food Team 94–6, 97, 98
Ringold, D. 114
Rist, G. 67
role definition 19, 23, 24–5
Ron, J. 101, 104

Sachdev, I. 71
Samuel, J. 21–2
Sarelin, A. 114
school enrolment 71
Schubart Park Residents Association v City of Tshwane Metropolitan Municipality 40–1
scope of meaningful engagement 42
Scruggs, L. 108–9
Sengupta, A. 67
Sichra, I. 70–1
SIDA 20–1
Simmons, B. 107–8
skilled birth attendants (SBAs) 46, 47, 53, 55, 56, 57–9, 63, 64
social accountability 114
social change 6–7, 24; transformative potential of social change theory 8–12
social movements 113
social norms around childbirth 63–5
social rights 1; adjudication of socio-economic rights 2, 26–44; impact assessment 2–3, 101–16
social rights litigation 105–6, 115, 116
social security laws 108–9
South Africa 27; Bill of Rights 27, 34; Constitutional Court 2, 27, 31–2, 32–3, 34–44; evictions law 2, 34–43
spoilers of change 12–13, 25; ActionAid 22; donor states 20–1; UNDG 19; UNICEF 14–15, 16
staff training 97–8
state: developmental 9; modern welfare state 28–9; policy reforms *see* policy reforms; role in development 9
strategy, mainstreaming 96–7
structural adjustment programmes (SAPs) 51
structural injunctions, participatory 32–3
structural reform litigation 34–5
structures, human rights 106–9, 115, 116

submersion model of education 82, 83–4
supervisory oversight 43
Svensson, J. 114
Sweden 20–1

targeting 93–4
teachers 80–1
temporary resettlement 39–40
traditional birth attendants (TBAs): assumptions about poor outcomes 54–7; banned 47–8, 51–4, 64; training 54–5
traditional healers 55
traditional leaders 52–3
training: mainstreaming 97–8; TBAs 54–5
transformation 13–17, 25; potential of human rights and social change theories 8–12
transition model of education 82, 83
transnational collaborations 9
transnational human rights obligations 5
treaty ratifications 103, 105, 106–9, 115, 116
true believers 7, 13, 14, 17, 20

Uganda 114
United Nations: Committee on the Rights of the Child 68; Declaration on the Rights of Indigenous Peoples 74; Food and Agriculture Organisation (FAO) 2, 86–100; mainstreaming within 87–90; System Staff College 98
United Nations Children's Fund (UNICEF) 9, 11, 12–13, 24, 54, 88–9, 98; organisational change 13–17
United Nations Country Teams (UNCTs) 17–20
United Nations Development Assistance Framework (UNDAF) 17–18, 89
United Nations Development Group (UNDG) 89–90; organisational change 17–20
United Nations Development Programme (UNDP) 67, 88–9
United Nations Population Fund (UNPFA) 54, 89
urban migration 81

vaginal trauma 55
values 96–7
Vandenhole, W. 9, 17
vernacularisation 99–100
Voluntary Guidelines on the Responsible Governance of Tenure of Land, Fisheries and Forests in the Context of National Food Security (VGGT) 91, 95
Voluntary Guidelines to Support the Progressive Realization of the Right to Adequate Food in the Context of National Food Security (Right to Food Guidelines) 91, 92, 94, 95

welfare state 28–9
women: maternity care 2, 45–65; position of childbearing women in Malawi 59–63; rights 107–8
World Bank 111
World Food Programme (WFP) 89
World Food Summits 90, 91

World Health Organisation (WHO) 54, 55, 89, 98

Yapita, J. 71
Young, K. 113

Zakari, Mr 113

For Product Safety Concerns and Information please contact our EU
representative GPSR@taylorandfrancis.com Taylor & Francis Verlag GmbH,
Kaufingerstraße 24, 80331 München, Germany

Printed and bound by CPI Group (UK) Ltd, Croydon, CR0 4YY

11/05/2025

01866595-0002